Nancy Fraser, Social Justice and Education

The American scholar and activist Nancy Fraser has written about a wide range of issues in social and political theory, and is well-known for her philosophical perspectives on democratic theory and on feminist theory. Her work on justice and identity politics has been particularly widely cited, and she has also been active in developing a 'feminism for the 99%'. Although education has not been a direct focus for much of her work, her thinking has been widely disseminated within the critical study of education. This volume illustrates the way in which education researchers have taken up and developed Fraser's theories in the areas of alternative education, higher education, inclusion and disability, and the effects of neoliberalism upon public (state) education, as they ask how social justice within the education system can be enhanced. These insightful essays cover a range of countries and topics, as the authors work with Fraser's concepts, to argue for the development of a more equitable education system. The chapters in this book were originally published as articles in Taylor and Francis journals.

Carol Vincent is a Professor of Sociology of Education at UCL Institute of Education, London, UK. She has written and researched extensively about the relationship between families and the education system, education policy, and responses to social and ethnic diversity. Her most recent books are *Friendship and Diversity* (2018, with Sarah Neal and Humera Iqbal), and *Tea and the Queen? Fundamental British Values, Schools and Citizenship* (2019).

Education and Social Theory
Series Editor: Stephen J. Ball, *Institute of Education, University College London, UK*

Social theory can help us to make sense of many aspects of contemporary education by providing analytic concepts and insights. Social theories are tools of analysis and interpretation for educational researchers that enable us to make sense of the processes, effects, and outcomes of educational experiences and institutions.

Drawing together selections from the best work previously published in Taylor and Francis journals to create powerful and effective collections, this series highlights and explores the social theories critical to educational writers, researchers and scholars. Each book focuses a different key writer or field of theory, with the overarching aim of providing an overview of the social theories important to education research, but also of showing how these theories can be applied in a practical manner in the current education landscape.

Books in the Series:

Foucault and Education
Putting Theory to Work
Edited by Stephen J. Ball

Marxisms and Education
Edited by Noah De Lissovoy

Revisiting Actor-Network Theory in Education
Edited by Tara Fenwick and Richard Edwards

Feminist Posthumanisms, New Materialisms and Education
Edited by Jessica Ringrose, Katie Warfield and Shiva Zarabadi

Freud, Lacan, Zizek and Education
Exploring Unconscious Investments in Policy and Practice
Edited by Claudia Lapping

The Education Assemblage
Edited by Greg Thompson

Bourdieu and Education
Edited by Diane Reay

Judith Butler and Education
Edited by Judith Butler

Nancy Fraser, Social Justice and Education
Edited by Carol Vincent

Nancy Fraser, Social Justice and Education

Edited by
Carol Vincent

LONDON AND NEW YORK

First published 2019
by Routledge
2 Park Square, Milton Park, Abingdon, Oxon, OX14 4RN

and by Routledge
605 Third Avenue, New York, NY 10017

First issued in paperback 2020

Routledge is an imprint of the Taylor & Francis Group, an informa business

© 2019 Taylor & Francis

All rights reserved. No part of this book may be reprinted or reproduced or utilised in any form or by any electronic, mechanical, or other means, now known or hereafter invented, including photocopying and recording, or in any information storage or retrieval system, without permission in writing from the publishers.

Trademark notice: Product or corporate names may be trademarks or registered trademarks, and are used only for identification and explanation without intent to infringe.

British Library Cataloguing-in-Publication Data
A catalogue record for this book is available from the British Library

ISBN 13: 978-0-367-72890-8 (pbk)
ISBN 13: 978-1-138-39194-9 (hbk)

Typeset in Times New Roman
by codeMantra

Publisher's Note
The publisher accepts responsibility for any inconsistencies that may have arisen during the conversion of this book from journal articles to book chapters, namely the inclusion of journal terminology.

Disclaimer
Every effort has been made to contact copyright holders for their permission to reprint material in this book. The publishers would be grateful to hear from any copyright holder who is not here acknowledged and will undertake to rectify any errors or omissions in future editions of this book.

Contents

Citation Information vii
Notes on Contributors ix

Introduction 1
Carol Vincent

1 Conceptualizing social justice in education: mapping the territory 13
 Sharon Gewirtz

2 Equality, Recognition and the Distributive Paradigm 29
 Chris Armstrong

3 Schooling and social justice through the lenses of Nancy Fraser 40
 Amanda Keddie

4 The scholarship of teaching and learning from a social justice perspective 57
 Brenda Leibowitz and Vivienne Bozalek

5 Beyond the binary: rethinking teachers' understandings of and engagement with inclusion 71
 Stuart Woodcock and Ian Hardy

6 Education markets, the new politics of recognition and the increasing fatalism towards inequality 91
 Sally Power and Daniel Frandji

7 Alternative education and social justice: considering issues of affective and contributive justice 103
 Martin Mills, Glenda McGregor, Aspa Baroutsis, Kitty Te Riele and Debra Hayes

8 The political economy of language education research (or the lack thereof): Nancy Fraser and the case of translanguaging 119
 David Block

9 Mixed-income schools and housing: advancing the neoliberal
   urban agenda 140
   Pauline Lipman

10 Public education in neoliberal times: memory and desire 156
   Jessica Gerrard

11 Considering Nancy Fraser's Notion of Social Justice for Social Work:
   Reflections on *Misframing* and the Lives of Refugees in South Africa 170
   Dorothee Hölscher

   Index 189

Citation Information

The following chapters were originally published as articles in Taylor and Francis journals. When citing this material, please use the original citation information, including page numbering for each article, as follows:

Chapter 1
Conceptualizing social justice in education: mapping the territory
Sharon Gewirtz
Journal of Education Policy, volume 13, issue 4 (1998) pp. 469–484
DOI: 10.1080/0268093980130402

Chapter 2
Equality, Recognition and the Distributive Paradigm
Chris Armstrong
Critical Review of International Social and Political Philosophy, volume 6, issue 3 (Autumn 2003) pp. 154–164
DOI: 10.1080/1369823032000233591

Chapter 3
Schooling and social justice through the lenses of Nancy Fraser
Amanda Keddie
Critical Studies in Education, volume 53, issue 3 (October 2012) pp. 263–279
DOI: 10.1080/17508487.2012.709185

Chapter 4
The scholarship of teaching and learning from a social justice perspective
Brenda Leibowitz and Vivienne Bozalek
Teaching in Higher Education, volume 21, issue 2 (February 2016) pp. 109–122
DOI: 10.1080/13562517.2015.1115971

Chapter 5
Beyond the binary: rethinking teachers' understandings of and engagement with inclusion
Stuart Woodcock and Ian Hardy
International Journal of Inclusive Education, volume 21, issue 6 (June 2017) pp. 667–686
DOI: 10.1080/13603116.2016.1251501

Chapter 6

Education markets, the new politics of recognition and the increasing fatalism towards inequality
Sally Power and Daniel Frandji
Journal of Education Policy, volume 25, issue 3 (May 2010) pp. 385–396
DOI: 10.1080/02680930903576404

Chapter 7

Alternative education and social justice: considering issues of affective and contributive justice
Martin Mills, Glenda McGregor, Aspa Baroutsis, Kitty Te Riele and Debra Hayes
Critical Studies in Education, volume 57, issue 1 (February 2016) pp. 100–115
DOI: 10.1080/17508487.2016.1123079

Chapter 8

The political economy of language education research (or the lack thereof): Nancy Fraser and the case of translanguaging
David Block
Critical Inquiry in Language Studies, volume 15, issue 4 (December 2018) pp. 237–257
DOI: 10.1080/15427587.2018.1466300

Chapter 9

Mixed-income schools and housing: advancing the neoliberal urban agenda
Pauline Lipman
Journal of Education Policy, volume 23, issue 2 (March 2008) pp. 119–134
DOI: 10.1080/02680930701853021

Chapter 10

Public education in neoliberal times: memory and desire
Jessica Gerrard
Journal of Education Policy, volume 30, issue 6 (November 2015) pp. 855–868
DOI: 10.1080/02680939.2015.1044568

Chapter 11

Considering Nancy Fraser's Notion of Social Justice for Social Work: Reflections on Misframing *and the Lives of Refugees in South Africa*
Dorothee Hölscher
Ethics and Social Welfare, volume 8, issue 1 (March 2014) pp. 20–38
DOI: 10.1080/17496535.2012.744845

For any permission-related enquiries please visit:
http://www.tandfonline.com/page/help/permissions

Notes on Contributors

Chris Armstrong is a Professor of Political Theory, in the Department of Politics and International Relations at the University of Southampton, UK.

Aspa Baroutsis is a Postdoctoral Research Fellow at Griffith Institute for Educational Research at Griffith University, Australia.

David Block is ICREA (Institució Catalana de Recerca i Estudis Avançats) Research Professor in Sociolinguistics at the Universitat de Lleida, Spain.

Vivienne Bozalek is the Director of Teaching and Learning at the University of the Western Cape, Cape Town, South Africa.

Daniel Frandji is a sociologist working at University of Lyon, UMR Triangle, UMS LLE, France.

Jessica Gerrard is a Senior Lecturer in Education, Equity and Politics at the Melbourne Graduate School of Education at the University of Melbourne, Australia.

Sharon Gewirtz is a Professor of Education at King's College London, UK.

Ian Hardy is an Associate Professor in the School of Education in the Faculty of Humanities and Social Sciences at the University of Queensland, Brisbane, Australia.

Debra Hayes is a Professor of Education and Equity in the Faculty of Education and Social Work at the University of Sydney, Australia.

Dorothee Hölscher is a Lecturer at the School of Human Services and Social Work at Griffith University, Australia, and a Research Associate with the Department of Social Work at the University of Johannesburg, South Africa.

Amanda Keddie is a Professor of Education in the Faculty of Education at Deakin University, Melbourne, Australia.

Brenda Leibowitz was the Professor of Teaching and Learning in the Education Faculty at the University of Johannesburg, South Africa. Sadly, she passed away in 2018.

Pauline Lipman is a Professor of Educational Policy Studies at the University of Illinois-Chicago, USA.

Glenda McGregor is the Deputy Head of the School of Education and Professional Studies at Griffith University, Australia.

Martin Mills is Professor and Director of the Centre for Research on Teachers and Teaching, UCL Institute of Education, UK.

Sally Power is a Professor, and the Director of WISERD Education, in the School of Social Sciences at Cardiff University, UK.

Kitty Te Riele is an Honorary Professor at Victoria University, Melbourne, Australia.

Carol Vincent is a Professor of Sociology of Education at UCL Institute of Education, London, UK.

Stuart Woodcock is a Senior Lecturer in the Faculty of Human Sciences at Macquarie University, Sydney, Australia.

Introduction

Carol Vincent

Nancy Fraser has maintained an impressively full career of both activism and scholarship, whilst based at the New School for Social Research in New York City, most recently as the Henry and Louise A. Loeb Professor of Philosophy and Politics. Her work on social and political theory, feminist theory and social justice is particularly notable for its sweep and scope. In a recent contribution, Bernstein (2017 p. 17) observes that her work has five interdependent themes: interrogating the idea of the public sphere; justice, redistribution and recognition; a rethinking of Karl Polanyi's 'The Great Transformation', which emphasises the human and environmental aspects of markets; prospects for a radical feminism; and a critique of neoliberal capitalism. Of these, the first two are the most familiar and most used within education. Her work, conceptualising, social justice as having first two and then three dimensions – redistribution, recognition and representation – has been hugely appealing to writers and researchers within education as can be seen in the papers in this collection. Fraser's nuanced work, oriented as it is around social justice, capitalism and the nature of the state and democracy, Fraser's nuanced work is a natural resource for educational researchers (Blackmore 2016).

As Bernstein notes, a major shift distinguishing Fraser's earlier from her more recent work is that the former took for granted a frame based on national sovereignty, with territorially bound, relatively autonomous states directing national economies – what she calls the 'Keynesian-Westphalian frame'. Her later work addresses the 'new spatialities' of globalisation (Lingard 2018 p. 725) and argues that social justice has to be considered within a post-Westphalian world. Thus, she further developed her original two-dimensional theory of social justice that emphasised redistribution (economic justice) and recognition (cultural justice), and added another dimension: representation, defined as political justice. All three are intertwined and are necessary for social justice.

In addition to the sweep of Fraser's work, there are another two dimensions that are particularly admirable, as well as attractive for other scholars. The first, as indicated earlier, is her willingness to revise her work as social, economic and political conditions change, throwing up new problems and contexts. The second is her emphasis on the necessity of critical theory and of it having both theoretical and practical orientations. Recent writing, for example, has focused on Trump's America, and the possibilities of building a 'progressive-populist' movement in the US (Fraser 2017). She aims to develop a 'critical social theory with a practical intent […] to conceptualize society in a way that made visible its historical fault lines, revealing the contradictions and the emancipatory potentials that mark a given time and place' (Fraser and Naples 2004 p. 1107).

In this introduction, I offer a brief summary of some of her key writings and then go on to outline the other contributions to this volume.

Recognition, redistribution and representation

Fraser argues that post-war feminism started from the assumptions of the permanence of the Keynesian state and that the focus for feminists then was the enlargement of the welfare state to encompass redistribution in terms of gender as well as class (Fraser and Naples 2004 p. 1111). She is well-known for her scepticism of identity politics that 'valorize[ed] culturalized differences [rather] than promoting economic equality' (ibid). She argues that this focus on recognition in the 1980s and 1990s effectively meant feminists took their eyes off the ball by not responding faster or more fiercely to the growth of neoliberal economics: 'Effectively mesmerized by the politics of recognition, we unwittingly diverted feminist theory into culturalist channels at precisely the moment when circumstances required redoubled attention to the politics of redistribution' (Fraser and Naples 2004 p. 1112).

Her ideas were at least partially shaped in response to Iris Young's (1990) *Justice and the Politics of Difference*, which argues that social justice is too often understood reductively as distributive justice. Young's argument was that differentiation on the various axes of oppression, such as class, gender, age, disability, ethnicity, sexuality and perceived racial group, generates distinct versions of what 'justice' looks like (Troyna and Vincent 1995, Gewirtz, this volume). Accordingly, Young maintained that distributive justice alone is inadequate, and that the concepts of domination and oppression provide a firmer basis for a politics of social justice, as they offer 'an institutional and ideological means for recognizing and affirming diverse social groups by giving political representation to these groups, and celebrating their distinctive characteristics and cultures' (Young 1990, p. 240). Fraser acknowledges that Young's book addresses both redistribution and recognition – the economic and the cultural – but disagrees with her treatment of the relationship between the two. She interrogates Young's emphasis on and theorising of cultural recognition (Fraser 1995 p. 169) arguing that her engagement with the politics of difference – the cultural paradigm – marginalises her emphasis on the 'political economy paradigm' (1995 p. 170) and that Young's understanding of these two forms of oppression – economic and cultural – ignores the tension between them. Fraser posits an analytical distinction between the economic and cultural as necessary to reveal underlying tensions. For example, culturally rooted oppression (e.g. against some ethnic groups) requires recognition and the affirming of cultural pluralism, thereby *promoting* group differentiation, but in relation to economically rooted oppression (e.g. class), the remedy would be to *undermine* the differentiation between the economically oppressed and others. Fraser later clarified that she accepted 'all real-world instances of subordination as involving both dimensions of (in)justice' (Fraser 2007 p. 306), and develops a 'bivalent conception that treats distribution and recognition as distinct perspectives on, and dimensions of, justice. Without reducing either one of them to the other, it encompasses both dimensions within a broader, overarching framework' (1998 p. 5). Fraser calls her stance 'perspectival dualism'. All cases should be assessed as 'simultaneously economic and cultural, albeit not necessarily in equal proportions, […] [from] both the standpoint of distribution and the standpoint of recognition, without reducing either one of these perspectives to the other' (1998 p. 8).

She further refines an understanding of the politics of recognition as one that moves away from 'validating group identity' to 'establishing status equality' (Fraser in Dahl et al. 2004 p. 377) as the former tends to reify group differences (e.g. suggesting that there is a 'right' way to be and act as, say a lesbian), whilst the latter 'locates the injustice in institutionalized hierarchies of cultural value that prevent some members of society from participating as peers in social interaction' (Fraser in Dahl et al. 2004 p. 377).

Thus, Fraser's theory of justice has at its core, the concept of parity of participation – the interaction of all adult members of society as peers, with equal moral worth (Zaretsky 2017 p. 274). In a debate with Axel Honneth, Fraser argues that

> it is unjust that some individuals and groups are denied the status of full partners in social interaction […] What makes misrecognition morally wrong, in my view, is that it denies some individuals and groups the possibility of participating on a par with others in social interaction. (1998 p. 3)

Participatory parity is an absence of structural exclusion across major arenas of social interaction, an exclusion that (at this point in her theorising) can be rooted in the political economy, the status order or both.

Fraser began to see her two-dimensional model of justice as inadequate, as 'a transitional aspect... of a deeper change in the circumstances of justice' (Fraser and Naples 2004 p. 1116). That transition describes a trajectory from the Keynesian post-war paradigm that had focused on redistribution, 'relegating to the margins' (ibid) problems of status (recognition), through the destabilisation of that paradigm in the last decades of the twentieth century as recognition claims surfaced, to the latest phase: the 'acceleration of globalization [that] has fundamentally transformed the circumstances of justice—by altering the scale of social interaction and decentering the sovereign state frame' (1117).

This development made it necessary to emphasise representation as 'furnish[ing] the stage on which struggles over distribution and recognition are played out' (Fraser 2007 p. 313). Processes of globalisation include population movements, and Fraser argues that disputes about justice are, primarily, disputes about *who* is a member of a community and *which* is the relevant community; 'the obstacle to justice [being] neither economic or cultural, but political' (p. 314). Thus, she argues that there are two levels to (mis)representation: *ordinary-political misrepresentation* which signals issues of voter registration, voting systems, quotas for political representatives and related issues to do with the full representation of a particular group. The second level is a deeper one of *misframing:* 'when a community's boundaries are drawn in such a way as to wrongly exclude some people from a chance to participate *at all* in its authorized contests over justice' (Lovell 2007 p. 22) as they are constituted as outside the frame of consideration in matters of redistribution, recognition and ordinary-political representation. Fraser states that globalisation has highlighted and intensified misframing. The emphasis on the national sovereignty of the Keynesian-Westphalian frame 'blocks many who are poor and despised from channeling the forces that oppress them', as their claims are only recognised as legitimate within their own, often precarious, nation states. This containment protects and insulates from any claim both 'powerful predator states' and 'the governance structures of the global economy which set exploitative terms of interaction' (Lovell 2007 p. 23).

The difficulties of transitioning from "thinking about justice in the frame of the modern territorial state to that of a global order" (Lara and Fine 2007 p. 44) have been noted. The division between Westphalian and post-Westphalian – although Fraser is certainly not the only theorist using it – has also been criticised for leaving globalisation as too amorphous a concept and for a lack of historical nuance (e.g. Lawson 2008 p. 890 argues that the 'Westphalian political imaginary' had a relatively short period of dominance in the twentieth century). Nevertheless, Lovell describes Fraser's productive emphasis on 'the political dimension [as] implicit in, indeed required by, the grammar of the concept of justice. Thus, no redistribution or recognition without representation' (Lovell 2007 p. 23).

Public sphere

I first came to Nancy Fraser's work through her criticism of Habermas' discussion of the public sphere. At the time I was writing about parents' relationships with the education system and trying to define a role for parents that went beyond the school-approved one of audience and supporter and the government-approved one of consumer. Researching parent activist groups (Vincent 2000), I was attracted by Fraser's complication of the public sphere.

Fraser aligns herself with those who argue that the work of political philosopher, Jurgen Habermas, idealises the liberal public sphere, through the elevation of rational deliberation, apparently leading to a consensus around the 'common good' (1990 pp. 59–60). She argues that the apparent 'accessibility, rationality and suspension of status hierarchies' (1990 p. 60), which distinguish Habermas' notion of the public sphere, were themselves strategies for distinction. Habermas' understanding of the public sphere has, Fraser argues, four assumptions: (i) participants in the public sphere can, in deliberative mode, bracket status differentials and debate as if they were social equals, (ii) a single comprehensive public is preferable in terms of democracy than a nexus of multiple publics, (iii) the inclusion of private interests in the public debate is undesirable and (iv) the assumption of a functioning democratic public sphere requires a sharp separation between civil society and state (Fraser 1990 pp. 62–63).

Fraser contests each of these points arguing in relation to the first two that even once all groups within a population are formally included that there are 'informal impediments to participatory parity' (pp. 63–64), and that 'social inequalities can affect deliberation even in the absence of any formal exclusions'. I was reminded of her critique recently when researching the promotion of so-called 'fundamental British values' in schools in England, a requirement that I argued could be characterised as liberal nationalist.[1] Liberal nationalists such as Miller (1995), Tamir (1993) and Soutphommasane (2012) argue that a developed sense of shared national identity is necessary to develop the required solidarity amongst citizens to generate a cohesive society. In order that the national identity is not exclusive on minority ethnic or religious grounds, these commenters argue for a national debate, assuming that different social groups can take part in a collective debate 'on an equal footing' (Miller 1995 p. 153) where all voices are heard, an example of Habermas' bracketing of status differentials for the purposes of deliberative dialogue. However, following Fraser, if such a debate is to be within the formal political arena, this then overlooks social and economic barriers that might prevent people participating in, valuing or trusting a process of formal representation, and if the arena is to be (or also to be) civil society, much the same objection can be made. As Fraser notes, 'discursive arenas are situated within a larger societal context that is pervaded by the structural relations of dominance and subordination' (1990 p. 65).

Indeed, Fraser argues that the exclusion of women and other groups was central to the whole process of constituting the liberal masculine, bourgeois public sphere, a process of structural exclusion. Presenting an idealised public sphere, as Habermas does, obscures the vitality of the power struggles for a voice and for inclusion, which are inherent in the idea of 'competing publics' (Lara and Fine 2007 p. 38). Fraser posits the idea of 'subaltern counterpublics'. This term describes the meeting places, literature and actions of subordinated social groups who form an alternative public in which to conduct deliberative conversations away from the 'gaze' of the dominant group. She gives the examples of minority ethnic, feminist and LGBTQ+ groups, noting the success of feminist groups (for example) 'inventing new terms for describing social reality' (1990 p. 67) (current examples would be 'everyday sexism' and anti-'slut shaming' campaigns). Counterpublics allow subordinate group members to define their needs and agendas, and deliberate on how best to frame these (also Mansbridge 1990). Fraser notes that such groupings are not always 'virtuous' but they do lead to an expansion of discursive space. This – the legitimacy (or not) of non-virtuous voices in the public sphere – is perhaps a point worthy of more consideration, given, for example, the current rise of far-right groups operating as tight-knit, well-networked counterpublics. How as a society, do 'we' address the rise of voices preaching exclusion and hatred? And how can teachers address and counter such views in the classroom?

Taking up what she sees as Habermas' third assumption (as above), Fraser also argues that the assumed rightness of public interests and the apparent unacceptability of private ones in public deliberation are frequently used to close down the claims of some, by rendering them illegitimate, whilst valorising others (1990 p. 73). I found this argument particularly useful whilst analysing the exclusion of parents from school decision-making as they are commonly positioned as too narrowly particular, too focused on their own child(ren) and thus unable to see beyond their own self-interest. However, as Mansbridge (1990) argues, in alignment with Fraser, private (self-interested) and public (altrustic) concerns intermingle in most people's motivations in complex ways, and suppressing particularity will detract from people's willingness to participate. Additionally, what looks like the ability to transcend particular attachments, 'in a single all-encompassing "we"' (Fraser 1990 p. 72), is often a reflection of already-existing privilege.

Fraser's reaction to Habermas fourth point argues that the assumption of a strong split between state and civil society leads to 'weak publics' in civil society, and asks, 'Where in society are direct democracy arrangements called for and where are representative forms more appropriate? How are the former best articulated with the latter' (1990 p. 76). These are questions very relevant today as the growth of populist movements illustrates that large sectors of the population in the US, the UK and elsewhere feel that their voices and concerns are easily dismissed and ignored by an elite.

Progressive neoliberalism and social reproduction

Fraser's most recent work has refocused on her early concern with the glossing over of the political economy in academic analyses (Fraser and Pettifor 2018 p. 158). Her understanding of political economy is far from narrow and includes conceptualising capitalism as 'an institutionalized social order' (2016b p. 166) in which racialised and gendered subjection play a constitutive role. Her recent analyses consider the fundamental role social reproduction plays in making capitalism possible (2016a), and the depth of 'capitalism's systemic entanglement with racial oppression' (2016b p. 1640).

To take the first of these, Fraser's argument is that social reproduction has been from the beginning separated from economic production, obscured and marginalised, placed within the domestic sphere and associated with women (2016a p. 102) – a 'peculiar relation of separation-cum-dependence-cum-disavowal' (p. 103). Fraser charts the relations between capitalism and social reproduction describing the most recent regime of 'financialised capitalism' as creating 'a crisis of care'. She analyses the largely unwaged work of social reproduction as entangled with neoliberal demands that women engage with paid work.

> Globalizing and neoliberal, this regime promotes state and corporate disinvestment from social welfare, while recruiting women into the paid workforce—externalizing carework onto families and communities while diminishing their capacity to perform it. (2016a p. 112)

Fraser argues that this situation can be understood in terms of the rise of 'progressive neoliberalism':

> a kind of unholy alliance between those dynamic sectors of finance capital, IT, the kind of post-material, symbolic part of the economy that is cosmopolitan, that is interested in globalisation, and so on, in an alliance with what I think of as the liberal mainstream currents of progressive social movements: lean-in feminism, meritocratic anti-racism, green capitalism, multiculturalism. (Fraser and Pettifor 2018 p. 162, also Fraser 2016c)

Progressive neoliberalism's interaction with 'financialised capitalism' (Fraser and Jaeggi 2018) creates a situation in which,

> [Financialised capitalism]'s dominant imaginary is liberal-individualist and gender-egalitarian—women are considered the equals of men in every sphere, deserving of equal opportunities to realize their talents, including—perhaps especially—in the sphere of production. Reproduction, by contrast, appears as a backward residue, an obstacle to advancement that must be sloughed off, one way or another, *en route* to liberation'. (2016a p. 114)

She describes the benefits that have accrued to affluent, middle-class women, but the resulting care gap left by the expectation of women working, longer working hours and reduced public provision (and the absence of any greater expectation that men take on caring responsibilities). This gap is filled by poorer women, often from the global south (see also Ehrenreich and Hochschild 2003). Fraser indicates that deep structural transformation of the social order is required to address this situation.

With regard to the entanglement of racial oppression and capitalism, Fraser argues that nation states have 'fabricated two distinct categories' (2016b p. 173), one of 'unfree, dependent and unwaged labour' (2016b p. 165) which she describes as expropriated (examples being slavery, but also in current times, sex trafficking and corporate land grabs). Such peoples, usually racialised others, are positioned as lesser beings to those who have the status of free individuals and citizens as 'workers', whose labour is exploited. 'The subjection of those whom capital expropriates is the hidden condition of possibility for the freedom of those it exploits' (2016b p. 166). Fraser traces the relationships between expropriation and exploitation through phases of capitalism and argues that the dynamics of the current capitalist regime – 'financialised capitalism' – has led to a blurring, in the relationship between the two, thanks to:

> The universalisation of expropriation by debt [...] Governments everywhere from Latin America, to Africa, to Greece have had to cut social spending and open their markets to foreign capital, vampirising their people for capital's benefit. (https://www.epw.in/engage/article/populism-contemporary-historical-moment-conversation-nancy-fraser)

As unionised labour diminishes in force and low-wage precarious jobs increase in countries like the UK and the US, workers there, 'previously shielded by their status as citizen-worker' (2016b p. 176), are increasingly subject to expropriation. Importantly however, Fraser acknowledges that 'the expropriation/exploitation continuum remains racialized, as people of color are still disproportionately represented at the expropriative end of the spectrum' (ibid). Despite this though, the rise in expropriation results in an increased commonality of condition that can lead to either growing solidarity between workers in different parts of the world or chauvinism, the latter seeming to be the more likely result. Fraser understands the 'reactionary populism' of Trump and the increasing populist and nationalist rhetoric around the globe as a rejection of 'financialised capitalism' and 'the liberal cosmopolitanism identified with it' (2016c p. 282): a resistance, in other words, to capital's attempt to achieve a trade without borders, a perception of diversity without friction. In response she calls for 'a new feminism and a new Left' (2016c p. 283, also 2016b).

Applying Fraser to education

Fraser's recent writing on capitalism's structural racialised and gendered oppressions offers more food for thought for education researchers struggling to address social justice within education systems that have, in much of the world, been subject to the sustained impact of neoliberal policies. Jill Blackmore, observing that the growth of neoliberal education policies has resulted in an emphasis on parental choice of educational provider, supply-side diversity and a creeping privatisation of public-sector education, suggests that Fraser's tripartite definition of social justice could give us some guidance as to where to start suggesting a range of 'accountabilities' (2016 p. 60) for schools. These include amongst others: well-resourced public schools, community representation, and a curriculum and pedagogical relationships based on 'the recognition of difference and inclusivity' (2016 p. 117).

Most of the researchers included here also take up this challenge of applying Nancy Fraser's work to understand the contours and challenges of moving towards a more socially just education system. Not all papers address education but all offer a useful point of debate with or application of Fraser's work.

Sharon Gewirtz's paper discusses the first of Fraser's very useful debates with other scholars – that with Iris Young, and Young's attempt to emphasise relational justice. In her commentary on their debate, Gewirtz argues that Young's five faces of oppression can inform a comprehensive research agenda for education policies but that Fraser's critical theory of recognition can expand one of Young's 'faces' – cultural imperialism, by adopting 'what Fraser refers to as a more differentiated theory of difference' (Gewirtz p. 26). This again raises the question I noted earlier of what counts as 'virtuous' and non-virtuous voices, or as Gewirtz puts it, 'which aspects of difference ought to be abolished (either because they are themselves oppressive or because they interfere with redistribution), which should be affirmed and which universalized' (ibid).

Chris Armstrong's paper does not apply Fraser's work to education, but helpfully includes a discussion of some key issues by focusing on how equality relates to difference. He engages with Fraser's debate with Young and Honneth to argue that Fraser's work initially appeared to relegate equality to one half of her two forms of injustice, so that matters of redistribution involved an ethic of equality, but failures of recognition were best remedied by cultural change (Armstrong p. 30). However, Armstrong suggests that through the overarching notion of 'parity of participation', which posits that 'the equal worth of persons' requires 'the absence of certain forms of economic inequality, and the presence of a culture of equal respect for diverse groups' (p. 33), Fraser clearly sees 'equality as first and foremost a moral concept' (p. 34), a 'complex, clustered concept', which provides the social and material conditions that are necessary for democratic citizenship (p. 36).

Amanda Keddie's paper draws on Fraser's discussion of her three-dimensional approach to social justice building on the original distinction between redistribution and recognition. Keddie identifies criticism of this model (by, for example, Iris Young and Judith Butler) as the 'most enduring criticism of her work' (p. 42). Applying Fraser's work to education, Keddie notes 'distributive principles have long-framed equity and schooling policy and initiatives' (ibid), but failed to consider 'cultural disadvantages'. Writing in relation to indigenous communities in Australia, she finds apposite Fraser's concern that 'current forms of identity politics have curtailed justice in simplifying and reifying group identity' (p. 43) and that what is needed is 'an alternative approach to recognition – which focuses on overcoming status subordination' (ibid). She continues by drawing on Fraser's principle of participatory parity – ' justice for all is possible when the structures of the economy reflect an equitable distribution of material resources, when the status order reflects equitable patterns of cultural recognition and when the constitution of political space ensures equitable representation' (Keddie p. 42). Keddie concludes that the clarity of Fraser's three-dimensional model can be difficult to apply to the messy, lived realities of education but offers 'a productive lens' for thinking about the ways in which different dimensions of injustice hinder 'the schooling participation, engagement and outcomes of marginalised students' (p. 53).

Writing in a South African context, **Leibowitz and Bozalek** use Fraser's tripartite account of participatory parity to argue that her work adds an important critical orientation to the context of higher education. They consider how maldistribution, misrecognition and misframing can impact on student participation – each perspective being understood from both an affirmative and transformative perspective. They also argue for the use of a 'pedagogy of discomfort' (Boler and Zembylas 2003), adding that it is necessary for staff as well as students to have such experiences. They illustrate their argument with reference to three courses which encourage academics and students to reflect on their practices and experiences as teachers and learners. They hint at resistance to discomforting pedagogies (something that Zembylas 2017 also discusses) and illustrate the difficulties of promoting progressive policies.

Woodcock and Hardy draw on Fraser to develop our understandings of inclusion. Drawing on research with Canadian elementary and high school teachers they note that teachers have often changing and contradictory ways of understanding inclusion. However, Fraser's dimensions of redistribution, recognition and representation can offer clarity through their insightful focus on 'the very social fabric that underpins current discriminatory practices' (p. 76). Woodcock and Hardy argue further that in education there has been a privileging of inclusion as focusing on special education needs and that Fraser's work allows us to see the 'significance of issues of disputation and power – politics – in relation to conceptualizing "inclusion"' (p. 73). They found that their teacher respondents paid little attention to the significance of distributive issues in relation to inclusion and that their focus on recognition tended to assume and reify particular characteristics of group identity, which led to instances of misrecognition. However, the teachers placed a relatively strong focus on issues of representation (p. 84). Woodcock and Hardy conclude by arguing that inclusive practices need to challenge status subordination and that Fraser's work is helpful to understand the importance of 'establishing the circumstances for people to be adequately resourced, recognised, and represented in learning [that] constitutes an alternative politics to [status] subordination' (p. 88).

Sally Power and Daniel Frandji's paper interrogates the role of published school performance ratings ('league tables') as a form of cultural injustice. They argue that schools that do poorly in league tables suffer from all three forms of Fraser's misrecognition – cultural domination, non-recognition and disrespect (Power and Frandji p. 94) – and discuss the possibility for a 'new politics of recognition' (p. 95) through using 'value-added' measurements. But this is far from a complete solution. As they note, a focus on school effectiveness can displace a politics of redistribution, and celebrating the relative success of disadvantaged children as exceptional can serve to make their educational inferiority appear the norm. Following Fraser, Power and Frandji argue that these issues arise when a 'cultural injustice of misrecognition' is divorced from an 'economic injustice of maldistribution' (p. 100).

Martin Mills and colleagues in their research on alternative education provision in Australia argue that Fraser's focus on recognition, redistribution and representation overlooks other important dimensions. Taking up Fraser's argument that all aspects of justice have to be attended to, i.e., to achieve 'parity of participation', they identify two more dimensions drawing on the work of Lynch and Sayer, respectively: affective and contributive justice. They conclude that affective justice (the quality of relationships, care and support) was of prime concern to teachers in the alternative settings studied and is crucial to student success. However, they also argue that these students are often presented with restrictive curricula that risk 'condemning [young people] to a lifetime of political and social marginalisation' (p. 115), rather than the opportunities for meaningful learning that would demonstrate a commitment to contributive justice. They end with a call for greater attention to be paid in *mainstream* settings to Fraser's three dimensions of justice as well as affective and contributive justice, as this could prevent some students' trajectories to alternative provision.

David Block takes up Fraser's more recent writing on progressive neoliberalism and ties this back to Fraser's earlier work on recognition and redistribution. He notes Fraser as presenting mainstream campaigns for the rights of women, minority ethnic groups and LGBTQ movements as having nothing to say on the political economy and the damage wreaked by neoliberalism, and therefore as 'enter[ing] into a unacknowledged, though significant, collusion with the current economic status quo' (p. 120). Block applies these arguments to research in translanguaging (how users move between and draw upon different linguistic resources to make meaning). He argues that translanguaging scholars often propose social and cultural solutions to address 'ethno-linguistic racism' but ignore the economic underpinning of language marginalisation. Block concludes therefore that working through education exclusively is a 'weak pillar on which most critical education stands', arguing that deep economic restructuring is also required (p. 136).

On this point, **Pauline Lipman** in her discussion of reforms to the schooling and housing policies in Chicago, USA, presents an example of what Fraser more recently called 'progressive neoliberalism'. Lipman problematises the way in which national and local housing and education policies in the first decade of this century proposed to reduce poverty and raise the educational performance of low-income students and families through creating mixed income communities and schools. Cities, she notes, are crucial sites for the articulation of neoliberal initiatives, presented, in this case, as progressive moves to create better conditions for low-income families – 'race and class uplift' (p. 149) – social class integration and greater social cohesion. The 'seemingly democratic and inclusive discourse'

(p. 145) of mixed income strategies, however, does not address the 'root causes of poverty and unequal opportunities to learn' (p. 141). Instead 'behaviour modification' (p. 149) rather than economic redistribution seems to be the goal. Furthermore, the policies for gentrification and new schools did not allow space for the representation of those affected, and ignored 'the power of marginalized communities to define their own needs' (p. 151).

Jessica Gerrard's critical consideration of both neoliberalism and 'the public' (as in public education) is very much in the spirit of Nancy Fraser's work. She starts by discussing the importance of 'the public' school invoked as a rallying cry to critics of neoliberalism wanting to 'claim…a purpose for education that extends beyond capital' (p. 157). She continues by making two main points: first is that some features of neoliberalism are not just a 'contemporary particularity' (p. 161), a point visible through the lens a longer historical perspective. Developing workers, for example, is a long-established concern of state education. Without these perspectives, 'long-held tensions between the instantiation of public state education and private and market interests' are obscured (p. 161). Her second point is that public education is often assumed to be an education for the 'common good' which is a 'contentious…slippery and indeterminate' concept (p. 163), here she uses Fraser's arguments that the so-called 'mainstream public sphere' was often exclusive and lacking in accountability. The task now is to 'wrestle public education' (p. 167) away from the confines of contemporary politics which understands what is possible only in the register of neoliberalism.

Dorothee Holscher's paper details the workings out of an offer by a South African church to shelter a group of refugees following violent pogroms. Her focus is on social work, not education. However, her account raises a key issue for the provision of public services, such as education, in our contemporary times: how we conceive social justice in relation to those caught up in global population mobilities. Holscher uses Fraser's concept of misframing, arguing that this is a particularly stark issue for refugees and migrants, who remain outside membership of a community and are therefore denied its benefits whilst their legal status is considered by a state bureaucracy that is often hostile to them. Thus, the refugees experienced structural violence at the hands of the South African government as well as the interpersonal violence which led them to seek shelter in the church. Holscher identifies the relationship between misframing and other injustices:

> Through misframing, a situation of voicelessness had been created among the refugees concerned vis-à-vis South African citizens and institutions of the South African state. This voicelessness then filtered out to justify, deepen and reproduce other substantive injustices, namely maldistribution and misrecognition, thus undermining the church's initial attempts of engaging in transformative framing practices, and illuminating pertinent aspects of the vicious circularity of social injustice. (p. 178)

In England, examples of structural violence to refugees and migrants include the creation by the state of a 'hostile environment', leaving families existing in limbo with no access to benefits and not allowed to work whilst their immigration status is in doubt. The work of one London primary school helping such families was highlighted recently (Elgot 2017). A case of interpersonal violence also hit the headlines recently with the prolonged bullying of Syrian refugee children at a school in Huddersfield in the north of England. In the first example, the primary school is proactively trying to address the effects of misframing. In the second, the school staff allegedly did little to halt the attacks (Parveen 2018). Relevant here is Holscher's considerations of the role of bystanders faced with situations of misframing. What part should professionals and others who are not excluded play? Holscher warns against expecting practitioners to 'solve' complex and intractable situations, suggesting that they aim to produce 'enclaves of just practice' (p. 185). She notes how some church members were themselves complicit in misframing and lacked awareness of the political dimensions of the problem. She concludes that the concept of misframing allows us to understand the 'multiple and intersecting exclusionary processes experienced by refugees participants' (ibid) and provides a conceptual framework in which 'the more substantive injustices of maldistribution and misrecognition occur' (ibid).

Thus, Holscher and the other contributors here identify the scope of Fraser's key contributions: that is, an understanding of different dimensions of social justice as intersecting, accompanied by a willingness to analytically disentangle them in order to clarify and challenge injustices, whilst simultaneously maintaining a recognition that as economic and political circumstances change, so will the differing manifestations of injustice. This approach provides fertile ground for education researchers to work with Nancy Fraser's comprehensive and insightful theorising.

Note

1. Since 2014, teachers in England (but not the other countries of the UK) have been required to promote the 'fundamental British values' which the government defines as democracy, the rule of law, individual liberty, mutual respect and tolerance of those with different faiths and beliefs. Schools are inspected on this promotion by the national school's inspectorate, Ofsted.

References

Bernstein, R. (2017) From Socialist Feminism to the Critique of Global Capitalism, in Bargu, B. and Bottici, C. (eds.), *Feminism, Capitalism, and Critique: Essays in Honor of Nancy Fraser.* Springer.

Blackmore, J. (2016) *Educational Leadership and Nancy Fraser.* London, Routledge.

Boler, M., and Zembylas, M. (2003) Discomforting Truths: The Emotional Terrain of Understanding Difference, in P. Trifonas (ed.), *Pedagogies of Difference: Rethinking Education for Social Change.* Falmer, Routledge, pp. 110–136.

Dahl, H.M., Stoltz, P., and Willig, R. (2004) Recognition, Redistribution and Representation in Capitalist Global Society: An Interview with Nancy Fraser. *Acta Sociologica,* 47, 4: 374–382.

Ehrenreich, B., and Hochschild, A. (eds.). (2003) *Global Woman: Nannies, Maids, and Sex Workers in the New Economy.* London, Granta Books.

Elgot, J. (2017) 'It's like family to me': The School Feeding Its Poorest Families. *The Guardian,* 26 December.

Fraser, N. (1990) Rethinking the Public Sphere: A Contribution to the Critique of Actually Existing Democracy. *Social Text,* 25/26: 56–80.

Fraser, N. (1995) Debate: Recognition or Redistribution? A Critical Reading of Iris Young's Justice and the Politics of Difference. *Journal of Political Philosophy,* 3, 2: 166–180.

Fraser, N. (1998) Social Justice in the Age of Identity Politics: Redistribution, Recognition, Participation, WZB Discussion Paper, No. FS I 98–108, Wissenschaftszentrum Berlin für Sozialforschung (WZB), Berlin.

Fraser, N. (2007) Identity, Exclusion, and Critique: A Response to Four Critics. *European Journal of Political Theory,* 6, 3: 305–338.

Fraser, N. (2016a) Contradictions of Capital and Care. *New Left Review,* 100: 99–117.

Fraser, N. (2016b) Expropriation and Exploitation in Racialized Capitalism: A Reply to Michael Dawson. *Critical Historical Studies,* 3, 1: 163–178.

Fraser, N. (2016c). Progressive Neoliberalism versus Reactionary Populism: A Choice that Feminists Should Refuse. *NORA-Nordic Journal of Feminist and Gender Research*, 24, 4: 281–284.

Fraser, N., and Naples, N. (2004). To Interpret the World and to Change It: An Interview with Nancy Fraser. *Signs: Journal of Women in Culture and Society*, 29, 4: 1103–1124.

Fraser, N. (2017) From Progressive Neoliberalism to Trump – and Beyond. *American Affairs*, 1, 4: https://americanaffairsjournal.org/2017/11/progressive-neoliberalism-trump-beyond/

Fraser, N., and Jaeggi, R. (2018) *Capitalism: A Conversation in Critical Theory*. London, John Wiley & Sons.

Fraser, N., and Pettifor, A. (2018) Understanding Capitalism: Nancy Fraser in Conversation with Ann Pettifor. *IPPR Progressive Review*, 25, 2: 154–165.

Lara, M., and Fine, R. (2007) Justice and the Public Sphere: The Dynamics of Nancy Fraser's Critical Theory, in T. Lovell (ed.), *(Mis)recognition, Social Inequality and Social Justice: Nancy Fraser and Pierre Bourdieu*. London, Routledge.

Lawson, G. (2008) A Realistic Utopia? Nancy Fraser, Cosmopolitanism and the Making of a Just World Order. *Political Studies*, 56, 4: 881–906.

Lingard, B. (2018) Miseducation. *British Journal of Sociology of Education*, 39, 5: 723–728.

Lovell, T. (2007) Introduction, in T. Lovell (ed.), *(Mis)recognition, Social Inequality and Social Justice: Nancy Fraser and Pierre Bourdieu*. London, Routledge.

Mansbridge, J. (1990) *Beyond Self-Interest*. Chicago, University of Chicago Press.

Miller, D. (1995) *On Nationalism*. Oxford, Clarendon Press.

Parveen, N. (2018) Syrian Schoolboy 'suffered years of abuse' in Huddersfield School. *The Guardian*, 5 December.

Soutphommasane, T., (2012) *The Virtuous Citizen: Patriotism in a Multicultural Society*. Cambridge University Press.

Tamir, Y. (1993) *Liberal Nationalism*. Princeton, Princeton University Press.

Troyna, B., and Vincent, C. (1995) The Discourses of Social Justice in Education. *Discourse: Studies in the Cultural Politics of Education*, 16, 2: 149–166.

Vincent, C. (2000) *Including Parents?* Milton Keynes, Open University Press.

Vincent, C. (2019) *Tea and the Queen? British Values, Schools and Citizenship*. Bristol, Policy Press.

Young, I.-M. (1990) *Justice and the Politics of Difference*. Princeton, Princeton University Press.

Zaretsky, E. (2017) Nancy Fraser and the Left: A Searching Idea of Equality, in B. Bargu and C. Bottici (eds.), *Feminism, Capitalism, and Critique: Essays in Honor of Nancy Fraser*. Springer.

Zembylas, M. (2017) Wilful Ignorance and the Emotional Regime of Schools. *British Journal of Educational Studies*, 65, 4: 499–515.

Conceptualizing social justice in education: mapping the territory

Sharon Gewirtz

> Within recent studies of education policy, social justice has been an under-theorized concept. This paper is an attempt to begin to remedy this situation. It critically examines some of the most prominent ways in which social justice has been and is being thought about within various traditions of social theory and concludes by sketching out a framework for conceptualizing social justice in the context of education policy research. However, the main purpose of the paper is not to provide a definitive conceptualization of social justice but to open up a debate which might usefully inform the work of the education policy research community.

Introduction

Within recent studies of education policy, social justice has been an under-theorized concept. Some work simply marginalizes or rejects social justice concerns, either because of a sceptical postmodernist denial of the tenability and desirability of universalistic principles, or because of an uncritical, problem-solving orientation, or because of a commitment to 'value-free' research. However, there is also a significant group of writers who are unambiguously committed to social justice in education, as evidenced in the growing number of empirical studies which draw attention to the ways in which inequalities are produced and reproduced by post-welfarist education policies. But within this work there is very little *explicit* discussion of what social justice means or ought to mean. This paper represents an attempt to begin to remedy this situation. Its central purpose is not to come up with a definitive conceptualization of social justice in education, but to start to map the territory in order to initiate a productive debate which might usefully inform the work of the education policy research community.

However, whilst not claiming to arrive at a definitive conceptualization, I do want to advocate the relevance for education policy of a particular approach to social justice. This is the model propounded by the socialist feminist theorist, Iris Young. In *Justice and the Politics of Difference,* Young (1990) argues for an extension of the boundaries of what is usually thought of as social justice. She suggests that social justice should not be used exclusively in the narrow conventional sense of referring to the way in which goods are distributed in society but should be expanded to include 'all aspects of institutional rules and relations insofar as they are subject to potential collective action' (Young 1990: 16). Young's approach to justice rests on a conceptualization of *injustice* based on a detailed explication of 'five faces of oppression': exploitation, marginalization, powerlessness, cultural imperialism and violence. She argues that 'Distributive injustices may contribute to and result from these forms of oppression, but none is reducible to distribution and all involve social structures and relations beyond distribution' (Young 1990: 9). I do not have the space in this paper for a detailed exposition of Young's approach to justice. Rather what I want to do is demonstrate the value of her conceptualization by doing two things. First, I will outline a variety of other approaches to conceptualizing social justice which emphasize important aspects of justice but which ultimately are partial and limited; and I will argue that Young's more complex and multi-dimensional approach acknowledges and incorporates the strengths of these other conceptualizations whilst avoiding their limitations. Second, I will confront some of the challenging criticisms of Young's model mounted by Nancy Fraser (1997). I will argue that whilst some of Fraser's arguments necessitate an elaboration of certain aspects of Young's conceptualization, they do not succeed in undermining its validity as a whole.

I will begin by outlining what I see as the two major dimensions of an expanded conceptualization of social justice – the *distributional* and *relational* dimensions – and by justifying my advocacy of this two-fold categorization. In the following two sections I will provide some examples of the different kinds of conceptualization which fall within each category, drawing attention to some of their strengths and limitations. I will then outline Iris Young's approach to combining the distributional and relational dimensions of social justice into a single framework, before going on to examine some of the criticisms which have been levelled at her work by Nancy Fraser. In the final section, I will draw on insights derived from the earlier discussion to sketch out how education policy research might pursue a social justice agenda rooted in a 'thick' and sophisticated conceptualization of social justice.

Two dimensions of justice

The first dimension, *distributional* justice, refers to the principles by which goods are distributed in society. This is the conventional conception of social justice, classically defined by Rawls (1972: 7) as follows:

> the subject matter of justice is the basic structure of society, or more exactly, the way in which the major social institutions... distribute fundamental rights and duties and determine the distribution of advantages from social co-operation.

For Rawls, the concept of justice refers to 'a proper balance between competing claims'. Although I am referring to distributional justice as *only one dimension* of justice, distributional justice is commonly thought of as *synonymous with* social justice. A society perceived to be just clearly cannot exist without a fair distribution of resources, both material and non-material. Therefore, as researchers concerned about social justice, we need to be clear about the principles which currently govern the distribution of goods in society, and we also need to be clear about our own beliefs about what ought to constitute fairness. However, as Young (1990) has so convincingly argued, to 'read' social justice as being *exclusively* about distribution is severely limiting and it is important that we conceptualize social justice in a broader way. I want to argue that what we include under the umbrella of justice be expanded to include another dimension, which I refer to as a relational justice.

The *relational* dimension refers to the nature of the relationships which structure society. A focus on this second dimension helps us to theorize about issues of power and how we treat each other, both in the sense of micro face-to-face interactions and in the sense of macro social and economic relations which are mediated by institutions such as the state and the market. For Rawls, justice is about the distribution of rights, duties and the social and economic goods accruing from social cooperation. It does not appear to be about the *form* of social cooperation itself. Relational conceptions of social justice do, however, focus on the form of social cooperation. These conceptions refer to the political/relational system within which the distribution of social and economic goods, rights and responsibilities takes place. In one sense this arena can be conceived of as another dimension of distributive justice in that, in part, it refers to the way in which relations of power are distributed in society. But it is not just about the *distribution* of power relations, nor is it just about the *procedures* by which goods are distributed in society (commonly referred to as *procedural* justice). Relational justice might *include* procedural justice, but it is about more than this. It is about the *nature* and *ordering* of social relations, the formal and informal rules which govern how members of society treat each other both on a macro level and at a micro interpersonal level. Thus it refers to the practices and procedures which govern the organization of political systems, economic and social institutions, families and one-to-one social relationships. These things cannot unproblematically be conceptually reduced to matters of distribution. The relational dimension incorporates what Fraser (1997) refers to as cultural justice, examples of which would be cultural autonomy, recognition and respect. But it is a much broader category. It also includes aspects of what Fraser calls economic justice, examples of which would be the reorganization of the division of labour and subjecting investment to democratic decision making (Fraser 1997: 15).

One way of distinguishing between the distributional and relational dimensions is by thinking of them as rooted within two contrasting ontological perspectives. The distributional dimension is essentially individualistic and atomistic, in that it refers to how goods are distributed to individuals in society. In Miller's well-known formulation it means 'ensuring everyone receives their due' (Miller 1976: 20). By contrast, the relational dimension is holistic and non-atomistic, being essentially concerned with the nature of interconnections between individuals in society, rather than with how much individuals get.

As I have already noted and as will become more apparent, the two dimensions are intimately connected and the distinction is in some senses somewhat blurred. Conceptualizations which I categorize as being essentially distributional clearly imply particular relational characteristics. And similarly, conceptualizations I ascribe to the relational dimension can be thought of as having a distributional component. It could be argued that in separating out social justice into these two dimensions I am creating a false distinction. Such an argument would go something along these lines:

> Social justice is about the distribution of goods. Whilst goods are more usually narrowly conceived as referring to material things, the definition of goods can and has been extended, as it was by Rawls, to include non-tangible things, for example particular forms of relationships. If relationships are goods, then the distinction disintegrates.

Whilst this argument might be logical, I would nevertheless argue that it is extremely worthwhile to think about the two dimensions as separate, albeit strongly connected. If we were to prioritize matters of distribution and treat relationships as merely goods to be distributed then we may neglect proper consideration of the nature of those relational goods which are to be distributed. By isolating relational justice as a separate dimension we are forced to think in greater depth about the nature of the relationships which structure society. For example, concepts like respect and dignity cannot be viewed unproblematically as goods to be distributed. A focus on relational justice can force us to think carefully and systematically about what treating each other with respect and conferring dignity on others actually means in different contexts.[1] In addition, as Fraser's work demonstrates, such a distinction enables us to examine conflicts which can arise when a politics of redistribution and recognition are pursued at the same time (see below).

I now want to look at some of the key ways in which distributive justice has been conceptualized, before turning to the relational dimension.

Distributive justice

Dominant notions of distributive justice have tended to fall within two categories. There is the traditional 'weak' liberal definition of justice as *equality of opportunity* and the more radical 'strong' liberal version of justice as *equality of outcome*. The equality of opportunity conceptualization is neatly summarized by Kathleen Lynch (1995: 11) as follows: 'Unequal results are justified if everyone has an equal opportunity to succeed'. There are competing conceptions within the liberal tradition of the precise conditions which need to be met for equality of opportunity to exist. But usually equality of opportunity is viewed as being dependent upon the existence of equal formal rights, equality of access and equality of participation. Equality of outcome differs from equality of opportunity in that it seeks to ensure equal rates of success for different groups in society through direct intervention to prevent disadvantage, for example via positive discrimination or affirmative action programmes.

Both of these liberal conceptions of social justice are limited, however, to the extent that they do not confront what Lynch (1995: 24) refers to as 'the fundamental problems of hierarchies of power, wealth and other privileges':

> The fact remains that in a highly unequal society, someone has to occupy the subordinate positions even if the identity of those occupying them may change from white to black, from citizens to migrant workers. (Lynch 1995: 12, 14)

It is in response to the limitations of liberal conceptualizations of equality that Lynch proposes a further 'equality objective' which she refers to as *equality of condition*:

> If equality of condition were adopted as an objective, it would involve the development of an egalitarian society which would be committed to equality in the living conditions of all members of society (both citizens and non-citizens) taking due account of their heterogeneity be it arising from gender, ethnicity, disability, religion, age, sexual orientation or any other attribute. It would not simply be concerned with equalising the position (access, participation and outcome) of marginalised groups at each level within the hierarchies of wealth, power and privilege. Rather, it would involve the equalisation of wealth, power and privilege. It would mean having substantial equality in working conditions, job satisfaction and income across different occupations; an educational system devoted to developing equally the potentials of every member of society; a radically democratic politics which aimed at the equal participation and influence of all citizens; and a restructuring of family and personal life for the sake of enriching the personal relationships of every individual (Lynch 1995: 24–25).

One of the attractions of Lynch's 'equality of condition objective' is that it encompasses both distributional and relational dimensions of social justice and therefore offers a more holistic conceptualization than the narrower, more atomistic liberal conceptions. It is a conceptualization which is complemented and extended by Young's formulation – *justice as freedom from oppressive relations* – which I discuss below. But first, I want to identify a number of conceptualizations which are more firmly (if still ambiguously) rooted within the relational dimension.

Relational justice

Currently vogue relational conceptualizations of justice *are justice as mutuality* and *justice as recognition*. I want to start by outlining two versions of justice as mutuality – one neo-Fabian, the other postmodernist.

Neo-Fabian versions of mutuality

Now extremely influential in mainstream social policy discourse is Etzioni's notion of communitarianism, the idea that a good society is one in which there is an ethic of mutuality in which citizens are bound together through a system of duties and obligations. For Etzioni (1996) communitarianism is concerned with achieving a balance between centrifugal forces drawing individuals towards autonomy with centripetal forces drawing them towards the collectivity. Etzioni argues that a lack of equilibrium between the two forces will either threaten the common good, through too much emphasis on the individual, or threaten autonomy, through too much emphasis on social duties. Communitarianism, according to Etzioni, operates at the midpoint between the anarchy of excessive individualism and the collectivism of excessive order.

Strongly linked to ideas of communitarianism are discourses of citizenship, stakeholding, inclusivity and social capital. I do not have the space here to discuss all of these narratives of mutuality. Instead, in order to provide a sense of neo-Fabian conceptions of mutuality, I will focus on some of the recommendations of the Commission on Social Justice (CSJ),[2] whose report (CSJ 1994) drew heavily on a selection of these narratives. For example, Putnamm's (1993) notion of social capital is taken on board by the CSJ and summarized as follows:

> Social capital consists of the institutions and relationships of a thriving civil society – from networks of neighbourhoods to extended families, community groups to religious organisations, local businesses to local public services, youth clubs to parent–teacher associations, playgroups to police on the beat. Where you live, who else lives there and how they live their lives – cooperatively or selfishly, responsibly or destructively – can be as important as personal resources in determining life chances... The moral and social reconstruction of our society depends on our willingness to invest in social capital. We badly need to mend a social fabric that is so obviously torn apart. (CSJ 1994: 308–9)

For the CSJ, investment in social capital is partly about redistribution of resources to ensure, for example, that children do not grow up in poverty. It is also about the redistribution of responsibilities, obligations or duties around, for example, childrearing. But it is not just about redistribution. It is also about shifts in the nature of participation, it is about a restructuring of power relations in society.

Ideas of relational justice are manifested in a range of policy proposals put forward by the CSJ. For example, the CSJ advocates the setting up of a 'Citizens' Service':

> a new voluntary community service scheme reflects our ambition to create a 'something for something' society, rich in civic wealth and social capital, where rights are matched by responsibilities, where mutual respect and individual fulfilment proceed side by side, where independence and mutuality are not opposed but can be combined. (362)

The notion of a 'something for something society' owes much to Etzioni's belief that there is a moral deficit in society arising from an imbalance between rights and responsibilities.

For Etzioni, provisions are needed which will enable individuals to accept greater responsibility towards themselves and others as a way of recompensing the community for any excess of rights received. The same thinking underpins New Labour's Welfare-to-Work scheme, within which the right of unemployed people to state benefits is to be counterbalanced by a duty to take up one of the offers provided by the state.

These versions of mutuality are essentially neo-Fabian and reformist. They differ from traditional Fabianism in some respects in that they embody a degree of scepticism towards the paternalism of old-style Beveridgean welfare bureaucracies (CSJ 1994: 104–6). However, the discourses of inclusion and accountability are Fabian in the sense that they are about reimporting a social conscience into capitalism, curbing its worst excesses, without seeking to dismantle capitalist power structures.

Let me now turn, to a somewhat different approach to the concept of social justice as mutuality, that adopted within certain variants of postmodernist thought.

Postmodernist versions of mutuality

It is now commonplace to identify two broad types of postmodern thought – one sceptical, the other affirmative. Sceptical postmodernism – what Ebert (1991: 115) refers to as 'ludic postmodernism' – emphasizes 'fragmentation, disintegration, malaise, meaninglessness, a vagueness or even absence of moral parameters and social chaos' (Rosenau 1992: 15). It dismisses the notion of social and political projects on the basis of the belief that there is no truth and therefore 'all that is left is play, the play of words and meaning' (Rosenau 1992: 15). Sceptical postmodernists can be contrasted with 'affirmative' or 'resistance' post-modernists (Ebert 1991) who are open to positive political or social action.

Affirmative postmodernist versions of mutuality arise from attempts to over come the fragmentation, disintegration and chaos which are emphasised by the sceptics. The challenge is how to balance two apparently oppositional moral obligations – difference and solidarity – to construct a politics

> which works with and through difference, which is able to build those forms of solidarity and identification which make common struggle and resistance possible but without suppressing the real heterogeneity of interests and identities. (Hall 1988: 28)

Peter Leonard (1997: 158) neatly summarizes the difficulties involved. He argues that exclusivity may blind the new social movements

> to the possibilities of wider solidarities. At the same time, exclusivity may lead to a demand for conformity within the identity group, thus reproducing the very mechanism of singular and stereotypical identity formation which social movements are, at another level, committed to opposing. The consequences of an identity politics which fails to acknowledge the wider discourses and structures of oppression and their impact on large populations is a fragmentation of opposition. Although emphasis on the local community and the diverse claims to welfare of different groups is a strength in terms of its recognition of diversity and the importance of democratic control of welfare initiatives at the base, its limitations are also clear. Emphasis on difference may be utilized by the state as a relatively safe, money-saving rationale for concentrating small-scale *adjustments among* competing social groups (micro redistributions of resources) resulting in the fragmentation of populations into ever-smaller communities of interest. Collective resistance may thereby be dispersed and weakened and the possibilities of constructing solidarities diminished.

Leonard (1997: 165) attempts to resolve the tension between solidarity and difference in relation to the field of welfare practice by drawing on the work of socialist feminists to argue that whilst it is vital to recognize difference it is important also to recognize that there is a degree of similarity in people's experiences which may be rooted in common experiences of class, gender and 'race'. He suggests that an emphasis on 'commonality, solidarity and interdependence' may enable subjects to participate in collective resistance in pursuit of claims for welfare. More specifically, Leonard proposes 'a discourse on interdependence' which is opposed both to the atomism implicit in the extreme relativism of sceptical postmodernism and the atomism explicit in neo-liberal discourses:

> A concept of mutually interdependent subjects... is crucial to a politics of collective resistance and, in particular, community action. The point is to extend the actual experience and realization of interdependence beyond the boundaries of a politics of particular identities, 'imagined communities' or single-issue social movements. Only by such an extension to include, at least potentially, all the communities and social identities that experience the present social order as domination, is postmodern particularist politics likely to have any possibility of rectifying its present weakness – its inability to challenge the politics, economic priorities and mass culture of late capitalism. (1997: 158–9)

What is the difference between this and the ethic of mutuality proposed by neo Fabians? The distinction is unclear in Leonard's version which talks in vague terms about challenging the politics, economic priorities and mass culture of late capitalism. Neo-Fabian communitarians might well be committed to challenging the same things. However, whilst the neo-Fabian version supports capitalism and celebrates alliances between the dominant and the dominated, the postmodern version seeks to solidify an alliance of 'otherness' which could, possibly, challenge the political and economic structures of late capitalism, rather than seek to curb their worst excesses.

What postmodernist versions of relational justice fail to do is to specify in any developed sense the *particular* conceptions of social justice which need to inform collective resistance to the dominations experienced by various groups of marginalized others. Leonard identifies some potential targets of that resistance, namely the disciplinary power of professionals, the commodification of culture and the manufacture of desire, and the economic discourse of global market necessity. But he does not identify precisely what conceptions of social justice underpin his choice of targets. Young's more sophisticated conceptualization of justice – *justice as freedom from oppressions* – which could help inform collective political action is outlined below. But first, let us turn to another postmodernist conceptualization – *justice as recognition*.

Justice as recognition

This conception of relational social justice, which is strongly linked to postmodernist notions of mutuality, arises from feminist insights taken on board by affirmative postmodernists in their attempts to reconcile 'the ethical paradox of postmodernity' (Bauman 1992): 'how can we act ethically (according to some notion of the Good) in any collective way if we have already abandoned a belief in universal moral rules? (Leonard 1997: 149). The answer lies in a *politics of recognition* (Fraser 1997), an *openness to unassimilated otherness* (Young 1990) or what Leonard calls *an ethics of otherness.* What is being challenged is what Hewitt (1997) refers to as the *transcendent universalist* assumptions which underpinned the expansion of state welfare provision in the Keynesian era. Transcendent universalism

> applies principles of equality, rights and justice to individuals, treating their needs as commensurable and providing social provisions characterised by their sameness. Transcendent universalism thereby cuts through individual and social differences. (Hewitt 1997: 1)

This is rejected by feminists and affirmative postmodernists in favour of an *immanent universalism* 'arising from the struggle for recognition between individuals who differ by gender, race, class or life-style – differences producing concrete subjects with real needs' (Hewitt 1997: 2). It 'entails being able to perceive commonality through difference' (Benjamin 1990: 171).

A politics of recognition or an ethics of otherness involves not only a commitment to respond to others and otherness but also a commitment to avoiding practising the power of surveillance, control and discipline upon others. Drawing on a Foucauldian critique of power as exercised by professional experts, it attempts to identify an alternative stance that, for example, education or welfare professionals can take up which is resistant to surveilling and disciplining others. Practically, according to Leonard (1997: 152–3), this entails listening before we act, and he gives the example of the response of white people to the plight of Aboriginal peoples:

> When we face the enormity of the cultural losses experienced by many Aboriginal peoples at the hands of the state health, welfare and education services, we may feel compelled to act, to put things right again in their interests. But we are told to listen first, to glimpse the overwhelming pain which cultural loss brings and to remember that it was the modern responsibility to act which led to the cultural losses in the first place. We may act if the Other wishes us to, and on their terms, but only after reflection, trying to relax the imperative to organize and classify with our plans and projects.

This ethic of otherness has implications for the micro practices of welfare work. Rather than the welfare professional surveilling, controlling and disciplining their clients, what is proposed – and practised by some feminist counsellors and therapists – is the

> co-authorship of a joint narrative about problems, needs and claims. Because every narrative (of the professional as well as the client) is open to interpretation, we are speaking here of efforts to establish a dialogue of the interpretations of narratives where recognition of the diversity of subjects is established as a priority. (Leonard 1997: 164).

Justice as recognition is valuable because it can inform more socially just micro practices of welfare. It can also contribute to the building of an immanent universality – a 'universality in the sense of the participation and inclusion of everyone in moral and social life' which does not leave 'behind particular affiliations, feelings, commitments, and desires' (Young 1990: 105). However, like postmodern versions of justice as mutuality, it does not provide a sufficient conceptual basis for a politics of collective resistance. I now want to turn to a conceptualization of social justice which builds on postmodern insights around mutuality and recognition but which, I would suggest, can more usefully inform anti-oppressive political and social activities.

Justice as freedom from oppressive relations

It could be argued that one of the key limitations of the neo-Fabian conception of mutuality is that, by attempting to promote a coincidence of interests between capitalists and other citizens, it ignores the injustices inherent within capitalism; for, however benevolent capitalists are and however heightened their sense of social conscience, capitalism will always entail essentially exploitative practices. The postmodernist conceptions of relational justice identified above – mutuality and recognition – also fail to properly address capitalist structures of oppression. This is, at least in part, because they tend to focus on the level of 'unmediated face-to-face relations'. Harvey (1993: 106) explains why this is a problem:

> In modern mass urban society, the multiple mediated relations which constitute that society across time and space are just as important and as 'authentic' as unmediated face-to-face relations. It is just as important for a politically responsible person to know about and respond politically to all those people who daily put breakfast on our table, even though market exchange hides from us the conditions of life of the producers... Relationships between individuals get mediated through market functions and state powers, and we have to define conceptions of social justice capable of operating across and through these multiple mediations. But this is a realm of politics which postmodernism typically avoids.

A discourse of interdependence, an ethic of otherness, and a politics of recognition are all important in so far as they provide an ethical and practical basis for relationships marked by a celebration and respect of difference and mutuality. These things are also valuable politically to the extent that they may help produce a sense of collective resistance to domination of various kinds. They are however also *limited* politically because they are not conceptions of social justice which can usefully inform the *direction* and *content* of collective action. A more useful conceptualization in this sense is provided by Iris Young who identifies 'five faces of oppression', summarized by Harvey as follows:

> *exploitation* (the transfer of the fruits of the labor from one group to another, as, for example, in the cases of workers giving up surplus value to capitalists or women in the domestic sphere transferring the fruits of their labor to men), *marginalization* (the expulsion of people from useful participation in social life so that they are 'potentially subjected to severe material deprivation and even extermination'), *powerlessness* (the lack ofthat 'authority, status, and sense of self ' which would permit a person to be listened to with respect), *cultural imperialism* (stereotyping in behaviours as well as in various forms of cultural expression such that 'the oppressed group's own experience and interpretation of social life finds little expression that touches the dominant culture, while that same culture imposes on the oppressed group its experience and interpretation of social life'); and *violence* (the fear and actuality of random, unprovoked attacks, which have 'no motive except to damage, humiliate, or destroy the person') (Harvey 1993: 106–7, citing Young 1990).

Young's multi-dimensional conception, I would suggest, represents a rich and holistic fusion of the distributional and relational dimensions of social justice. Although Young explicitly criticises the distributive paradigm of justice, her framework incorporates aspects of liberal notions of distributional justice through the identification of marginalization, powerlessness and violence as modes of oppression, for it is these things which constitute the barriers to the equality of opportunity advocated by liberals. It also incorporates postmodernist conceptualizations of mutuality and recognition by identifying cultural imperialism, alongside marginalization, powerlessness and violence as modes of oppression. But Young's conceptualization, by identifying exploitation as a face of oppression, also addresses the limitations of liberal and postmodern conceptualizations. It seems to me, that because it is rooted in a political-economic analysis of social life, it constitutes a more useful underpinning to political action than the other conceptions I have identified. It focuses on the 'multiple mediated relations' of mass urban society as well as upon unmediated face-to-face relations and thereby specifically can help inform identification of the necessary targets of any collective political action, whilst not losing sight of the importance of mutuality and recognition. As Harvey (1993: 107) notes, it is also useful because it

> emphasises the heterogeneity of experience of injustice – someone unjustly treated in the workplace can act oppressively in the domestic sphere and the victim ofthat may, in turn, resort to cultural imperialism against others.

Young's attempt to integrate the distributional and relational dimensions of justice is not however universally acclaimed. In the next section I want to look critically at some of the objections raised by one of Young's main critics, Nancy Fraser. The relative detail in which I focus on the Young–Fraser debate reflects both the complexity of the arguments and the importance of the contribution made by Young *and* Fraser to understandings of the nature of the relationship between conceptualizations of social justice and political and social action.

The redistribution–recognition dilemma: Fraser's critique of Young

Fraser (1997: 16) takes Young to task for not recognizing the 'redistribution–recognition dilemma' which she explains as follows:

> Recognition claims often take the form of calling attention to, if not performatively creating, the putative specificity of some group and then of affirming its value. Thus, they tend to promote group differentiation. Redistribution claims, in contrast, often call for abolishing economic arrangements that underpin group specificity. (An example would be feminist demands to abolish the gender division of labor.) Thus, they tend to promote group dedifferentiation. The upshot is that the politics of recognition and the politics of redistribution often appear to have mutually contradictory aims. Whereas the first tends to promote group differentiation, the second tends to undermine it. Thus, the two kinds of claim stand in tension with each other.

Fraser objects to what she sees as the way Young lumps all modes of collectivity into one category – the social group – which consists of 'a collective of persons differentiated from at least one other group by cultural forms, practices or ways of life'. Fraser believes that this definition blurs two distinct kinds of groups which she refers to as 'culture-based groups' and 'political-economy-based groups'. According to Fraser, culture-based groups are rooted in a culture alone, and 'the best familiar model' for this kind of group is the ethnic group. Political-economy-based groups on the other hand are rooted in political economy and the best model for this kind of group is class. Fraser (1997: 196) argues that in Young's work, the ethnic group is implicitly and inappropriately used as the paradigm for all social collectivities and that this has 'unfortunate political consequences':

> The politics of difference embraced by Young is a vision of emancipation especially suited to the situation of ethnic groups. Where the differences in question are those of ethnic cultures, it is *prima facie* plausible to consider that justice would be served by affirming them and thereby fostering cultural diversity. Where, in contrast, cultural differences are linked to differentially desirable locations in the political economy, a politics of difference may be misplaced. There justice may require precisely undermining group differentiation by, for example, restructuring the division of labor. In that case, redistribution could obviate the need for recognition.

Fraser goes on to argue that Young's account of cultural imperialism contains an implicit bi-partism because some modes of cultural imperialism are culturally rooted whilst others are economically rooted. Fraser believes that different solutions are necessary for the different types of imperialism. In the case of culturally-rooted cultural imperialism, 'affirmation of cultural difference is a plausible remedy for oppression'. In the case of economically-rooted cultural imperialism, however, political-economic restructuring is necessary. 'In that case, consequently, the politics of difference could be counterproductive because it tends to preserve those group differences that redistribution could very well undermine. Recognition, in sum, could work against redistribution' (Fraser 1997: 199–200).

To support her argument that Young's politics of difference 'may be less globally applicable than Young thinks', Fraser considers what she refers to as 'some real-world applications that concern different cases of oppressed groups'. First, she takes the case of working-class nonprofessionals, arguing that this is an affinity group based on the shared experience of powerlessness and non-respectability and that this group would not survive as a group if its economic oppression were solved by redistribution:

> Suppose, for example, that the division of labor between task-defining work and task-executing work were abolished. In that case, all jobs would encompass both sorts of work, and the class division between professionals and non-professionals would be abolished. Cultural affinities that differentiate professionals from non-professionals would probably wither away as well, since they appear to have no other basis of existence. Thus, a politics of redistribution that successfully combated the political-economic oppression of powerlessness would effectively destroy this group as a group... The politics of difference, in contrast, would not foster the overcoming of oppression in this case. On the contrary, by entrenching the very specificities that redistribution would eliminate, it would work against the overcoming of oppression. (Fraser 1997: 200–1)

In the case of gays and lesbians, by contrast, 'the politics of difference is absolutely crucial for remedying oppression' (Fraser 1997: 202). This is because, Fraser argues, sexuality

> is a mode of social differentiation whose roots do not lie in the political economy because homosexuals are distributed throughout the entire class structure of capitalist society, occupy no distinctive position in the division of labor, and do not constitute an exploited class. Rather, their mode of collectivity is that of a despised sexuality, rooted in the cultural-valuational structure of society. From this perspective, the injustice they suffer is quintessentially a matter of recognition.

Between these two extremes of class and sexuality are 'the hardest cases' of gender and 'race'. Because oppression of these groups is 'complex', 'multiple' and 'multiply-rooted', redistribution *and* recognition are required remedies (Fraser 1997: 202).

In response to these tensions, Fraser develops two different, and I would argue conflicting, strategies aimed at 'softening' them in order to 'minimize conflicts between redistribution and recognition in cases where both must be pursued simultaneously' (Fraser 1997: 31). The first draws on a distinction between affirmative and transformative remedies to injustices. She defines these in the following way:

> By affirmative remedies for injustice I mean remedies aimed at correcting inequitable outcomes of social arrangements without disturbing the underlying framework that generates them. By transformative remedies, in contrast, I mean remedies aimed at correcting inequitable outcomes precisely by restructuring the underlying generative framework. (Fraser 1997: 23)

The distinction is applied both to economic (or distributional) and cultural (or recognitional) injustices. The affirmative remedy to economic injustice is represented in the policies of the liberal welfare state which seeks to 'redress end-state maldistribution, while leaving intact much of the underlying political-economic structure' (Fraser 1997: 24–5). The transformative remedy, in contrast, is historically associated with socialism, involving the restructuring of production relations 'to change the social division of labor and thus the conditions of existence for everyone' (Fraser 1994: 25). The affirmative solution to cultural injustice is the approach of what Fraser refers to as 'mainstream multiculturalism'. It is to counter cultural oppression by 'revaluing unjustly devalued group identities, while leaving intact both the contents of those identities and the group differentiations that underlie them'. The transformative solution, on the other hand, involves deconstructing identities 'by transforming the underlying cultural-valuational structure' and by 'destabilizing existing group identities and differentiations'. Her model for the transformative remedy to cultural injustice is queer politics:

> The point is not to dissolve all sexual difference in a single, universal human identity; it is, rather, to-sustain a sexual field of multiple, debinarized, fluid, ever-shifting differences. (Fraser 1997: 24).

Fraser concludes from her analysis of affirmative and transformative remedies that the best way to 'finesse' the redistribution–recognition dilemma is likely to be 'socialist economics combined with deconstructive cultural polities'. This differs from Young's position which seeks to combine socialist economics with the affirmation of cultural difference.

Fraser's second attempt at softening the redistribution–recognition dilemma is her 'critical theory of recognition' which distinguishes between four contrasting attitudes towards 'difference'. The first sees differences as artifacts of oppression and the proper response is to abolish them. The second sees differences as manifestations of cultural superiority. These differences, Fraser suggests, should not be celebrated as differences but should be extended to those who manifest inferior traits like competitiveness. The third views differences as simply variations which should neither be abolished nor extended but affirmed and valued (which is Young's position). The fourth attitude, and the one advocated by Fraser, is that there are different types of difference:

> Some differences are of type 1 and should be eliminated; others are of type 2 and should be universalized; still others are of type 3 and should be enjoyed. This position... militates against any politics of difference that is wholesale and undifferentiated. It entails a more differentiated politics of difference. (Fraser 1997: 204)

Fraser concludes that we should defend 'only those versions of the politics of difference that coherently synergize with the politics of redistribution' (Fraser 1997: 204).

So what should we make of Fraser's objections to Young? The most compelling and politically useful aspect of Fraser's contribution to the debate, as I see it, is her critical theory of recognition, for it is vital that we do not uncritically affirm and celebrate *all* expressions of difference. This is not simply because some expressions of difference are antagonistic to a politics of redistribution, but because some are oppressive in themselves (e.g. neo-Nazism). However, the critical theory of recognition does not undermine Young's freedom-from-oppressive-relations conceptualization of social justice, since that conceptualization is perfectly capable of accommodating 'a differentiated politics of difference'.

But, whilst Fraser's critical theory of recognition represents an important modification to Young's conceptualization, there are other aspects of Fraser's critique which are,

I would suggest, flawed and need to be rejected. Here I want to highlight what I see as the two central weakness of Fraser's critique. One is her caricatured portrayal of working-class culture. The other is her advocacy of cultural deconstruction.

As we have seen, Fraser's arguments are based on a bipolar categorization of oppression as either economically or culturally rooted. She acknowledges that 'in practice' cultural injustice and economic injustice 'are intertwined' but presents her two-fold categorization 'for analytical purposes'. This analytical distinction is useful in certain respects in that it highlights the way in which the celebration of *certain aspects* of cultural identity may interfere with strategies of redistribution. The problem arises when Fraser applies this analytical distinction to the 'real-world' which she appears to do inconsistently. Her account of women as an oppressed group is *relatively* nuanced (although nevertheless still over-simplified and inchoate) in so far as she argues that gender affinities are rooted in a diversity of bases including 'the division of labour', 'socialization' and 'culture'. However, her account of class oppression is much cruder. As we have seen, her contention is that the group affinities of working-class non-professionals are wholly rooted in political economy. This conclusion, it seems to me, is predicated on a reductionist, essentialist and static conception of class culture.[3]

The weakness in Fraser's economistic interpretation of class culture becomes apparent when one attempts to apply her analysis to the site of education. The logic of Fraser's argument is that the education system, teachers and schools should not celebrate or affirm working-class cultural affinities because this would interfere with a politics of redistribution. If working-class identities can really be reduced to a sense of powerlessness and non-respectability, as Fraser suggests, then indeed it would be inappropriate for curricula and pedagogies to affirm them. However, there are few who would accept this negative and narrow characterization of working-class cultural affinities, and there are clearly dimensions of working-class subjectivities which could be affirmed and celebrated without interfering with a politics of redistribution. One example would be the valuing of locality and friendship which underpins the orientation of many working-class families to school choice (Gewirtz *et al.* 1995). This is an aspect of working-class culture which is linked to the division of labour in at least two ways: at least in part, it is a response to the time and material poverty experienced by working-class families as a consequence of their positioning within the division of labour (most working-class parents are simply not able to transport their children to schools beyond the immediate locality); and, arguably, it is also based on the realistic view that for most working-class families, which school a child attends is not going to make an awful lot of difference to their future economic status. Yet the valuing of locality and friendship, whilst *in these respects* is clearly rooted in the political-economic structuring of society, is not something that one would particularly want to see abolished if the division of labour was abolished, nor is there any reason why these values should *have* to disappear. Locality and friendship are positive values which are worthy of celebration, and indeed they would be quite capable of surviving in the absence of capitalist political-economic structures. The lesson to be drawn from this example is that theorizing about social justice needs to be based on a more nuanced conceptualization of class culture. Some aspects of class cultural identities should be discouraged, others should be affirmed and celebrated, and others should be extended. In other words, Fraser's analysis appears to suffer because she fails to apply her own critical theory of recognition to working-class cultural affinities.

The other aspect of Fraser's critique I want to take issue with is her advocacy of cultural deconstruction or 'transformative recognition'. Not only does the strategy of cultural deconstruction seem *practically unrealistic,* it is also not clear that it is *necessary.* As I argued above, whilst affirmation of cultural differences may in some circumstances interfere with a politics of redistribution (as in the case of affirming a sense of working-class powerlessness and unrespectability) there is no reason to suppose that affirmative recognition will always conflict with redistribution (as indicated in the example of friendship and locality as values underpinning school choice for many working-class families). Furthermore, Fraser's advocacy of cultural deconstruction smacks of a form of the very cultural imperialism it is meant to undermine. Whilst, as Young (1990: 48) has pointed out '[i]n complex, highly differentiated societies like our own, all persons have multiple group identifications' and group differentiation is 'cross-cutting, fluid and shifting', some cultural groups, or individuals within them, may simply not wish to 'be weaned from their attachment to current cultural constructions of their interests and identities' (Fraser 1997: 31). One of the reasons why some may resist Fraser's preferred strategy is that, as Anne Phillips (1997: 152) has pointed out,

> it looks like an assimilationist project that ultimately expects all barriers and divisions to dissolve. The weight attached to transformation inevitably suggests a process of convergence between what are currently distinct values or identities, a cultural 'melting pot' out of which new – but then no longer 'cultural' – identities will be forged.[4]

So where does all this leave Young's freedom-from-oppressions conceptualization of social justice? It seems to me that Fraser's exposition of the redistribution-recognition dilemma leaves Young's conceptualization largely intact. I would want to elaborate the framework in only one respect in response to Fraser's objections. That is, in thinking about the third face of oppression, cultural imperialism and how we oppose it, we need to adopt what Fraser refers to as a more differentiated theory of difference. In other words we need to consider which aspects of difference ought to be abolished (either because they are themselves oppressive or because they interfere with redistribution), which should be affirmed and which universalized.

Conclusion: social justice and education policy research

The thrust of my argument in this paper is that the breadth and richness of Young's conceptualization of social justice makes it a useful framework for thinking about an agenda for social justice research in relation to education policy. Young's model incorporates what is good in liberal and postmodern conceptualizations of social justice, but overcomes their limitations. In addition, I have argued that whilst Fraser's concerns about the tensions between redistribution and recognition are valid in certain respects, they do not undermine the validity or attractiveness of Young's framework as a whole. But, I have suggested that we ought to take on board Fraser's concerns about the need to theorize about difference in a way that enables us to 'make normative judgments about the relative value of alternative norms, practices and interpretations, judgments that could lead to conclusions of inferiority, superiority and equivalent value'. In other words, we need to avoid a 'politics of difference that is wholesale and undifferentiated' (Fraser 1997: 204). However, modified to take account of Fraser's concerns, Young's framework provides us with a wide-ranging set of questions which need to be – and indeed are in some quarters being – addressed by education policy research. These might be formulated in the following way:

How, to what extent and why do education policies support, interrupt or subvert:

1. Exploitative relationships (capitalist, patriarchal, racist, heterosexist, disablist, etc.) within and beyond educational institutions?
2. Processes of marginalization and inclusion within and beyond the education system?
3. The promotion of relationships based on recognition, respect, care and mutuality or produce powerlessness (for education workers and students)?
4. Practices of cultural imperialism? And which cultural differences should be affirmed, which should be universalized and which rejected?
5. Violent practices within and beyond the education system?

Clearly this framework is broad and needs further clarification and explication. But, as I said at the beginning, my interest is in mapping out the territory in a relatively loose way in order to start a discussion. I have not intended to provide a definitive conceptualization of social justice. I would suggest that amongst the issues we need to debate now are whether there are aspects of the conceptualization I have identified which ought not to be included, or whether there are ingredients which have been omitted but ought to be included. Is such a broad interpretation of social justice valid and valuable, or are we better off restricting ourselves to more conventional distributional conceptualizations? If we agree that Young's conceptualization is a useful starting point, does the agenda I have set out ask the right questions in the right way or are there other questions we need to ask? Should we think about our own research practices in relation to the five faces of oppression identified by Young? If so, how? We then need to think about how successfully our own research to date has contributed to a social justice agenda of whatever type we identify as being appropriate. What have been the strengths and the limitations? What work still needs to be done?

Acknowledgements

I am very grateful to Alan Cribb for his extremely insightful comments on an earlier draft of this paper and to Carol Vincent for her very helpful editorial guidance.

Notes

1. See Young (1990, Chapter 1) for a more extensive discussion of why justice cannot and ought not be reduced to the distributional paradigm.
2. The CSJ was set up by the late leader of the UK Labour Party, John Smith, with a brief to develop a practical vision of social and economic reform for the next century.
3. Indeed, Fraser admits as much in a footnote, when she argues that she is 'conceiving class in a highly stylized, orthodox, and theoretical way in order to sharpen the contrast to the other ideal-typical kinds of collectivity' she discusses. She goes on to argue that she herself prefers 'a less economistic interpretation, one that gives more weight to the cultural, historical, and discursive dimensions of class emphasized by such writers as E. P. Thompson' (f.n. 15, p. 34). But Fraser's appreciation of the complexity of class culture appears to be confined to that footnote. It does not emerge in her discussion of class in the 'real-world'.
4. Moreover, it seems to me that the idea of transformative recognition and Fraser's critical theory of recognition are mutually antagonistic. Not only does Fraser's explication of her critical theory of recognition fail to mention cultural *deconstruction, but it accepts* the validity of cultural affirmation in certain situations. Such a position is incompatible with her advocacy of transformative recognition which eschews affirmation as a superficial remedy for cultural injustice.

References

Bauman, Z. (1992) *Intimations of Postmodemily* (London: Routledge).
Benjamin, J. (1990) *The Bonds of Love: Psychoanalysis, Feminism and the Problem of Domination* (London: Virago).
Commission on Social Justice (1994) *Social Justice: Strategies for National Renewal* (London: Vintage).
Ebert, T. (1991) Political semiosis in/of American cultural studies. *American Journal of Semiotics*, 8 (1/2), 113–135.
Etzioni, A. (1996) The responsive community: a communitarian perspective. *American Sociological Review*, 61, 1–11.
Fraser, N. (1997) *Justice Interruptus: Critical Reflections on the "Postsocialist" Condition* (London: Routledge).
Gewirtz, S., Ball, S. J. and Bowe, R. (1995) *Markets, Choice and Equity in Education* (Buckingham: Open University Press).
Hall, S. (1988) New ethnicities, ICA Document 7 (London: ICA).
Harvey, D. (1993) Class relations, social justice and the politics of difference, inj. Squires (ed.), *Principled Positions: Postmodernism and the Rediscovery of Value* (London: Lawrence and Wishart).
Hewitt, M. (1997) Welfare, recognition and the politics of difference: a response to postmodern critiques of universalism. Paper presented to the Social Policy Association Annual Conference, Lincoln, 15–17 July.
Leonard, P. (1997) *Postmodern Welfare: Reconstructing an Emancipatory Project* (London: Sage).
Lynch, K. (1995) The limits of liberalism for the promotion of equality in education. Keynote address at the Association for Teacher Education in Europe, 20th Annual Conference, Oslo, 3–8 September.
Miller, D. (1976) *Social Justice* (Oxford: Clarendon Press).
Phillips, A. (1997) From inequality to difference: a severe case of displacement? *New Left Review*, 224, 143–153.
Putnamm, R. (1993) The prosperous community: social capital and public life. *American Prospect*, 13 (Spring).
Rawls, J. (1972) *A Theory of Justice* (Oxford: Clarendon Press).
Rosenau, P. (1992) *Postmodernism and the Social Sciences* (Princeton: Princeton University Press).
Young, I. M. (1990) *Justice and the Politics of Difference* (Princeton: Princeton University Press).

Equality, Recognition and the Distributive Paradigm

CHRIS ARMSTRONG

Introduction

In this article I shall examine how some recent work on equality has thrown light on the thorny issue of how equality relates to the recognition of difference. It has been argued that, whilst equality is a concept appropriate for dealing with matters of distributive justice, it is out of place in the discussion of other forms of injustice. Hence, the extent to which equality can function as an overarching normative concept is limited. In this article I shall cast doubt on these claims by examining Nancy Fraser's arguments on recognition and redistribution. Although Fraser initially claimed that equality was best limited to matters of distributive justice, her position has been softening. The way in which her arguments have recently changed is particularly interesting for those who wish to rehabilitate the idea of equality as an overarching normative concept, that can be mobilised in opposing a wide variety of forms of injustice.

Equality, Recognition and Difference

It has been suggested that theories of equality are ill-suited for dealing with real-world issues of human difference and diversity. This charge was perhaps put most forcefully within feminist theory, where it formed the core of what came to be known as the 'equality / difference debate'. The argument often advanced against equality was that it was an inherently assimilationist idea. Being equal demanded that we each display a certain set of characteristics, or live up to a certain conception of the individual or citizen. Thus Jane Flax asked whether, for women, 'equality can mean anything other than assimilation to a pre-existing and problematic male norm' (1992: 196; but see Armstrong 2002). The problem, as Joan Scott suggested, was how 'we recognise and use notions of sexual difference and yet make arguments for equality' (1988: 88).

Since the early days of the equality–difference debate, this alleged opposition between equality and difference has been shown to be, in many ways, overdrawn (see, for example, Meehan & Sevenhuijsen 1991; Holli 1997; Squires 1999; Walby 2001). Attempts to rehabilitate equality from a feminist perspective have recently been made by Davina Cooper (2000) and Kate Nash (2002). In recent years, however, similar points have been remade within what has been called the redistribution–recognition debate. Iris Young famously argued that egalitarians had focussed to too great an extent on inequalities in the possession of material goods, and insufficiently on issues of such as power, oppression, and sexual and racial injustice. Young's critique of what she called 'the distributive paradigm' in theories of equality (1990: 15–37) actually incorporated two points, although the relation between them was perhaps uneasy. One was that the distributive paradigm had wrongly neglected a whole series of important issues; the other was that that paradigm was inherently *unsuited* to dealing with those issues. An implication of Young's strategy, then, seemed to be that we must abandon the conception of equality as a broad ethical category in favour of an expanded conception of *justice* which is opposed to oppression in all its forms. Indeed, more recently the ideal of *inclusion* has played a similar role in her thought (see Young 2000). Either way, she has seemed to consign equality to a quite subordinate role in her work.[1]

Nancy Fraser's solution to these problems was quite different and led to a lengthy debate with Young. Fraser's initial contribution suggested that moral language was divided into two classic paradigms: a paradigm of recognition and a paradigm of redistribution. Most importantly for our purposes, the two paradigms had quite different regulatory principles (Fraser 1995a; see also Fraser 1997). First, matters of redistribution were clearly governed by some kind of 'politico-economic restructuring', which could well involve an ethic of equality (Fraser 1995a: 73). Egalitarianism, Fraser agreed, provided the proper and logical language for debates about socio-economic injustices, as conducted by theorists such as Marx and later Rawls and Dworkin (Fraser 1997: 13). Failures of recognition, however, were best remedied by 'cultural or symbolic change', aimed at 'valorizing diversity' (1995a: 73). They were ill-served by the language of equality, which was out of place in discussions of the hugely important issues of social or cultural recognition.[2]

Fraser's view has been very influential and a number of versions or revisions of her thesis have been developed. Isin and Wood (1999), for example, situate redistribution within a realm of citizenship and recognition within in a realm of identity. On the other hand, many feel that the distinction that Fraser's view makes between material and social forms of injustice is either untenable (which I take to be Young's position; see Young 1997), or unwise insofar as it draws our attention away from actual linkages between the two forms of injustice (Phillips 1999).[3] There is good reason to ask why, if we are seeking to reunite the disparate strands of theorising about justice, it is best to begin by erecting a categorical distinction between the material and the social, even if Fraser aims ultimately to bridge that distinction. (Fraser 2000a: 199–200 states that as one of her major theoretical aims.) In this respect the debate between Young and Fraser threatens to re-enact the earlier, and similarly intractable, 'dual systems' debate within feminism, which asked whether women's oppression was basically material or cultural/social in origin. Despite the fecundity of that debate, it was never clear that an answer was either possible or strictly necessary (see, for example, Sargent 1981). To add to these difficulties, Fraser has recently implied that we might need to work with a tripartite, rather than a bipartite, distinction – a distinction between the realms of recognition, redistribution and the political. This further division seems altogether unnecessary, not least because the cultural and economic obstacles to full citizenship are, in many ways, deeply political facts (Fraser 2000b: 116).[4]

Although Fraser's view was adopted in some measure by other theorists (but see Yar 2001), there was, even at the time, good reason to be sceptical about it. In particular, it was not obvious why equality claims could not be used to advance the goal of recognition. In Axel Honneth's highly influential work on recognition, for instance, it seems that for both political and social forms of misrecognition, equality is, directly or indirectly, the appropriate remedy (Honneth 1992). I say 'directly or indirectly' because strictly speaking, Honneth recommends equality only as the remedy for social misrecognition. For political matters, his recommended remedy is universal rights, supported by the principle of the equal right of all citizens to participate as full members of the community. Although this disrupts Honneth's neatly triadic typology, I would describe this too as an equality claim. Only in the arena of 'personal' or bodily needs is equality out of place, because, rightly or wrongly, Honneth seems to identify equality as an essentially political concept. Thus equality provides at least two of the three desirable forms of recognition. Indeed, it is interesting to note the extent to which Honneth's arguments about the equal right to participate prefigure Fraser's arguments about parity of participation (on which I comment below).

These doubts are significant, and may have prompted Fraser's recent restatement of her position on the languages of justice. Although I shall suggest that Fraser does not take her arguments far enough, or fully spell out their conclusions, I shall argue that she comprehensively undermines her earlier relegation of the idea of equality to a sub-category of the language of justice. In effect, Fraser's position implies that equality *can* provide an important, overarching language for the discussion of both material and social injustices – in short, that equality in some form can provide an overarching conception of justice. I shall go on, then, to examine Fraser's more recent contribution to the debate.

Fraser on Parity of Participation

If we examine what has been happening in Nancy Fraser's more recent work, we find that equality has been subtly rehabilitated. She has argued – I believe correctly – that we need to transcend the material/cultural dichotomy. As she argues, 'the two problematics need to be integrated in a single, comprehensive framework' (Fraser 2001: 22). In fact, she shows a reluctance to declare that equality is the overarching concept of her recent work, and claims that what she is doing (rather like Young) is uniting the language of recognition and redistribution under 'an expanded understanding of justice' (2001: 23) that is not explicitly egalitarian in nature. But I would draw attention to two important shifts in her thinking.

First, it appears that Fraser has now abandoned her contention that the language of equality can play no useful part in demands for recognition. In this respect, her work may have been influenced by engagement with Axel Honneth's notion of recognition, which indicates that norms of equality are a key tool for those who would claim social and political recognition. Indeed, arguably Fraser now differentiates her position from Honneth in only a trifling way. Whereas Honneth argues that we are 'entitled' to social esteem, Fraser rejects this as absurd and claims instead that we should all have an *equal right* to pursue social esteem. Honneth has not replied to Fraser's claim, but it is certainly conceivable that his intention was really no different from hers (Fraser 2001: 28). Either way, Fraser now uses the notion of '*status equality*' to describe a situation of mutual recognition (2001: 24). The operative ideal has become 'status equality in the sense of parity of participation' (2001: 25), so that claims for recognition can now be understood as claims for a kind of equality. Equality, remember, provides the obvious language for claims for redistribution – but now it provides at least part of the language of claims for recognition too.

Second, when we look beneath the surface of Fraser's so-called 'expanded understanding of justice', we find that it is a clearly egalitarian ideal. The idea of 'parity of participation' now functions as the overarching conception of justice which both recognition and redistribution are supposed to serve. As Fraser argues, her expanded notion of justice 'requires social arrangements that permit all (adult) members of society to interact with one another as peers' (2001: 29). These social arrangements are both cultural and material. As she rightly notes elsewhere, 'equal participation is also impeded when some actors lack the necessary resources to interact with others as peers' (Fraser 2000b: 116). Without these resources, a person cannot be 'a full member of society, capable of participating on a par with the rest' (2000b: 113). It is hard to see how we can have 'parity' as 'peers' without the kind of interpersonal comparisons that have often been the stock-in-trade of egalitarian politics. Moreover, the idea of an equal ability to participate seems to depend for its justification upon a notion of the moral equality of persons. It is not clear why Fraser uses the idea of 'parity' of participation rather than 'equality' of participation, but 'parity' seems clearly to be an egalitarian ideal.

To sum up, equality appears to have been rehabilitated in Fraser's recent writings in two ways. First, her overarching notion of parity of participation is based on broadly egalitarian ideas, and can even be interpreted *as* an egalitarian idea. Second, with regard to both material and cultural forms of disadvantage, remedies for social ills should be sought through recourse to largely egalitarian principles. Defending the equal worth of persons, that is, requires both the absence of certain forms of economic inequality, and the presence of a culture of equal respect for diverse groups. I believe that Fraser is just about right on this, but the most important point to note for now is that all of this must be seen to overturn her earlier arguments about the limited role of the idea of equality.

Equality and Distribution

We have seen that Fraser has more or less abandoned her doubts about the scope of equality as a critical concept and that she has rehabilitated the ideal of equality. But her position draws our attention to a broader issue within some branches of political theory. It is instructive to ask why theorists such as Fraser argued in the first place that equality had such a limited role within the language of justice. The most obvious answer is that equality was seen as fundamentally a distributive category. This was the charge made by Iris Young, although I would argue that Young was ambiguous on what she meant by the 'distributive paradigm',[5] and on whether it required us to abandon the concept of equality. On the one hand, prominent egalitarian theorists were criticised for adhering to a narrow and inadequate theoretical model. But it is not clear whether Young believed that the baby of equality needed to be thrown out with the bathwater of the distributive paradigm. Rather than either completely jettisoning or explicitly calling for a reconceptualisation of equality, she left the concept floating in a sort of limbo in her work. It has played a role in the background, but one subordinate to apparently less problematic notions such as justice and, more recently, inclusion.

To be sure, Young has laid down a series of persuasive challenges to egalitarian theorists, and it is regrettable that they have failed to respond to these adequately.[6] At least five charges might be adumbrated under her critique of the distributive paradigm, each of which is persuasive in some measure. First, we have a critique of the economism of mainstream egalitarian theories. Second, there is the parallel charge that egalitarian theorists have neglected some important issues, especially power. Third, a somewhat contrary charge is that egalitarian theories have misrepresented the nature of some social relations by conceiving them in terms of goods that can be distributed and redistributed. A fourth charge is that many egalitarian theories are superficial, in that they concentrate on the effects of institutional structures rather than on the nature of those structures. Finally, egalitarian theories are charged with being excessively statist, and with disempowering individuals and groups by presuming too great a role for central allocative agencies. I am happy to accept that these are highly pertinent critiques of many existing theories of equality. But it does not follow that equality should be consigned to the intellectual dustbin. Nor, ultimately, does Young declare that it should. As I have already indicated, she leaves the status of equality oddly undetermined.

The correct response to Young's criticisms, I would argue, is to reiterate that equality is first and foremost a moral concept. As Samuel Scheffler has recently put it, equality 'is not, in the first instance, a distributive ideal … It is, instead, a moral ideal governing the relations in which people stand to one another' (Scheffler 2003: 21). Equality is only distributive in a derivative and partial sense, in the sense that a variety of distributive measures are likely to be enlisted to forward it, but that these may be accompanied by measures which it makes relatively little sense to describe in distributive language.

This distinction is important, because it opens up two possibilities. The first of these is that equality may require a variety of different distributive measures. There is nothing intrinsic to the idea of equality that demands that it be translated into a single distributive principle. Secondly, it is important to note that equality as a moral concept may have implications that are not best understood as distributive in any meaningful sense. As John Baker has argued in support of Young's position, 'Nor is equality entirely a matter of distributions, in the sense that certain kinds of relationship, such as domination, oppression and subservience, are clearly relations of inequality even if it is not very helpful to portray them as unequal distributions of some good' (Baker 1997: 59). Furthermore, the remedies for these social maladies may not be distributive either. For example, the equal moral worth of persons may, as Fraser implies, require certain cultural conditions that are not best achieved by way of distributive measures.

It may well be the case, however, that many egalitarian thinkers have treated equality as if it *were* a distributive concept, and it is perhaps for this reason that theorists such as Young and Fraser have made the mistake of assuming it to be of limited applicability – and even of limited *appeal* – as a moral concept. As Scheffler has noted, in the so-called 'equality of what?' debate, 'the idea that justice requires the equal distribution of *something* is often simply taken for granted as the starting-point of discussion' (Scheffler 2003: 17, emphasis original). But that assumption leads to a series of difficulties.

Most worrying is the assumption that there must be one clear principle that should determine the distribution of all goods. For Ronald Dworkin, for example, equality requires that we are rewarded or punished for the consequences of our genuine choices only, for in this way ambition and judgement alone will be rewarded. Accordingly, Dworkin argues that equality of resources is the single, purely distributive expression of the equal moral worth of persons (Dworkin 1981; see also Fraser 2001: 39).

There are two problems with Dworkin's view. First, such a principle may have limited practical applicability. For instance, as Fraser suggests, it may not be the best way to deal with questions of cultural recognition. Second, it may threaten the recognition of key differences. It seems to me that, with regard to differences that matter, this is where the major problems start. For, as I have argued elsewhere (Armstrong 2003), the theorisation of equality characteristic of luck egalitarianism in particular entails that, in order for individuals to benefit from egalitarian policies, they need to display certain concretely defined qualities, over and above broad ones such as common humanity. These qualities most often include rationality and ambition, and such demands may be problematic and disciplinary in their own right.[7] The model of equality used becomes, in one way or another, one of just reward for the exercise of rational judgement. Just as importantly for defenders of difference, in the urge to drive out all extraneous influences on distribution, these accounts make it more difficult to justify tailoring distributions to specific groups, since any departure from the uniformity of a distributive system begins to look like discrimination.

However, these problems are much less applicable to theories which define equality in terms of some general state of affairs within a society. Understood in this way, equality might be conceived as the absence of oppression or domination, or it might require that there are not huge disparities of wealth, for example, such that a common life or meaningful participation in politics or a decent universal enjoyment of citizenship becomes impossible. As Scheffler has argued, 'equality so understood is opposed not to luck but to oppression, to heritable hierarchies of social status, to ideas of caste, to class privilege and the rigid stratification of classes, and to the undemocratic distribution of power' (2003: 22). This, I would argue, is a much more promising position from which to (re)start the politics of equality.

Unlike some more procedural notions of equality, there is, on this model, no impulse to discover one regulatory principle for all social costs and benefits. Rather, a whole network of possibly conflicting distributive principles might be required to advance the goal of equality, as well as an arsenal of non-distributive measures (I have in mind here Baker's idea of equality as a complex, clustered concept: Baker 1997). Thus equality as a monolithic regulative ideal is replaced by a more complex concept, which is most likely to be united under a conception such as 'equal citizenship' or 'equality of status'. Egalitarian theorists who defend more complex conceptions of equality include Michael Walzer, with his theory of complex equality (Walzer 1983). It may also include David Miller's theory of equality of status (Miller 1999)[8] and Elizabeth Anderson's idea of democratic equality (Anderson 1999). The focus in these theories, as in Fraser's, is on providing the social and material conditions that are necessary for us to enjoy a certain idea of democratic citizenship, which after all requires certain forms of both mutual respect and self-respect. Indeed in these terms, Fraser's position seems more analogous to that of Rawls (1971), although it might require different cultural and distributive changes.[9]

Conclusions

By way of conclusion, I would like to reiterate that the critique of equality as an ideal inherently unsuited to questions of recognition was never sufficiently nuanced. In particular, that critique was very much misplaced when it was applied to conceptions of equality that defined equality in terms of freedom from social oppression, or from systematic and pervasive imbalances of power which, for example, impede individuals' chances of participation. Fraser's recent work gives a very good indication of this, insofar as she has, in one way or another, reached much the same conclusion. What this suggests is that we need to reappraise the claim that equality cannot function as a key normative concept for radical political theorists. It also suggests (cf. Voet 1998), that further investigation into the idea of difference-sensitive citizenship should be a priority for those who want to retain the moral and political force of the concept of equality.

NOTES

1. I say 'seemed', because equality does seem to retain a background role in Young's theory, although a proper analysis of this must be set aside for my present purposes. For instance, in the course of rejecting Fraser's distinctions, she argues that 'we need to show how recognition is a means to, or an element in, economic and political equality' (Young 1997: 156), indicating that it may well have a proper subsidiary role. One of the most suggestive uses of the language of equality occurs in Young (2002a).
2. Perhaps in order to avoid operating too obvious a material–social dichotomy, Fraser sometimes uses the term 'social inequalities' to describe 'distributive' inequalities in the possession of material goods. For purposes of this essay, I use the more common typology of material or economic inequalities on the one hand, and social, cultural or political inequalities on the other.
3. Pointing out these common linkages, however, still leaves us with the task of explaining their nature. As Phillips (1999) shows, drawing firm theoretical conclusions from them is not an easy task.
4. Fraser tentatively suggests the move, arguing that it falls in more comfortably with Weber's classic disitinctions between 'class, status, party'. But it is notable that the only instance of 'political' obstacles to parity of participation that she mentions are specific 'electoral rules' (Fraser 2000b: 116). On this basis, the definition of the political sphere at hand looks quite narrow and legalistic, with a surprisingly undertheorised relationship between the 'political' and both economic and cultural relations within society as whole.
5. We can express concern about the distribution of childhood illness amongst certain social groups, for instance, without making any of the problematic assertions that Young associates with the 'distributive paradigm'. At least some, though by no means all, of the quotations Young uses in her critique of the distributive paradigm could be taken in this more neutral sense. See Young 1990: 15–38. Indeed, if we were to rule out any concern with the 'allocation' or 'distribution' of social goods amongst people, we would have to

rule out what Nozick (1974) called 'patterned' theories of justice altogether. Fraser (1995b) observes some further ambiguities.
6. David Miller is one honourable exception to this, although I find his answer unpersuasive. Essentially, Miller reaffirms the identity between justice and distribution (1999: 14–17). But now, equality is bifurcated into 'social' and 'distributive' variants. The latter is a part of social justice, which is basically distributive, but social equality is non-distributive in nature and not a part of social justice. As though this were not complicated enough, social equality can apparently make (distributive) claims on social justice, although the connection between the two is otherwise unclear. See Miller 1999: 15–16, 240–241. Overall, my feeling is that Miller defends the idea that justice is basically distributive in nature only by removing from the realm of justice things that many of us would want to keep there (such as a concern for social equality, and also for individual development), and at the expense of overall coherence. See also Young 2002b.
7. I have in mind here the literature inspired by Foucault's discussion of liberal 'governmentalities', and particularly its depiction of an 'enterprising self', though I cannot develop this point in detail here. See for example Rose (1992).
8. Although I have some serious doubts about Miller's position, including the reservations noted above.
9. On this view, Rawls's *Theory of Justice* actually sits at the more 'complex' end of the spectrum, and is primarily an attempt to develop the various preconditions of free and equal 'democratic' citizenship, via a mixture of cultural/political assumptions, and a *set* of distributive principles (most famously maximin and fair equality of opportunity). See Cohen 1989. For the view that Rawls's theory is not properly understood as the progenitor of luck egalitarianism, with its search for a single pristine distributive principle, see Daniels 2002 and Scheffler 2003.

REFERENCES

Anderson, E. 1999. 'What is the point of equality?'. *Ethics,* 109/2, 287–337.
Armstrong, C. 2002. 'Complex equality: beyond equality and difference'. *Feminist Theory,* 3/1, 67–82.
   2003. 'Opportunity, responsibility and the market: interrogating liberal equality'. *Economy & Society,* 32/3, 410–27.
Baker, J. 1997. 'Studying equality'. *Imprints,* 2/1, 57–71.
Bock, G. & S. James, eds. 1992. *Beyond Equality and Difference: Feminist Politics and Female Subjectivity*. London: Routledge.
Cohen, J. 1989. 'Democratic equality'. *Ethics* 99/4, 727–51.
Cooper, D. 2000. '"And you can't find me nowhere": relocating identity and structure within equality jurisprudence'. *Journal of Law and Society,* 27/2, 249–72.
Daniels, N. 2002. 'Democratic equality: Rawls's complex egalitarianism'. Freeman 2002: 241–76.
Dworkin, R. 1981. 'What is equality? Part 2: equality of resources'. *Philosophy and Public Affairs.* 10/4, 283–345.
Flax, J. 1992 'Beyond equality: gender, justice and difference'. Bock & James 1992: 193–210.
Fraser, N. 1995a. 'From redistribution to recognition? Dilemmas of justice in a "postsocialist" age'. *New Left Review,* 212, 68–93.
   1995b. 'Recognition or redistribution? A critical reading of Iris Young's *Justice and the Politics of Difference*'. *Journal of Political Philosophy,* 3/2, 166–80.
   1997. *Justice Interruptus: Critical Reflections on the "Postsocialist" Condition*. London: Routledge.

2000a. 'Radical academia, critical theory and transformative politics: an interview with Nancy Fraser'. *Imprints*, 4/2, 197–212.

2000b. 'Rethinking recognition'. *New Left Review*, 3, 107–20.

2001. 'Recognition without ethics?'. *Theory, Culture and Society*, 18/2–3, 21–42.

Freeman, S., ed. 2002. *The Cambridge Companion to Rawls*. Cambridge: Cambridge University Press.

Heelas, P. & P. Morris, eds. 1992. *Values of the Enterprise Culture: The Moral Debate*, London: Routledge.

Holli, A.M. 1997. 'On equality and Trojan horses: the challenges of the Finnish experience to feminist theory'. *European Journal of Women's Studies*, 4, 133–64.

Honneth, A. 1992. 'Integrity and disrespect: principles of a conception of morality based on the theory of recognition'. *Political Theory*, 20/2, 187–201.

Isin, E. & P. Wood, 1999. *Citizenship and Identity*. London: Sage.

Meehan, E. & S. Sevenhuijsen, eds. 1991. 'Introduction'. *Equality, Politics and Gender*. Sage: London.

Miller, D. 1999. *Principles of Social Justice*. Cambridge, MA: Harvard University Press.

Nash, K. 2002. 'Human rights for women: an argument for "deconstructive equality"'. *Economy and Society*, 31/3, 414–33.

Nozick, R. 1974. *Anarchy, State and Utopia*. Oxford: Blackwell.

Phillips, A. 1999. *Which Equalities Matter?* Cambridge: Polity Press.

Rawls, J. 1971. *A Theory of Justice*. Oxford: Oxford University Press.

Rose, N. 1992. 'Governing the enterprising self'. Heelas & Morris 1992: 148–62.

Sargent, L., ed. 1981. *Women and Revolution: The Unhappy Marriage of Marxism and Feminism*. London: Pluto Press.

Scheffler, S. 2003 'What is egalitarianism', *Philosophy & Public Affairs* 31/1, 5–39.

Scott, J. 1988. 'Deconstructing equality versus difference: or, the uses of poststructural theory for feminism'. *Feminist Studies*, 14/1, 358–71.

Squires, J. 1999. *Gender in Political Theory*. Cambridge: Polity Press.

Voet, R. 1998. *Feminism and Citizenship*. London: Sage.

Walby, S. 2001. 'From community to coalition: the politics of recognition as the handmaiden of the politics of equality in an era of globalization'. *Theory, Culture and Society*, 18/2–3, 113–35.

Walzer, M. 1983. *Spheres of Justice: a Defense of Pluralism and Equality*. New York: Basic Books.

Yar, M. 2001. 'Beyond Nancy Fraser's "perspectival dualism"'. *Economy and Society*, 30/3, 288–303.

Young, I.M. 1990. *Justice and the Politics of Difference*. Princeton, NJ: Princeton University Press.

1997. 'Unruly categories: a critique of Nancy Fraser's dual systems theory'. *New Left Review*, 222, 147–60.

2000. *Inclusion and Democracy*. Oxford: Oxford University Press.

2002a. 'Status Inequality and Social Groups'. *Issues in Legal Scholarship*, article 9, ⟨http://www.bepress.com/ils/iss2/art9/⟩.

2002b. 'Review of David Miller, *Principles of Social Justice*'. *Political Theory*, 30/5, 754–9.

Schooling and social justice through the lenses of Nancy Fraser

Amanda Keddie

> This review essay draws on Nancy Fraser's work as featured in *Adding insult to injury: Nancy Fraser debates her critics* to explore issues of schooling and social justice. The review focuses on the applicability and usefulness of Fraser's three-dimensional model for understanding matters of justice in education. It begins with an overview of the principles of economic, cultural and political justice as they are reflected in specific examples of equity and schooling policy and practice. This is followed by (1) a consideration of Fraser's concerns that current forms of identity politics are reifying group identity and displacing matters of distributive justice and (2) with an account of her concerns about the political justice issues of representation and misframing in the contemporary global era. With reference to the sphere of Indigenous education, the review examines some of the problematics involved in pursuing distributive, recognitive and representative justice. Fraser's 'status model' is presented as a way through these problematics because it engages with a politics that begins with overcoming status subordination rather than with a politics of group identity. Against this theoretical backdrop, the final section of the review briefly considers some of the future challenges for schooling and social justice.

Introduction

> I think first and foremost [we are] about advocacy. It's about who are the students at our school? What are the issues for those students? What might be the barriers to their learning . . . to their ability to take advantage of the opportunities of education? And then to find [out] how we act on that - what can we actually do about that. ('Penny', secondary teacher)

Penny is a secondary teacher at a small English language school for refugee and immigrant students in a suburban area in Queensland. These comments were made in response to a question about schooling, equity and social justice posed to her as part of a study that examined these issues (see Keddie, 2012). Her comments are presented here because they seem to resonate with how many 'progressive' teachers articulate their thoughts about these issues. For these teachers, school is a site of possibility and 'advocacy' that can transform circumstances of disadvantage and overcome 'barriers to learning'. This is a view that is usefully theorised drawing on the principle of 'participatory parity' offered by US political philosopher Nancy Fraser (2007, p. 27), who explains justice as requiring:

> ... social arrangements that permit all to participate as peers in social life. On the view of justice as participatory parity, overcoming injustice means dismantling institutionalized

obstacles that prevent some people from participating on a par with others, as full partners in social interaction.

Creating social arrangements that foster such parity, as Penny suggests, centres upon knowing 'who' students are and 'acting' on this information to improve their capacity to 'take advantage of the opportunities of education'; it is about recognising how students are differently positioned in terms of their equity needs and on providing differential support to address these needs. Grappling with the complexities of such recognition and provision is a major issue for teachers – especially for those, like Penny, who are committed to supporting a more just education for disadvantaged or marginalised learners. Indeed, amid the unprecedented and rising levels of ethnic, racial, religious and class diversity within western classrooms, engaging with the politics of student difference has never been more difficult and contentious. Such contention is particularly evident in the lack of shared understanding about issues of justice within schools and amongst teachers. Although most teachers, for example, would agree that it is important to remove the barriers or obstacles that prevent some students from participating on par with their more privileged peers, there is far less agreement about what these obstacles might be and how they might best be overcome.

This lack of agreement brings to light the moral imperatives shaping equity work in schools – that is, how teachers' views about what might constitute the social good shape the ways in which they understand and approach student difference and disadvantage (see Giroux, 2003). For example, some teachers might understand student disadvantage on the basis of race or ethnicity to be associated primarily with economic obstacles or barriers, whereas others might associate this disadvantage more with cultural or political barriers. These understandings will impact on how equity is addressed – where disadvantage is thought to be an economic issue, redistributive measures might be prioritised (i.e. the greater allocation of material or human resources), where it is thought to arise from cultural barriers, recognitive measures might be prioritised (i.e. increased cultural recognition and valuing) and where it is thought of as a political issue, representative measures might be prioritised (i.e. increased avenues to accord equitable representation/political voice). Such understandings and priorities will also be shaped and further complicated by how student identity is constructed – for example, essentialising racial or cultural identity may reify difference and otherness and create further inequities, as might a focus on a specific barrier to justice at the expense of a focus on other barriers.

The aim of this review essay is to explore some of the key theoretical developments that have been useful in understanding and addressing these issues through the lenses of Nancy Fraser's work. With such developments in mind, the essay proposes some future challenges for the field of schooling and social justice. *Adding insult to injury: Nancy Fraser debates her critics* (Olson, 2008a) provides an excellent account of such developments and challenges. From her important 1995 essay *From Redistribution to Recognition?* to her recent work on political misframing, this edited collection charts the unfolding of important debates shaping social justice philosophy, theory and politics in contemporary times. The book's major contribution is an articulation of the complexity and scope of justice issues and the development of Fraser's three-dimensional model to support a comprehensive understanding of such issues. As alluded to in the opening reflections, these dimensions acknowledge socio-economic, cultural and political injustice. For Fraser, socio-economic injustices arise when the structures of society generate maldistribution or class inequality for particular social groups; cultural injustices arise when institutionalised or hierarchical patterns of cultural value generate misrecognition or status inequality for particular social groups; and political injustices arise when some individuals or groups are not accorded equal voice in decision-making about justice claims. In line with the notion of participatory parity, Fraser argues that justice for all is possible when the structures of the economy reflect an equitable distribution of material resources, when the status order reflects equitable patterns of cultural recognition and when the constitution of political space ensures equitable representation.

Although the first two dimensions (economic and cultural) of Fraser's model are featured and discussed in the earlier sections of *Adding Insult to Injury*, the later sections of the book track the arguments that prompted her to add the third dimension (political). The book provides a rich and detailed account of debates and counter-debates associated with Fraser's theorising that have appeared in other publications since 1995. For example, it features early concerns with her work – articulated in separate chapters by Iris Young and Judith Butler about the model's dichotomising/polarising of economic and cultural justice as analytically distinct. For these theorists, this distinction does not reflect the complex political realities and intersections of justice claims. Other concerns about Fraser's earlier work are associated with how she theorises the integration and pursuit of justice on these two dimensions. Here, Fraser's rejection of an affirmative approach to group recognition, as in tension with the principles of distributive justice, is challenged in a chapter by Elizabeth Anderson who highlights how affirmative action can support distributive principles. A further chapter by Ingrid Robeyns offers Amartya Sen's capability framework as more effective than Fraser's in theorising how matters of distributive and recognitive justice might be pursued simultaneously. In the later sections of the book, the failure of Fraser's two-dimensional model to account for matters of political justice is highlighted in chapters by Leonard Feldman and Kevin Olson. These commentators argue that political injustices are 'analytically distinct from, and cannot be reduced to, inequities of economy or culture' and thus should be assigned a privileged place in Fraser's theorising (Olson, 2008b, p. 6). Further shortcomings to Fraser's work are noted in chapters by Nikolas Kompridis and Rainer Forst who question the philosophical underpinnings of her critical theorising around recognition, justice, public claims-making and participatory parity.

It is beyond the scope of this review essay to engage with all of these important criticisms. Suffice to say, Fraser provides detailed responses to, and reconciliations of, the major criticisms of her work in *Adding Insult to Injury* – indeed, as she concedes, they have clearly developed and extended her theorising. Perhaps the most enduring criticism of her work (highlighted by Young and Butler) relates to the model's polarising of economic, cultural and political justice issues as analytically distinct – this criticism prevails despite Fraser's insistence of the 'interimbrication' and overlap of these issues. The conclusion to this review essay considers how this criticism might be addressed in relation to research and theorising within education.

This review focuses on two key developments in Fraser's work that are explored in two separate chapters in the book – (1) her 're-thinking' of recognition to support the simultaneous pursuit of economic and cultural justice and (2) the augmenting of her model to include the dimension of political justice. These two developments have presented particular challenges within equity and schooling policy and practice.

This review focuses on the applicability and usefulness of Fraser's three-dimensional model for understanding and approaching matters of justice in education. As such it builds on the already expansive body of research and writing across a vast array of educational areas and disciplines that draws on her work (see, e.g., Atweh, 2009; Gilbert, Keddie, Lingard, Mills, & Renshaw, 2011; Huttunen, 2007; Keddie, 2012; Mills, 2012; Power & Frandji, 2010; Tikly & Barrett, 2011). This review begins with an overview of the principles of economic, cultural and political justice as they are reflected in specific examples of equity and schooling policy and practice. This is followed by a consideration of the concerns that feature in Fraser's chapter *Rethinking recognition: overcoming displacement and reification in cultural politics* (2008a). In this chapter, she argues that current forms of identity politics have curtailed justice in simplifying and reifying group identity – encouraging separatism and intolerance – and in marginalising and displacing matters of distributive justice. This part of the review draws attention to these concerns within the sphere of Indigenous education and considers how problems of reification and displacement might be overcome through an alternative approach to recognition – which focuses on overcoming status subordination. For Fraser, this approach is not about recognising group identity simply on the basis of marginality or privilege, but rather on dismantling the concrete arrangements that impede parity. The next section of the review considers the concerns that feature in Fraser's chapter *Reframing justice in a globalising world* (2008b). In this chapter, she specifies matters of political justice as analytically distinct from economic and cultural justice, thus augmenting her model to include a third dimension. Drawing on this theorising, the review examines some of the key tensions associated with political representation (again) referring to the sphere of Indigenous education, namely the problematics of voice in linking representation to identity in reductionist and simplistic ways. Moving beyond such problematics is argued to necessitate, as with the previous section, an approach that focuses on overcoming status subordination and transforming the social arrangements that silence or misrepresent marginalised students. The final section of the review briefly considers some of the future challenges for schooling and social justice in the light of such key developments.

Schooling for social justice: redistribution, recognition and representation
Distributive principles of justice have been a significant feature of equity and schooling policy and practice in western contexts for some time. Generally, these principles recognise, on the one hand, that schools are not equitable in their distribution of material benefits and, on the other hand, that students are not equitably positioned in their capacity to take up these benefits. Education determines employment credentialing and students' subsequent access to the labour market (Connell, 1994; Gale & Densmore, 2000; Mills & Gale, 2010). A key platform of socially just schooling then must be to prepare students for their future productive participation within this market. For Sarra (2003, see also Ladson-Billings, 1995), crucial here is assisting marginalised students to achieve on the 'same measuring sticks' of educational achievement (e.g. standardised tests) as their more privileged counterparts so that they can 'mix it with anybody' and 'eventually access society in the same way that any other [student] would'. Principles of distributive justice recognise the links between poverty, poor schooling performance, early school leaving and future economic deprivation and social discontent/dysfunction. Achievement at school is central to disrupting these links – as De La Rosa (1998, p. 268) argues in relation to the United States – 'the continuing dropout dilemma presents staggering social and economic repercussions... dropping out of school is the surest way of perpetuating the cycle of poverty and crime that many students are born into'.

Although highly varied, distributive principles have long framed equity and schooling policy and initiatives across contexts such as the United States, the United Kingdom and Australia. They are generally focused on the allocation of extra funding and resources to students on the basis of economic need to support increased school participation and achievement. In Australia, for example, the *Disadvantaged Schools Program*, instituted by the federal government in 1972, allocated additional funds to schools on the basis of students' socio-economic deprivation – ameliorating some of the negative impacts of poverty on students' educational outcomes. Similar distributive principles are evident in the recent *National Partnership Scheme* in Australia with funding allocated to schools on the basis of their location within low socio-economic communities. Individualised resource allocation and funding for economically deprived students such as the *Free School Meal* and the *Pupil Premium* programmes in the United Kingdom are also reflective of distributive principles.

Other distributive measures take a more integrated approach from the outset – evident in the United States, for example, with the *Head Start* programme launched nearly 50 years ago in 1965. *Head Start* was one of a number of programmes developed to address chronic poverty. It was designed to support the school readiness of children reared in poverty towards lifelong productivity (Bradley, Chazan-Cohen, & Raikes, 2009). It reflected an integration of education, health and social welfare needs through combining home-based and centre-based approaches that supported parents to create educationally stimulating environments for their children (Robinson et al., 2009). Similar distributive principles are reflected in initiatives in the United States and other western contexts aimed at supporting other 'at-risk' students, for example, students with violence and substance abuse issues; pregnant and parenting students; and refugee students. In these instances, the allocation of extra human and material resources to support these students' school retention, participation and achievement might include, for example, specialised counselling and therapy services, family services, parenting education, transportation assistance, housing assistance, childcare services; financial assistance; literacy support and translation services; and other community/social outreach services (Amin, Browne, Ahmed, & Sato, 2006; Carswell, Hanlon, O'Grady, Watts, & Pothong, 2009).

A distributive understanding of justice has been the predominant focus within equity and schooling policy and practice since its inception. This focus continues to be extremely important in pursing social justice particularly given that schools continue to perpetuate class disadvantage through the inequitable distribution of education's material benefits and given that poverty and early school leaving continue to be the most accurate predictor of educational disadvantage and future economic and social marginalisation. However, such a focus is also recognised as limited – a purely distributive approach fails to consider how matters of cultural disadvantage constrain students' educational outcomes.

Driven by concerns about the enduring educational disadvantage experienced by particular groups of students (especially on the basis of racialised difference), matters of cultural recognition, alongside matters of economic redistribution, have become important educational priorities. As with circumstances of poverty, issues of race are highly accurate predictors of educational underperformance, for example, Indigenous students in Australia, Canada, New Zealand and the United States and Black students of African descent in the United States and the United Kingdom are groups that consistently underperform relative to their more race- and class-privileged counterparts. Concerns about the underperformance of these students have illuminated the cultural exclusivity of western education contexts in their privileging of white and middle class ways of knowing and being and marginalising of 'other' ways of knowing and being. Such privileging reflects and reinscribes inequitable patterns of cultural recognition. Creating culturally inclusive and relevant learning environments that connect with the funds of knowledge specific to marginalised groups is seen to support greater participation, motivation and achievement for students from these groups (see, e.g., Banks, 2010; Bishop, 2003; Sleeter, 2005).

The significance of creating these learning environments is well established in equity policy. In Australia, for example, cultural inclusion is prioritised in the *National Goals for*

Schooling Framework. The Framework's particular focus is Indigenous marginality and the role of education in valuing the histories and cultures of this group (Ministerial Council on Education, Employment, Training and Youth Affairs, 2008). One of the key goals is that schools support all young Australians to become active and informed citizens who 'understand and acknowledge the value of Indigenous cultures' (p. 10). Following this, Australia's recently introduced National Curriculum has Aboriginal and Torres Strait Islander histories and cultures as one of the three cross-curricula priorities to support the integration of culturally inclusive content across relevant learning areas.

A similar focus on culturally inclusive learning is evident in the National Curriculum in England. The introduction of the Citizenship Curriculum in 2002 was framed by broader concerns associated with issues of cultural diversity and social justice, especially rises in community disharmony, social fragmentation, violence, racism and xenophobia. With the aim of developing responsible and active citizens who challenge inequity and discrimination, an important focus within this curriculum area is to foster students' greater valuing of cultural diversity (Figueroa, 2000; Osler & Starkey, 2005).

Connecting with the histories, cultures, contributions and perspectives of non-dominant groups through the curriculum is one of the many inclusive schooling practices that can support recognitive justice for marginalised students. Such practices are central to creating more equitable patterns of cultural recognition – which reflect greater respect and esteem for marginalised groups. It is clear then that both distributive and recognitive approaches can enhance the schooling participation, engagement and performance of marginalised students. However, such principles do not tend to acknowledge issues of political or representative justice. In further reference to how schooling might better connect with, and be relevant for, marginalised students (again especially in relation to issues of race), concerns with how political or representative disadvantage might constrain students' educational success have also been a feature of equity and schooling policy and practice.

The political constitution of most western schooling contexts – as in the broader social world – tends not to accord a voice to marginalised groups and, in this case, they are subject to political injustice or misrepresentation. Most schools across the globe not only privilege white, western and middle-class ways of knowing and being but, in contexts such as Australia, the United Kingdom and the United States (especially in particular areas), they also tend to be overwhelmingly populated by white, middle-class teachers and white students. There has been a long-held concern about how such contexts can undermine the autonomy of students whose racialised identities are other to the mainstream. In Australia, for example, the under-representation of Indigenous teachers (at less than 1% of all teachers) is seen to be a contributing factor to the poor academic performance of Indigenous students and their low levels of school retention (relative to their non-Indigenous counterparts). A recent federal government initiative seeks to address this imbalance with its mandate to increase the number of Indigenous teachers in Australian schools – the aims of this increase are to foster greater cultural awareness and understanding of Indigenous issues and to provide Indigenous students with positive role models (DEEWR, 2011).

Similar concerns have underpinned arguments in favour of segregated schools, on the basis, for example, of race, ethnicity or religion. These contexts are seen to provide a political space that represents the voices and thus the educational needs of particular minority or marginalised groups. They are seen as a positive and just alternative to the assimilationist discourses within mainstream education where marginalised students' voices are silenced and their cultures misrepresented or ignored (Ladson-Billings, 1995; Nelson-Brown, 2005). Although at odds with legislation in the United States (and Europe), which finds segregated schools (particularly on the basis of race) to be inherently discriminatory and inequitable, there has been a long history of, and government support in relation to, school segregation based on these arguments – particularly regarding gender and religious segregation.

Such issues and concerns illustrate the importance of an approach to equity in schools that reflects the multidimensionality of justice claims. Although the broad scope of such claims has been recognised within education policy and practice for some time, Fraser's model is a useful conceptual scaffold for thinking comprehensively about these issues as they relate to identifying and overcoming students' economic, cultural and political disadvantage and marginalisation. Her work also encapsulates some of the major tensions involved in pursuing justice on these dimensions that education theory, policy and practice continue to grapple with. These tensions (and the possibilities for overcoming them) are particularly well captured in the chapters *Rethinking recognition: overcoming displacement and reification in cultural politics* and *Reframing justice in a globalising world*. As briefly mentioned in the introduction, the first chapter focuses on Fraser's concerns that current forms of identity politics are producing problems of reification and displacement, whereas the second specifies matters of political justice. These problems and matters are examined drawing on examples from Indigenous education in Australia.

Rethinking recognition: problems of reification and displacement

As noted in the previous section, culturally responsive learning environments are an important aspect of a socially just education and well recognised as such within equity and schooling policy. In particular, the valuing of non-dominant or marginalised cultures (e.g. within the curriculum) reflects recognitive justice in its potential to destabilise the dominant social patterns that create inequitable status hierarchies (Fraser, 2008a). There is much evidence to suggest that such valuing improves marginalised students' schooling participation, motivation and outcomes (Bishop, 2003; Sleeter, 2005). However, there is also much evidence indicating the tensions and problematics involved in educators' efforts to create culturally responsive learning environments. Often these efforts reify culture as an essentially knowable and bounded entity that is delineable and congruent with particular population groups (see Benhabib, 2002; McConaghy, 2000). It is this reification, according to Fraser in her *Rethinking recognition* chapter, that has come to characterise many recent forms of identity politics where 'a single, drastically simplified group identity' is imposed. Such a politics 'denies the complexity of people's lives, the multiplicity of their identifications and the cross-pulls of their various affiliations'; it is particularly problematic in 'stressing the need to elaborate and display an authentic . . . collective identity' and in discouraging 'cultural criticism' and scrutiny in relation to intragroup conflict and injustice (2008a, pp. 133–134). For Fraser, such reification is a troubling consequence of the shift in justice and political claims-making over the past several decades from a predominant concern with redistributive justice to an overriding focus on recognitive justice. Within an environment of unprecedented cultural pluralism, claims for cultural recognition have proliferated in ways that have encouraged separatism and differentiation. Fraser welcomes the ways in which the burgeoning of identity politics around matters of cultural recognition since the 1970s has added a 'richer, lateral dimension to battles over the redistribution of wealth and power' (p. 129). However, along with reification, she notes another troubling consequence arising from this shift – a displacement of distributive justice claims, as she contends, from the turn of the century 'questions of recognition are serving less to supplement, complicate and enrich redistributive struggles than to marginalise, eclipse and displace them' (p. 130).

The tendency for current forms of identity politics to reify culture is explored in McConaghy's work in the area of Indigenous education in Australia (2000). She draws attention to how such reification or 'culturalism' within schools has perpetuated oppositional binaries between Aboriginality and non-Aboriginality. She argues that traditions of culturalism within Indigenous education have preserved the 'other' and marginal status of Indigeneity and remain a key mechanism through which colonial authority is exercised in and through education. Certainly, superficial engagement with Indigenous culture in schools, akin to the familiar 'holidays and heroes' or 'spring rolls in the tuckshop' approaches to multiculturalism (see Rasheed Ali & Ancis, 2005), is common in Australian schools. Here, culturally inclusive teaching is reduced to stereotypical representations of Indigenous histories and identities that wash-out their complexity and multiplicity.

That such reification has foreclosed cultural criticism and scrutiny is evident in McConaghy's view that curriculum frames purporting to be culturally inclusive tend to ignore important questions such as: What constitutes western or Indigenous knowledge? Whose and which knowledges should be privileged? and Who can know and speak with respect to these knowledges? Further resonating with Fraser's concern that reification discourages cultural criticism, McConaghy (2000) highlights the rarity of debate about the 'relative merits' of Indigenous theory and knowledges and the 'lack of aesthetic' for 'determining good or bad Indigenous knowledges' – such knowledges, she suggests, appear beyond critique as they are relegated to the realm of culture (see also Keddie, 2012).

An additional problematic of such reification is its tendency to reduce all Indigenous educational phenomena to problems of the 'cultural' – which isolates issues of racism from other political antagonisms, especially those associated with class and gender (Keddie, 2012; McConaghy, 2000). This is Fraser's concern with the current mode of identity politics, where a focus on the cultural has displaced struggles for distributive justice. The problem according to Fraser (2008a) arises from a 'hypostatising' of culture that abstracts it from its institutional matrix and its entwinement with distributive injustice. This abstracting is evident in the concerns many commentators express about culturally responsive teaching that compromises a focus on high academic outcomes – for example, teaching framed by low expectations that 'waters down' (or creates separate measures of) achievement for marginalised students. McConaghy (2000) draws attention here to the 'new racism' in education generated by these sorts of expectations and strategies where Indigenous culture is constructed as incommensurable with western schooling norms. Such teaching draws on deficit understandings of marginalised students where poor academic achievement is reduced/attributed to culture (see Antrop-Gonzalez & De Jesus, 2006; Sarra, 2003; Williamson & Dalal, 2007). Struggles for distributive justice are displaced when culturally responsive teaching is defined in opposition to an emphasis on academic achievement – as argued earlier, assisting marginalised students to achieve on the 'same measuring sticks' of educational achievement as their more privileged counterparts is crucial to enabling their future access to the material benefits of the social world and thus also crucial to supporting economic justice.

Further displacement problems arising from a predominant focus on cultural responsiveness at the micro-classroom level are indicated in Kanu's research (2007) with Indigenous students in Canada. She argues for a more 'systematic, holistic and comprehensive approach' that is cognisant of the socioeconomic disadvantage confronting these students (2007, p. 38):

> ... micro-level classroom variables such as culturally responsive curriculum and pedagogy alone cannot provide a functional and effective agenda in reversing achievement trends among

> Aboriginal students ... it is one thing to integrate Aboriginal perspectives into the school curriculum but quite another to ensure that all Aboriginal students, particularly those who are socioeconomically disadvantaged, are actually in the classroom to benefit from such integration. As such, macrostructural variables contributing to chronic absenteeism and dropout among Aboriginal students [are] significant factors to consider. Implications for policy and practice, therefore, include the need to explore the relationships between micro- and macro-level variables affecting schooling and the realization that meaningful and lasting intervention requires a systematic, holistic, and comprehensive approach.

The macrostructural variables that Kanu refers to here as perpetuating marginalised students' educational disadvantage are associated with issues of distributive justice – that is, the variables that relate to Indigenous students' lack of access to specific material resources that hinder their school access, participation and achievement. Her argument, along the lines of Fraser, rejects the abstraction of culture from its institutional matrix and recognises the entwinement of cultural and economic injustice – as she notes, enhancing the achievement of Aboriginal students requires that 'chronic absenteeism and dropout' (matters of economic/distributive justice) are considered alongside culturally responsive curriculum and pedagogy (matters of cultural/recognitive justice). The suggestion that policy and practice need to 'explore the relationships between the micro- and macro-level variables' affecting the schooling of Indigenous students highlights the injustices these students suffer on the basis of both economy *and* culture (Fraser, 2008a). This suggestion importantly does not treat misrecognition as a 'free-standing cultural harm' but understands its location within broader social–structural conditions where maldistribution seriously impedes these students' schooling participation and success.

Beyond reification and displacement

In moving beyond, or at least mitigating, the problems of reification and displacement that have tended to characterise contemporary identity politics, Fraser proposes an alternative approach – the 'status model' where recognition is treated as a question of social status. She argues here that 'everything depends on how recognition is approached'. For Fraser, recognition as a question of social status supports an integration of struggles for recognition with struggles for redistribution (2008a). Akin to, but developing, her earlier theorising around transformative justice (1997), this approach rejects a politics that begins with group identity – it engages instead with a politics that begins with overcoming status subordination. She explains this (2008a, p. 137) as allowing for a

> ... range of possibilities depending on what precisely the subordinated parties need in order to be able to participate as peers in social life. In some cases, they may need to be unburdened of excessive ascribed or constructed distinctiveness; in others, to have hitherto under-acknowledged distinctiveness taken into account ... In every case, the status model tailors the remedy to the concrete arrangements that impede parity.

For McConaghy (2000), this engagement is central to supporting Indigenous equity through schooling. Consistent with Fraser, she argues against the recognition of Indigenous or non-Indigenous identity – simply on the basis of marginality or privilege. Similar to the idea of recognition as a question of social status, she contends that recognition should be focused on better understanding and addressing the 'specific nature of specific oppressions at specific sites' (p. 8).

This focus brings to light the particular 'concrete arrangements' or specific oppressions that impede parity of participation for Indigenous students. In relation to cultural or recognitive justice, as mentioned earlier, the concrete arrangements impeding parity might be associated with the silencing or simplifying of marginalised knowledges within school curricula. A focus on overcoming status subordination here would necessarily involve greater recognition and valuing of these subjugated knowledges, which may bring into play as Fraser argues, 'hitherto under-acknowledged distinctiveness' – this distinctiveness is important in disrupting the social patterns that misrecognise and trivialise these knowledges (Fraser, 2008a).

To avoid reification, however, as Fraser also argues, this focus would also necessitate cultural criticism and scrutiny in relation to intragroup conflict and injustice. This focus may, in contrast, involve a rejection of excessive ascribed cultural distinctiveness – for example, the unproblematic exaltation of the minority other. For McConaghy (2000), and many others in the sphere of critical multiculturalism, this analytic is supported through a critical engagement with *all* relations and knowledges (i.e. within dominant *and* subordinate cultures) that oppress and marginalise. Such critical engagement draws attention to the dynamic, complex and contradictory ways in which privileged and marginalised cultures are constructed. It thus challenges notions of cultural authenticity and delineation. In particular, as it identifies and challenges oppressions created through dominant cultural norms, it also challenges oppressions generated through marginalised cultural norms. This approach is reflected in critical or deconstructive pedagogies that broaden knowledge and perspectives and challenge students to think critically about themselves and the broader social world (see Banks, 2007; Enns & Sincore, 2005; Garcia, 2002). Such a focus mitigates problems of reification that occur within curricula that superficially engages with marginalised knowledges. It begins with addressing the specific oppressions that create status subordination for Indigenous students rather than from a politics of group identity.

In relation to distributive justice, as noted in the previous section, arrangements impeding parity of participation might be associated with the deficit understandings and low expectations about Indigenous learners within culturally responsive teaching. These understandings/expectations impede parity because they undermine these students' academic achievement and thus displace struggles for economic justice. An alternative approach along the lines of Fraser's status model would position high academic expectations and pedagogic demandingness as a central part of culturally responsive teaching. This alternative focus would necessarily involve an 'unburdening' of 'constructed distinctiveness' that positions Indigenous culture as incompatible with and inferior to western schooling norms. Instead, it would favour a distinctiveness that supports compatibility with these norms to the extent that such distinctiveness supports these students to achieve at school in ways that maximise their future capacity to access the material benefits of the social world. Thus, it is a distinctiveness that begins with a focus on overcoming status subordination rather than group identity. In line with this logic, deploying appropriate human and material resources to prevent the chronic absenteeism and drop out of Aboriginal students, as mentioned in Kanu's work, would be focused on transforming the circumstances of poverty impacting on many Aboriginal students (through holistic approaches such as the *Head Start* program mentioned earlier) rather than on these students' distinctive Aboriginality. In these approaches recognition is approached in ways that mitigate the problems of displacement – that is they address struggles for redistribution.

Problems of reification and displacement as defined by Fraser have been major concerns in the pursuit of equity through education. An identity politics that reifies group identity and displaces a politics of redistribution is, as Fraser argues, deeply flawed. The status model offers a way of pursuing distributive and recognitive justice simultaneously through a focus on overcoming status subordination. Rather than adopting a politics of recognition that begins with group identity, this approach begins with a critical analysis of the concrete arrangements – the structures and relations of economic and cultural oppression – that impede parity. It targets precisely what subordinated parties need to be able to participate as peers in social life.

Reframing justice: issues of political representation

In Fraser's earlier work – as the preceding section illustrates– there is limited theorising around matters of political or representative justice. This absence has been a key criticism. As mentioned earlier, Feldman and Olson in *Adding Insult to Injury* argue that political injustices are analytically distinct from economic and cultural injustices. In his chapter *Participatory parity and democratic justice*, Olson draws attention to the distinct political character that is central to Fraser's notion of participatory parity. He argues that matters of political representation (i.e. being heard and accorded a voice) are crucial in any conception of justice – as he states, 'participation is distinctively *political* in character' (original emphasis, 2008c, p. 252) – and furthermore, that such participation or non-participation frames and informs how distributive and recognitive justice are understood and approached. Following this, for Olson, matters of political representation are not only analytically distinct from economic redistribution and cultural recognition but should be assigned a privileged place in Fraser's theory. Although the development of Fraser's ideas does not occlude the possibility of considering matters of political justice, her later work engages explicitly with these matters. Consistent with Olson's argument, her chapter *Reframing justice in a globalising world* explicates a three-dimensional theory of justice that specifies the political. As noted earlier, Fraser defines political injustices as arising when some individuals or groups are not accorded equal voice in decision-making – that is when the constitution of political space is such that all social actors are not equitably represented.

In this chapter, Fraser locates the significance of a focus on political justice within the global context. Fraser's argument is that the demise of the modern territorial nation state has changed the way we think about and consider justice issues – processes such as the rise of neoliberalism and global governance, transnational finance, migration and politics and global media flows have destabilised and prompted a questioning of previous paradigms and structures for understanding justice. In this 'post-westphalian' environment, she contends, there is greater uncertainty and disagreement about, for example, who might be entitled to consideration in matters of justice and how such injustices might be remedied. This uncertainty, in her view, brings to the fore problematics and tensions associated with representative justice.

According to Fraser, there are at least two types of political in/justice: first, *ordinary mis/representation* – which, she contends, has tended to be understood within nation state boundaries and relates to parity of political representation for minority groups within these boundaries and, second, *mis/framing* – where the focus is on the global and on the ways in which nation state boundaries include and exclude particular questions of justice. In relation to the latter type, Fraser argues that political space or frames can be powerful instruments of injustice as they 'furnish the stage on which struggles for justice are played out'; they 'establish the criteria of social belonging' and thus determine who and what counts in matters of distributive, recognitive and representative justice (2008b, p. 278).

In *Reframing justice* most of Fraser's theorising relates to the macro-politics of the global – especially the ways in which the 'gerrymandering' of political space impacts on 'who counts as a subject of justice' (p. 283). However, her analysis of political justice issues in this chapter has clear resonance with some of the key tensions of representation identified within the sphere of education at a more micro-political level. As noted earlier, issues of *ordinary* political justice are a focus of equity within education – in relation, for example, to concerns about the under-representation of minority groups within mainstream schooling contexts. Although not sharing the same macro-political focus (in relation to global exclusions), education theory, policy and practice have long been cognisant of similar *mis/framing* issues associated with such representation. Certainly, initiatives to increase the representation of Indigenous teachers in Australian schools, for instance, are informed by concerns about the exclusions of racialised boundaries within mainstream education. Such boundaries or frames – in their privileging of white and middle-class identities and knowledge – tend to omit or distort issues of economic, cultural and political justice for Indigenous students. In relation to matters of economic justice (as noted earlier), for example, the deficit thinking and low expectations associated with Indigenous learners that are common within mainstream frames have curtailed these learners' capacities to take advantage of the material benefits of schooling; in relation to matters of cultural justice, these frames have tended to trivialise Indigenous culture through tokenistic or superficial engagement; and in relation to matters of political justice, these frames have tended to silence or marginalise Indigenous voices – albeit often through a well-intentioned but paternalistic advocacy.

These frames clearly 'furnish the stage' on which struggles for justice are played out. Moving beyond their exclusions, for Fraser, requires re-constituting political space so that all are accorded a voice. Although again associated with the demarcation of global space, her 'all-affected principle' has been instructive here. This principle holds that 'all those affected by a given social structure or institution have moral standing as subjects of justice in relation to it' (p. 285). Moves to increase the representation of minority teachers in western schooling contexts reflect this principle. Recognising the exclusivity of mainstream frames and their effect on marginalised students, these moves create conditions of moral standing for minority groups. Although predominantly focused on quantifying minority group representation, increasing representation in this sense creates environments where genuine engagement with, and inclusion of, marginalised voices are possible.

The re-constitution of political space to be more inclusive of minority groups is, of course, crucial to supporting representative justice for students from these groups. It is well recognised that attending to, and thinking from the space of, marginalised groups can enable just and democratic societies because beginning from the lives and interests of these groups identifies and makes visible the workings of power and inequity (hooks, 1994; Mohanty, 2003). Greater minority group representation within schooling clearly supports this thinking and a challenging of exclusionary (mainstream) schooling frames.

However, it is also evident, as reflected in the previous section in relation to matters of cultural/recognitive justice, that efforts to increase minority representation within schools (e.g. through teacher quotas) are vulnerable to, and often shaped by, a politics of reification. One of the key problematics that continues to undermine political justice in education is the assumption that one needs to be a member of a particular group (whether on the basis of racial, cultural, gender or class difference) to authentically represent the interests of the group (Keddie, 2012; McConaghy, 2000). The 'cultural bio-determinism' within this politics – where one's membership to a certain identity group is seen as a literal determinant of their knowledge and actions in relation to the group – is seen to be highly problematic (see

Spivak, 1990). It restricts who can know and speak about issues of marginality and ignores the productive and important role that members of privileged groups must play to support marginalised groups. It also places undue expectation and responsibility on members of marginalised groups to authentically represent, and act on behalf of, the interests of their group (see Moreton-Robinson, 2000). It is evident then that the 'links between racialised identity, knowledge and legitimacy can no longer be sustained' (McConaghy, 2000, p. 2).

These contentions point to the problematic notion of voice in linking representation to identity in reductionist ways and reflect Fraser's concerns with reification. Such representation drastically simplifies group identity – which can set-up unhelpful binaries and essentialisms akin to the culturalism noted earlier where, for example, minority others are denigrated or unproblematically exalted. It is clear then that political justice is far more complicated than simply including marginalised voices. These voices are complex and multifaceted and, although they might represent the interests of a particular group, they cannot know or speak on behalf of all within the group and they will not necessarily support justice for marginalised groups. Consistent with the theorising presented in the previous section, working through such complexities, as Fraser contends, is supported by focusing on *how* such representation is approached. Focusing on overcoming status subordination, rather than group identity, allows for a range of possibilities depending on what precisely the subordinated parties need for parity of participation.

In relation to political justice, consistent with the earlier discussion, this may mean having 'hitherto under-acknowledged distinctiveness taken into account' but it may also mean 'unburdening' minority groups of their constructed distinctiveness. For example, initiatives aimed at increasing the number of minority teachers in schools or at creating segregated schools on the basis of race or ethnicity reflect a politics where difference or distinctiveness is affirmed. These initiatives appreciate that group identity is important in struggles for justice and that cultural distinctiveness is a means by which minority groups can assert their presence to achieve material and symbolic transformations (hooks, 1994; Spivak, 1987). However, such a politics need not ascribe to culturalism and reification – it can 'unburden' cultural distinctiveness when it recognises and values the complexity and multiplicity of marginalised voices and when it promotes understandings of oppression and marginalisation. Again, to refer to Fraser, the important issue here is *how* such distinctiveness is represented and mobilised – it can be mobilised as a strategy of the particular that is not about exclusions or the simplifying and hypostatising of culture but about overcoming status subordination (see also Spivak, 1987). McConaghy (2000) contends along these lines that there will be times when such distinctiveness is useful for particular political strategies, and there will be times when it is not. Referring to Indigenous education, the key question for her (2000, p. 261) is:

> ... when is it useful to use the notion of 'Indigenous culture' and 'Aboriginality', and when do these terms cease to become useful and instead work to limit, exclude and contain the possibilities that Indigenous people have for attaining institutional, disciplinary and political capacity?

In response to this question, for Fraser, the notion of 'Indigenous culture' or 'Aboriginality' would be useful when the focus is on overcoming the subordination of Indigenous people. In relation to political justice, although this view might support quotas to increase Indigenous representation in schools, it would reject the bio-deterministic premise that delimits who can speak for marginalised groups. Rather than beginning with an identity politics, the focus would alternatively be on genuinely including and engaging with marginalised voices in ways that problematise all modes of domination and oppression that compromise democratic relations.

Conclusion

In the introduction to *Adding Insult to Injury*, Olson (2008b) ponders the significant attention that Fraser's work has commanded since her ground-breaking essay *From Redistribution to Recognition?* – which was 'hailed as a major intervention even by those who disagreed with its core propositions' (p. 3). He attributes the wide resonance of her work across many disciplines and areas of study to her capacity to shift justice debates away from 'sterile' arguments that construct 'cultural politics' as antithetical to the politics of 'social democracy' towards more productive and useful questions of how to recognise and pursue justice in multidimensional ways. For Olson (2008b), a second reason that Fraser's work has wide resonance is in its capacity to 'make the presently chaotic scene surveyable and intelligible' – it affords 'a synoptic view of the political landscape [connecting] the dots among apparently discrete injustices [and] enabling us to consider how we might relate otherwise disparate, fragmentary struggles to the larger picture' (p. 2).

This is perhaps the key strength but also the weakness of Fraser's work. The danger in making 'chaos' 'intelligible' is that it necessarily delimits and contains. Such delimitation in the case of Fraser's three distinctive dimensions is problematic in underplaying the significance of their intersection and overlap. Matters of distribution, for example, are not purely about economics – they are informed and shaped by matters of cultural recognition and political representation. Fraser's work does attend to these intersections particularly in her later work around misframing and the propensity of political demarcation to intersect with and distort matters of justice on all three dimensions. Indeed, as she argues, this demarcation determines who and what counts in matters of distribution, recognition and representation. However, the overwhelming emphasis, especially in her earlier work, on the analytic distinctiveness of economic, cultural and political justice remains vulnerable to the criticisms originally articulated by Butler and Young – as falsely separating and polarising these areas of justice. As such, drawing on Fraser's model to make sense of the messy terrain of schooling and equity policy, research and practice requires a cautious approach that is cognisant of, and transparent about, the arbitrariness of this boundary making and the often lack of distinctiveness between and amid matters of economic, cultural and political justice. Presenting matters of injustice within these categories should not be about fixing them or diluting their complexity and interrelatedness. Fraser's model should not be offered as an ideal of justice that is static and uncomplicated but rather as a productive lens for thinking about and addressing some of the key ways in which different dimensions of injustice are currently hindering the schooling participation, engagement and outcomes of marginalised students. With this in mind, my own use of Fraser has always been enhanced through a multilayered theoretical approach (see Keddie, 2012) – it is one of the many useful and powerful lenses within my theoretical 'toolkit' that I draw on to help me comprehend the complex manifestations of injustice that characterise current equity and schooling landscapes.

It is clear, as Fraser argues, that contemporary global processes have profoundly changed the way we think about and consider justice claims. In education, as in the broader social world, these processes have transformed how equity is understood. There has been a long-held concern about how the neoliberal precepts within such processes – which have come to undergird much education policy and practice across western contexts – are undermining the important social justice role schools are expected to play. This concern, shared by many within and beyond the sphere of education, relates to how such precepts have re-articulated equity priorities in schools to a narrow focus on measuring access, retention and achievement on standardised tests. This view of equity continues to sideline the broader moral and social purposes of schooling (see Rizvi & Lingard, 2009). It has also led to prescriptive and parochial teaching that is at odds with the cosmopolitan sensibilities necessary for educators to productively engage with the unprecedented and rising levels of ethnic, racial, religious and class diversity within their classrooms (Luke, 2004; Rizvi & Lingard, 2009).

Such shifting frames for thinking about equity alongside this rising diversity mean that there will never be a sense of closure in our attempts to understand and address issues of equity through education. As McInerney (2003, p. 252) points out:

> ... the historically constituted nature of social inequalities means that there can never be any real sense of closure ... Shifts in the political, economic and cultural landscape disturb existing social patterns, produce new sets of demands for recognition among disaffected groups and generate new questions for educators working for social justice in schooling.

Amid this climate of uncertainty, what is certain is that we must continue to engage in an ongoing monitoring and critical examination of our presumptions for understanding and approaching matters of justice. This will be the key challenge in developing more productive responses to the new equity and social justice questions of contemporary education – which engage with the broader historical and political contexts that produce disadvantage in the first place (Rizvi & Lingard, 2009). Fraser's theorising is clearly useful in supporting this monitoring and engagement. Although not unproblematic, her work moves the terrain forward in providing a comprehensive and multi-dimensional approach to navigating through some of the 'chaos' of justice issues in education towards greater economic, cultural and political parity for all.

References

Amin, R., Browne, D.C., Ahmed, J., & Sato, T. (2006). A study of an alternative school for pregnant and/or parenting teens: Quantitative and qualitative evidence. *Child and Adolescent Social Work Journal, 23*(2), 172–195.

Antrop-Gonzalez, R., & De Jesus, A. (2006). Toward a theory of critical care in urban small school reform: Examining structures and pedagogies of caring in two Latino community-based schools. *International Journal of Qualitative Studies in Education, 19*(4), 409–433.

Atweh, B. (2009). What is this thing called social justice and what does it have to do with US in the context of globalisation. In P. Ernest, B. Greer, & B. Sriraman (Eds.), *Critical issues in mathematics education* (pp. 111–124). Greenwich, CT: Information Age Publishing.

Banks, J. (2007). *Educating citizens in a multicultural society* (2nd edn.). New York, NY: Teachers' College Press.

Banks, J. (2010). Multicultural education: Characteristics and goals. In J. Banks & C. Banks (Eds.), *Multicultural education: Issues and perspectives* (pp. 3–20). Hoboken, NJ: John Wiley & Sons.

Benhabib, S. (2002). *The claims of culture: Equality and diversity in the global era*. Princeton, NJ: Princeton University Press.

Bishop, R. (2003). Changing power relations in education: Kaupapa māori messages for 'mainstream' education in Aotearoa/New Zealand. *Comparative Education, 39*(2), 221–238.

Bradley, R., Chazan-Cohen, R., & Raikes, H. (2009). The impact of early head start on school readiness: New looks. *Early Education & Development, 20*(6), 883–892.

Carswell, S.B., Hanlon, T.E., O'Grady, K.E., Watts, A.M., & Pothong, P. (2009). A preventive intervention program for urban African American youth attending an alternative education program: Background, implementation, and feasibility. *Education and Treatment of Children, 32*(3), 445–469.

Connell, R. (1994). Poverty and education. *Harvard Educational Review, 64*, 125–149.
DEEWR. (2011). *7.5 million to help increase Indigenous teacher numbers*. Retrieved from http://ministers.deewr.gov.au/garrett/75-million-help-increase-indigenous-teacher-numbers
De La Rosa, D. (1998). Why alternative education works. *High School Journal, 81*(4), 268–272.
Enns, C., & Sincore, A. (Eds.). (2005). *Teaching and social justice: Integrating multicultural and feminist theories in the classroom*. Washington, DC: American Psychological Association.
Figueroa, P. (2000). Citizenship education for a plural society. In A. Osler (Ed.), *Citizenship and democracy in schools: Diversity, identity, equality* (pp. 47–62). Stoke on Trent: Trentham Books.
Fraser, N. (1997). *Justice interruptus: Critical reflections on the 'postsocialist' condition*. New York, NY: Routledge.
Fraser, N. (2007). Feminist politics in the age of recognition: A two-dimensional approach to gender justice. *Studies in Social Justice, 1*(1), 23–35.
Fraser, N. (2008a). Rethinking recognition: Overcoming displacement and reification in cultural politics. In K. Olson (Ed.), *Adding insult to injury: Nancy Fraser debates her critics* (pp. 129–141). London: Verso.
Fraser, N. (2008b). Reframing justice in a globalising world. In K. Olson (Ed.), *Adding insult to injury: Nancy Fraser debates her critics* (pp. 273–294). London: Verso.
Gale, T., & Densmore, K. (2000). *Just schooling*. Buckingham: Open University Press.
Garcia, K. (2002). Swimming against the mainstream: Examining cultural assumptions in the classroom. In L. Darling-Hammond, J. French, & P. Garcia Lopez (Eds.), *Learning to teach for social justice* (pp. 22–29). New York, NY: Teachers College Press.
Gilbert, R., Keddie, A., Lingard, B., Mills, M., & Renshaw, P. (2011). *Equity and education research, policy and practice: A review*. Carlton: Australian College of Educators.
Giroux, H. (2003). Public pedagogy and the politics of resistance: Notes on a critical theory of educational struggle. *Educational Philosophy and Theory, 35*(1), 5–16.
hooks, b. (1994). *Teaching to transgress: Education as the practice of freedom*. London: Routledge.
Huttunen, R. (2007). Critical adult education and the political-philosophical debate between Nancy Fraser and Axel Honneth. *Educational Theory, 57*(4), 423–433.
Kanu, Y. (2007). Increasing school success among aboriginal students: Culturally responsive curriculum or macrostructural variables affecting schooling? *Diaspora, Indigenous, and Minority Education, 1*(1), 21–41.
Keddie, A. (2012). *Educating for diversity and social justice*. New York, NY: Routledge.
Ladson-Billings, G. (1995). Toward a theory of culturally relevant pedagogy. *American Educational Research Journal, 32*(3), 465–491.
Luke, A. (2004). Teaching after the marketplace: From commodity to cosmopolitan. *Teachers College Record, 108*(7), 1422–1443.
McConaghy, C. (2000). *Rethinking indigenous education: Culturalism, colonialism, and the politics of knowing*. Flaxton, QLD: Post Pressed.
McInerney, P. (2003). Renegotiating schooling for social justice in an age of marketisation. *Australian Journal of Education, 47*(3), 251–264.
Mills, C., & Gale, T. (2010). *Schooling in disadvantaged communities*. New York, NY: Springer.
Mills, M. (2012). *The work of Nancy Fraser and a socially just education system, The handbook of education theories*. Charlotte, NC: Information Age Publishing.
Ministerial Council on Education, Employment, Training and Youth Affairs. (2008). *Melbourne declaration on educational goals for young Australians*. Carlton South: MCEETYA.
Mohanty, C. (2003). *Feminism without borders*. Durham, NC: Duke University Press.
Moreton-Robinson, A. (2000). *Talkin' up to the white woman: Indigenous women and feminism*. St Lucia, QLD: University of Queensland Press.
Nelson-Brown, J. (2005). Ethnic schools: A historical case study of ethnically focused supplemental education programs. *Education and Urban Society, 38*(1), 35–61.
Olson, K. (Ed.). (2008a). *Adding insult to injury: Nancy Fraser debates her critics*. London: Verso.
Olson, K. (Ed.). (2008b). Adding insult to injury: A introduction. In *Adding insult to injury: Nancy Fraser debates her critics* (pp. 1–8). London: Verso.
Olson, K. (Ed.). (2008c). Participatory parity and democratic justice. In *Adding insult to injury: Nancy Fraser debates her critics* (pp. 246–272). London: Verso.
Osler, A., & Starkey, H. (2005). *Changing citizenship*. Maidenhead: Open University Press.
Power, S., & Frandji, D. (2010). Education markets, the new politics of recognition and the increasing fatalism towards inequality. *Journal of Education Policy, 25*(3), 385–396.

Rasheed Ali, S., & Ancis, J. (2005). Multicultural education and critical pedagogy approaches. In C. Enns & A. Sincore (Eds.), *Teaching and social justice: Integrating multicultural and feminist theories in the classroom* (pp. 69–84). Washington, DC: American Psychological Association.

Rizvi, F., & Lingard, R.. (2009). *Globalizing education policy*. London: Routledge.

Robinson, J.L., Klute, M.M., Faldowski, R., Pan, B., Staerkel, F., Summers, J.A., & Wall, S. (2009). Mixed approach programs in the Early Head Start Research and Evaluation Project: An in-depth view. *Early Education & Development, 20*(6), 893–919.

Sarra, C. (2003). *Cherbourg State School, strong and smart, What Works Program; Improving outcomes for Indigenous students*. Retrieved from http://www.whatworks.edu.au/dbAction.do?cmd=displaySitePage1&subcmd=select&id=111

Sleeter, C. (2005). *Un-standardizing curriculum*. New York, NY: Teachers College Press.

Spivak, G. (1987). *In other worlds: Essays in cultural politics*. New York, NY: Methuen.

Spivak, G. (1990). *The post-colonial critic: Interviews, strategies, dialogues*. New York, NY: Routledge.

Tikly, L., & Barrett, A.M. (2011). Social justice, capabilities and the quality of education in low income countries. *International Journal of Educational Development, 31*(1), 3–14.

Williamson, J., & Dalal, P. (2007). Indigenising the curriculum or negotiating the tensions at the cultural interface?: Embedding Indigenous perspectives and pedagogies in a university curriculum. *The Australian Journal of Indigenous Education, 36*, 51–58.

The scholarship of teaching and learning from a social justice perspective

Brenda Leibowitz and Vivienne Bozalek

ABSTRACT
We argue that there is a reciprocal relationship between all scholarly activities, most importantly between teaching, learning, research and professional learning. The article builds on the work of others who call for a social justice approach to inform the SoTL. It focuses on the implications for professional learning, as an aspect of the SoTL which has been neglected. The tripartite account of participatory parity as advanced by Nancy Fraser is shown to be a valuable frame to describe instances of social justice, as well as the kind of institutional arrangements that should be instituted to support participatory parity. Alongside this, the notion of a 'pedagogy of discomfort' is shown to be an effective, but challenging means to advance awareness of justice and injustice amongst academics. The article draws on examples from three action based research projects run by the authors.

Introduction

In this article we wish to contribute to debates on the scholarship of teaching and learning (SoTL) by placing the concept within a social justice framework, most specifically that informed by the work of Nancy Fraser on participatory parity. We pose what we see as a relational or reciprocal view: that whatever aspects of teaching and learning one is dealing with and that one may be researching – whether the facilitation methods, the choice of research design, the graduate attributes enshrined in policy and programme documents, or the nature of the support for academics to engage in the SoTL – these should all be discussed in relation to the same social justice principles.

We begin this article with comments on the origins and definitions of SoTL before outlining the social and educational setting which has given rise to the approach towards the SOTL that we have taken. We then move to outline key concepts we are working with in relation to social justice, based on the views on social justice and participatory parity advanced by Nancy Fraser. We sketch in broad terms the implications of these principles for practice. After outlining the research design of the three research projects we refer to, in the penultimate section we illustrate how the principle of reciprocity plays itself out in professional development work with examples from our experience in this field, and finally, we summarise the implications for the professional development of academics.

The SoTL

The SoTL is an endeavour intersecting with various fields relating to the enhancement of higher education teaching and learning. It received its initial definition by Ernest Boyer (1990). Boyer's initial impetus was to advocate for integration of the work of an academic, and not for the autonomous status for the SoTL. He stressed the interrelationship between theory and practice: 'The arrow of causality can, and frequently does, point in *both* directions. Theory surely leads to practice, but practice also leads to theory. And teaching, at its best, shapes both research and practice' (Boyer 1990, 15/16). He placed emphasis on the scholarliness inherent in good teaching, thus on the notion of reciprocity between all matters of scholarship that we have been arguing for in the introduction to this article:

> good teaching means that faculty, as scholars, are also learners. … Through reading, through classroom discussion, and surely through comments and discussions and questions posed by students, professors themselves will be pushed in creative new directions. (Boyer 1990, 24)

The field of SoTL is distinguished from other forms of higher educational development in that it involves a degree of reflection, research or scholarship which is usually achieved in the process of academics researching their own teaching and learning contexts. In many cases, it also includes students as researchers of their own learning and as knowledge producers (Griffiths 2004). A definition that embodies SoTL is 'where academics frame questions that they systematically investigate in relation to their teaching and their students' learning' (Brew 2007, 1/2). Although there are a variety of conceptions of the SoTL, the idea that it is about academics and students engaged in research on their own teaching and learning is the view adopted for the purposes of this article.

Hutchings (2000) maintains that what distinguishes SoTL from other educational research is that it is conducted by specialists and non-specialists alike. Thus, despite the fact that not all teaching-based research refers to itself as 'SoTL', the SoTL banner remains a useful focus for theorising the research on teaching and learning (RTL) conducted by academics and the support for this work, and is for this reason the focus of this article. The increasing popularity of the SoTL and the manner in which it has been taken up has led to an emphasis on the value of SoTL to encourage academics' professional learning (Hutchings, Huber, and Ciccone 2011). Thus, there is a high stake attributed to the kind of research that is undertaken in the name of SoTL. Does this research live up to its potential? Kreber (2013b) argues that it does not, partly because of how narrowly it tends to be understood, within an 'evidence-led' instrumentalist paradigm, and that it 'has not adequately taken up the bigger questions of social justice and equality *in* and *through* higher education' (2013a, 5). We acknowledge that the field of SoTL includes a wide variety of pedagogical approaches (Hutchings, Huber, and Ciccone 2011). A significant view on the SoTL is that it ought to have a critical and transformative or social justice orientation (Gale 2009; Gilpin and Liston 2009; Kreber 2013a). Our position is that the social justice aspect of SoTL has received inadequate attention, and this is the lacuna that we wish to contribute to.

Research and teaching context

We have both worked in higher education in South Africa for the past four decades, thus during and post-apartheid. We have witnessed the oppression and injustice of the apartheid era and its continuing effects. The present dispensation has indeed contained forms of transformation in society and education, but overall there has been a disappointing lag in the movement towards change and equity (Cooper 2015; Department of Education 2008). Thus, whilst there have been significant changes and evidence of transformation in higher education, as we have argued elsewhere (Leibowitz and Bozalek 2014) there remain major disparities with regard to: the provisioning in higher education as well as with regard to the social, educational and cultural capital of students entering and exiting the system. There has been a publically expressed disappointment in the ability of universities to transform their institutional ethos into a more welcoming one (Tabensky and Matthews 2015) and one that not only turns its head in deference to and in imitation of dominant Western culture (Badat 2009). With regard to the teaching cohort in higher education, the most senior levels are predominantly white, middle class, and male, especially in the more historically advantaged institutions (HAIs), whereas the historically disadvantaged institutions (HDIs) have a large contingent of black teachers (see Cooper 2015 for more details on this). Inequality in the country has always tended to coalesce along lines of race and class, but in the present period class has tended to become slightly more salient, with more privileged students identifying themselves in terms of both race and class (Cooper 2015; Soudien 2008). Students and academics bring into the teaching and learning space vestiges of memories of oppression and oppressive thinking typical of the apartheid era. Jansen (2009) refers to this collective and enduring memory as 'knowledge in the blood' and Costandius (2012) describes how years of indoctrination would have influenced her thinking as a white Afrikaans speaking academic. Writings in the edited volume by Tabensky and Matthews (2015) suggest that many students or academics still do not feel 'at home' in higher education institutions in South Africa, and educational social mobility amongst academics remains a problem (Mabokela 2000). In short, social injustice persists with regard to matters of ethnicity and identity, thus of recognition, matters of distribution of material and cultural resources, and matters of power and voice, thus of framing (Bozalek and Boughey 2012). We will return to this tripartite account of social justice in the next section, with a discussion of the work of Nancy Fraser and participatory parity – suffice it to say that student and staff participation at university is impeded by social injustice in relation to these three dimensions.

With the democratic dispensation post-1994 and the opening up of South African society, increasing numbers of students and academics from the rest of Africa have entered the country. Despite official policies of welcome, this opening up has been met with outbreaks of xenophobia, in 2008 and 2015 (see Aljazeera 2015; Human Rights Watch 2008). These have admittedly affected people living in working class and rural areas rather than some of the more privileged spaces such as universities. This phenomenon serves to demonstrate that as change occurs, so other challenges appear, such as xenophobia. The point is simply that there is always a reason why teaching is challenged to respond to societal phenomena, and to be based on a sound ethical foundation and vision.

Social justice and teaching and learning

We see SoTL and social justice as interrelated. Moje (2007) makes the distinction in relation to general education between socially just pedagogy (equitable learning conditions for academic success) and a pedagogy for social justice (transformation of learners, knowledges and contexts through critical questioning and engagement).[1] Kreber (2013a) makes the same claim for a form of SoTL that she claims is 'authentic', *in* and *through* higher education. She sees authenticity as involving transformative learning, and as implicating both students and all academics in a process of becoming. Kreber argues that teachers achieve this authenticity through reflection: about the purpose of education, about student learning and development; and about knowledges, curricula and pedagogy. We extend this relational ontology even further, where the spheres affected by the need for reflection and reflexivity go so far as to include: the kind of research that is adopted by academics, and the principles for professional development and learning of the academics themselves. As an example of how we see academics as part of the same learning cycle as students, we found in the past that expecting students to undergo learning and unlearning processes, especially ones that are uncomfortable – what drawing from Boler and Zembylas (2003) we referred to as a 'pedagogy of discomfort – requires academics and those conducting change initiatives and researching these, to have similar learning experiences (Leibowitz et al. 2010).

This notion of reciprocity can be further extended, to inform the advocacy that academics engage in: how we agitate for better conditions for ourselves and students, so that teaching for social justice and in a socially just manner can be realised. Hutchings, Huber, and Ciccone (2011, 6) write that academics who work actively to enhance learning work 'against the grain' and that preparation and collaboration necessary to support educational innovation often goes against 'the inherited routines of academic life'. This has implications for academic developers, who should advocate for enhanced conditions for the SoTL in universities (Brew and Jewell 2012). In a compelling account of how opting for a teaching-focused position can marginalise an academic, Ragoonaden (2015) demonstrates how the high value of research outputs versus teaching is part of a larger hegemonic discourse of performativity. She maintains that university educators 'should be advocating for practices that benefit society as well as emergent transformative scholarly cultures in academia to build just, inclusive, democratic communities' (2015, 10/11). This points to a role for those who support the research of others, which Apple (2013, 43) describes in relation to educationists more generally as 'tense' and embodying 'dual commitments': to be role models and credible scholars, as well as to be activists and focusing on change in and through higher education.

Dimensions of social justice: participatory parity

In this section we advocate that social justice pedagogy be underpinned by the writing of political philosopher Nancy Fraser. Although Nancy Fraser is not a critical theorist in pedagogy, her work has been used by critical pedagogy, particularly in relation to her notion of participatory parity, which she equates with social justice (see for example Apple, Au, and Gandin 2009). The three dimensions of social justice as advanced by Nancy Fraser (2008, 2009) are a useful frame for exploring the implications of a socially just pedagogy. These dimensions are the economic, the cultural and the political, each of which either mitigates against or contributes to social justice. Fraser (2008, 2009) equates social justice with the ability to interact on an equal footing with social peers. In order to achieve participatory parity in a higher education context, *social arrangements* would have to be put in place which would make it possible for individuals to interact on a par with each other. All three of these dimensions are seen as being both analytically separate and entangled or intertwined but not reducible to the other. As Fraser (2008, 282) aptly puts it 'No redistribution or recognition without representation.' Thus, all social arrangements which are conducive to all three dimensions would have to be in place for social justice to be possible.

Each of the three dimensions of social justice can be viewed either from an affirmative or transformative perspective according to Fraser. From an affirmative perspective, social justice can be redressed by attending to the inequitable outcomes of social arrangements in ways which make ameliorative changes. Transformative approaches to social justice, on the other hand, address the root causes of the three dimensions through restructuring the generative framework which has given rise to impairment of participatory parity.

Considering socially just pedagogy from each of these dimensions: in higher education people can be prevented from participating as equals. Examples of the economic dimension include lack of access to material resources such as food, transport, housing, electricity, health care, social literacies, and funding, poorly paid or exploitative work such as continued casualisation that is now prevalent in higher education. Of concern for socially just pedagogy is how higher education students are charged differential fees which prevent those who do not have resources from access to higher education. Working class and poor students usually have to work to support themselves and family members, and they have less leisure time and less time for study than their middle class counterparts. Access to the Internet and Wi-Fi and ability to engage with digital literacies is important for participatory parity in higher education, both for students and for higher educators themselves. Affirmative approaches to dealing with these would be redistributing resources, by for example, providing national funding for study purposes without addressing inequities in the system itself. Social justice pedagogy would concentrate on transformative approaches which would examine how to change who gets to do what, (how responsibilities such as teaching and research are set and how research and teaching are valued (Bozalek and Carolissen 2012)).

In terms of the second dimension, of recognition and misrecognition, this relates to the cultural dimension. What is important for socially just pedagogy is how perceived attributes of people or practices are either valued (recognised) or devalued (misrecognised). This will impact on ways in which students and academics are able to participate in the pedagogical process. Fraser (2008, 2009) makes it clear that she is interested in institutionalised rather than psychological processes of valuing or devaluing – mis/recognition and status in/equalities. These forms of status inequality include: degrading students' prior knowledges, colonisation of settler groups where the values and attributes of certain other groups are backgrounded and rendered invisible in the curriculum. Part of the work of social justice pedagogy would be to alert people to these structural inequalities in the status order. In order to do this, it would be important to examine what knowledges are accorded less respect and esteem than others and who is valued or devalued in terms of cultural categories such as race, gender, sexuality, ability or nationality. Examples of institutional practices which would affect misrecognition would be institutional policies and practices which assume a normative social actor, such as white, male, middle class, heterosexual and where the attributes of other groups are implicitly regarded as deficient or inferior. Social justice pedagogies would consider ways of addressing these impediments to equal participation. Affirmative approaches would involve revaluing devalued categories such as indigenous knowledges or devalued social categories such as race, ability or class – this may, however, reify groups of people along a single axis, such as women or blacks, thus reducing the lived complexity of situations. A more transformative social justice pedagogy would alert students to the possibility of destabilising institutionalised cultural patterns through deconstructing binary categories.

The third political dimension which has more recently been added by Fraser (2008, 2009) to the other two dimensions to accommodate transnational flows and practices, focuses on who belongs, and is included and who is excluded from higher education pedagogies. Fraser distinguishes between two forms of misrepresentation – the ordinary political one which has the national territorial state as its frame, where particular groups of people on the basis of social markers such as gender, race and ability are prevented from participation in their national political processes. The second form of misrepresentation is more serious, and concerns how political boundaries are set and who can be a member or not. In this way, people can be excluded from participating at all, and those who are poor or devalued have no way of challenging their situations – this she refers to as *misframing*. Misframing is the most serious form of injustice as it can be regarded as a political death. Misframing in higher education occurs because of a focus on individual institutions rather than the system as a whole thus depoliticising and misframing the gross inequalities in the education system as a whole, and placing the responsibility on the individual institution as such to 'pull themselves up by their own bootstraps' (see Bozalek and Boughey 2012, for a fuller discussion of this). With affirmative approaches, individual institutions and nation states would be accepted as the spaces of higher education that socially just and social justice pedagogies should concentrate on. From a transformative perspective, structural injustices pertaining to international or global issues such as the digital divide and differential access to knowledge production and consumption, all impact groups of people *across* national territories and individual higher educational or disciplinary contexts. Fraser's 'all affected' principle addresses how these common issues affect the life chances and ability to participate as equals of those affected by these across geopolitical contexts. In this case, the most effective way of addressing these issues would be through international socially just pedagogy, which provide students and academics with various fora to develop a more collective voice to express their concerns.

Supporting the growth of academics as scholars of teaching and learning

We have chosen to illustrate this section of our argument with reference to three change initiatives that we have been involved in, in order to highlight the relationship between SoTL imbued with a social justice perspective and professional learning, because this is the domain of SoTL in relation to social justice that has been the most neglected. Our work to support the growth in SoTL amongst academics has been premised upon the notion that maldistribution, misrecognition and misframing affects academics in a like manner that it affects students. One could argue that this is less the case for academics, because to become an academic implies a greater level of social mobility, enculturation and access to dominant knowledges than would be the case for students. However in the previous section, we have argued that lack of participatory parity persists at this level, between institutions and within institutions. Furthermore, attention to the growth of academics as scholars of teaching and learning is extremely important in terms of sustainability, as academics would teach students in a socially just manner for many years, and would also be role models to students – role models in terms of how they behave, teach, relate and the way they conduct their research with students.

Three research-based interventions

The observations we make in this section derive from research-based interventions where we have both collaborated, mostly in teams with others. The first is a short course for academics, called *Citizenship, Social Inclusion and Difference (CSID)* which was designed to give academics the opportunity to engage with techniques they could use with their students, in order to explore matters of difference in the classroom. Our teaching and research approach was based on a conceptual framework informed by the notion of a 'pedagogy of discomfort' (Boler and Zembylas 2003). We led this as part of a team of five educators. The course followed on from an action research intervention that was conducted three times with students across barriers of discipline, institution, race and class (see Leibowitz et al. 2012, for a full account of the student-oriented intervention) and we used many of the same educational techniques and principles in work with students and academics. The data we draw upon stem from the responses to participant feedback questionnaires to participant feedback questionnaires, reflective essays which were a requirement for completing the course, one published paper (Clowes 2013) and one conference paper authored by the academics, about their experiences of participating in the course. A total of 28 academics participated over the three years. All the data were analysed in order to ascertain how academics responded to this approach in comparison to students. For this article we provide quotes from the one published article and one reflective essay, by one white female and one black female, as these represent the depth and complexity of many of the reactions to the course.

The second intervention is an inter-institutional course designed and facilitated by colleagues from four universities in the Western Cape region and supported by the Cape Higher Education Consortium (CHEC), a body which aims to foster inter-institutional academic programme collaboration between these four institutions. The short course was entitled *Research on Teaching and Learning: Preparing for your proposal (RTL)* and was intended to build on academics' abilities to conduct educational research in their own contexts. To facilitate this, we familiarised academics with various educational research techniques, culminating in the participants' writing of an educational research proposal. Key sources of data for this project were the drawings by each of the 28 participants in which they documented their experiences and aspirations with regard to the SOTL; transcriptions of audio-taped focus group discussions of all participants in which they discussed their drawings with each other; and feedback from all participants about the short course. Project team members conducted an analysis of all the data according to the topics of researcher identity, emotions and the use of drawings. Presentations by two project team members and five course participants were made at a panel at a local teaching and learning conference (CHEC 2013). This was an attempt to draw the 'students' into the research production process as part of their experience of being on the course.

The third intervention is a collaborative research project undertaken by 18 South African academic developers at eight institutions on the subject of professional development. The six-year-long project is entitled *Structure, Culture and Agency (S, C + A)*. The primary focus of this research project was academics' uptake of professional development opportunities at 8 South African universities, but a secondary focus was the collaborative research process for the 18 participants. The data we use in this case were collected for two papers, Leibowitz, Ndebele, and Winberg (2014) and another in process, co-drafted by 14 of the researchers. The research design in this case was a form of group reflection. At the end of the first year of the collaboration all researchers submitted an unstructured reflective text. This was analysed by three of the team members for the above publication, with a focus on researcher identity. At the end of the third year, a second round of reflective texts was submitted in response to four questions. This has been analysed by 14 of the team members, using the constructs of reflexivity – how individuals and groups mediate the systemic conditions (Archer 2007) and relational reflexivity – how individuals consciously generate group agency (Donati 2010). Evidently, each intervention had its own research design and conceptual framework. For this article, we focus on the findings which pertain directly to the SOTL and its linkages to participatory parity.

Outcomes and challenges

In order to reflect on the implications for a socially just approach to support the SoTL, we provide examples of positive outcomes as well as challenges experienced by academics who participate in opportunities to grow as scholars of teaching and learning. Some of the challenges and outcomes are influenced by issues of maldistribution, malrecognition and misframing in the strong sense of inequality pertaining to class, race or gender. Some pertain to more subtle elements, for example, to the unequal status of teaching versus research, and some due to even less overtly political phenomena, for example, due to the challenges of crossing theoretical or disciplinary paradigms.

Examples from the data of the dimension of recognition and misrecognition in the experience of academics learning to research teaching and learning abound, even though these are not always explicitly tied to issues of social status. On the *RTL* short course lecturers described themselves as 'inadequate' because of their lack of experience with research in general, with one describing her proposal apologetically as 'lumpy' (female black academic from an HDI[2]). On the *S, C + A* project, even very seasoned researchers who had to work within a new theoretical domain felt inadequate. One of the participants in this collaborative research project even used the term 'at home', a term that has gained so much currency in the South African literature on transformation and inclusion in order to express feeling included:

> I really enjoyed engaging with the group and drawing on their experience and knowledge. I felt very at home with the Project members. (Female white researcher from an HAI on S, C + A research project)

Vice (2015, 52) notes the interrelationship between feeling 'at home' and feeling productive and engaged, where she describes as feeling 'at home' as: 'we are in the "appropriate sphere of operation" of our agency'. Vice admits that the notion of feeling 'at home' is complex, as there are elements of feeling 'at home' that may be counterproductive. It is often maintained that there is a positive relationship between learning and discomfort. Nonetheless a certain degree of feeling at home is required, for an academic to flourish. In some instances feeling out of one's comfort zone and unable to participate is attributable to a sense of being a novice within a group:

> ... my own lack of knowledge about research and its processes caused me to feel unsure and sometimes even feeling totally stupid or ignorant which then kept me from participating or saying something. (Female white PhD student at HAI on S, C +A research project)

It is worth pointing out that both these statements were uttered by staff working in the field of academic professional development, who are not considered in their institutions to have academic status. This may have a constraining effect on their ability to work successfully with academics (Healey and Jenkins 2003). Maldistribution, misrecognition and misframing constitute social justice-related challenges for staff working in other support services too; for example, the library, as one of the participants in the RTL short course depicted in her drawing.

> This is me climbing over a chain nail fence – you can see through it from libraryland ... you *can* see it through, but there is a distinct barrier from the faculty neighbourhood. ... (Female white participant from HDI on *RTL* short course)

Redistribution as a dimension of social justice can be considered in relation to cultural and educational capital, as well as material goods. The sharing of research know-how and resources was appreciated by more than one educational developer in the S, C + A collaborative research project:

> I think this, for me, has been one of the most astonishing characteristics of this group of colleagues – their generosity of spirit and willingness to share resources, intellectual property, and give generously of their time. (female white researcher from HDI *on* S, C + A project)
> Through a collaborative process with two seasoned researchers resulting in a publication in a highly rated higher education journal my confidence in publishing was boosted. (Male black researcher from HDI on S, C + A project)

Amongst the resources to which academics have access is the valued knowledges or cultural resources. In the S, C + A collaborative project, the theory which was chosen to inform the conceptual framework of the project operated as a form of cultural capital, with some research participants having access to this, and others not:

> I gathered from the earlier paper that some of the project members found the social realism/critical realism theoretical framework which was used for the project difficult and challenging. I suppose I was lucky to have come into the project with some of that theory. (Female white researcher from HAI on S, C + A project)

This participant's observation regarding her theoretical knowledge is not a trivial point in relation to social justice, as cultural resources such as theories are circulated and shared in settings such as institutions or departments, and academics privileged to work in those settings – not unlike students privileged to study in particular institutional settings – benefit from such circulations. Access to theory was not expressed overtly as a social justice issue for those academics who teach in fields other than education, who find the transition to educational research a significant barrier. One academic in the *RTL* short course described his research journey as a hurdle, as 'crossing mount paradigm' (male white academic from HAI). However, if social arrangements and opportunities to access educational theory is *denied* to such an academic, this could indeed be described as a matter of social (in)justice. And certainly *within* research collaborations, one should attend to this as a crucial aspect of participatory parity, and hence social justice.

In the *S, C + A* research project material aspects of distribution or maldistribution that might impact on academics' participation were found to be: geographical proximity to the lead institution or to other researchers, or funding available to researchers in their own institutions, the latter which is often tied directly to institutional privilege (Bozalek and Boughey 2012).

Hindrances to participatory parity may be created by institutional affiliation or professional identity. Data from the *S, C + A* research project include the comment from an academic developer from a HDI who implied, by way of contrast, how his own lack of participation in the research project within which he participated was reversed:

> Coming from an academic institution where research and publishing by the academic developers has in the past not been emphasised, the need to reflect on, and share our practices through research and publications on our practices is made critical by my involvement in a study of national magnitude. (Male black researcher from HDI on S, C + A research project)

Thus far the experiences of academics who have been supported in one way or another to grapple with RTL have been discussed in relation to the tripartite account of participatory parity. However, the account of social justice pedagogy provided in the early section of this paper referred to the need to include elements of destabilisation and the creation of discomfort (Boler and Zembylas 2003). These more discomforting aspects of pedagogy were reported as extremely productive, though not always, of course, easy. One participant in the *CSID* short course found the destabilising process significant for her personal development:

> If it had not been for my involvement in this project, my life would probably have continued on a path of constant uncertainty and feelings of inadequacy – not so much because of others imposing these ideas on me, but because of me imposing it on myself (internalised oppression). I am grateful for having had the opportunity to be challenged in such a personal way, discomforting as it had been. (Female black academic from HAI on *CSID* short course)

This statement demonstrates clearly how the personal and professional lives and identities of academics are often highly interwoven (Bosetti 2015; Vice 2015). There were participants on the *CSID* short course who could see the linkages between the course, their own practice and their teaching, as this participant recorded in the final course evaluation: '[I learnt about] my part in perpetuating inequality and that I can change this through changing my teaching and learning.'

Opportunities for destabilisation, as productive as these may be, also contain inherent difficulties, as Clowes (2013), a female white academic at an HDI argues in her reflection as a participating academic on the *CSID* course. Clowes found the very process difficult, as the language used to discuss difference itself employs the same prioritisation of kinds of difference that are pervasive in post-apartheid society. In the article which she wrote about her experiences of participating in the course she contends that the participants in her cohort emphasised race over other aspects of difference such as gender, and that the facilitators endorsed this. Her struggle to convey her misgivings within the group were aggravated by her sense of risk that her dissension would be seen as lack of sensitivity to previously and presently oppressed black people. She concludes: 'South African educators need to find ways of talking about a shared future without reinscribing the same 'habits of practice' that constitute the very hegemonic discourses of inequality that require critique' (Clowes 2013, 717). Clowes' engagement with, but critique of, the methodology in the course suggests that there is much room for research into teaching and learning about social justice and in particular, but not solely, where educators are the target group.

Conclusion

In this article, we have attempted to flesh out implications of a social justice informed approach towards the SoTL for the support of academics to engage in the SoTL. These are for institutional arrangements which attend to the distribution of material as well as cultural resources amongst academics, and which attend to participatory process and a sense of inclusion and respect within research processes. Collaboration across institutional, disciplinary, national boundaries are necessary, provided that attention is paid to the opportunities for participatory parity, and where relevant, to opportunities for destabilisation and discomfort. Our examples are drawn from work in South Africa, but we contend that the SoTL and social justice for learners, educators and educational developers is an international issue.

We have found the tripartite approach to participatory parity as described by Fraser (2008, 2009) to be useful, in order to frame the discussion. Questions of participatory parity pervade all aspects of university life. We have attempted to illustrate how the social arrangements which are implicit in institutional, professional or disciplinary affiliation might serve to enable or constrain one's participation in research activities. We have not gone the next step, of demonstrating the benefit of engaging in social justice matters with academics, on the learning conditions for students – we recommend this as an important arena of study on the SoTL.

Regarding issues of social justice, we have tried to suggest the need for clear linkages between teaching and learning and research and suggest that processes and attributes based on one set of social justice principles should inform all of these relationships. If students are expected to collaborate and share, can their teachers do that? And do the teachers lead by example? If the students are expected to engage in troubling dialogues, do their teachers do that? Have the lecturers examined their long-held assumptions and deeply ingrained prejudices? If it is required that the curriculum makes place for scaffolding and enabling students to access the secrets of the disciplinary discourses of the academy, is provision made for academics to access learning theory and knowledge about research methods? To emphasise the interwovenness of all aspects of teaching and learning and the SoTL, we return to the words of Boyer, cited in the introduction to this article: 'good teaching means that faculty, as scholars, are also learners' (1990, 24).

This article is an attempt to respond to the dearth of articles written from a social justice perspective in the burgeoning field of SoTL, through its specific focus on the work of Nancy Fraser and participatory parity. It shows an attempt to go beyond the confines of educational theorising and to draw from the wisdom of other branches of knowledge such as philosophy and political science, to conceptualise what socially just pedagogies might involve. We would encourage further consideration of other approaches to social justice and socially just pedagogies in SoTL.

Notes

1. For the rest of this article, we use the term 'socially just pedagogy' as a shorthand, to refer to pedagogy *for* social justice as well.
2. HDIs and HAIs are South African terms used to denote universities that were mainly for black students and under-resourced, or mainly for white students and well resourced, during the apartheid era.

Disclosure statement

No potential conflict of interest was reported by the authors.

Funding

This research was funded by the National Research Foundation, Grant No: 90384.

References

Aljazeera. 2015. www.aljzeera.com/indepth/inpictures/2015/05/xenophobia-south-africa-15050
Apple, M. 2013. *Can Education Change Society?* London: Routledge.
Apple, M., W. Au, and L. Gandin. 2009. "Mapping Critical Education." In *The Routledge International Handbook of Critical Education*, edited by M. Apple, W. Au and L. A. Gandin, 3–19. New York: Routledge.
Archer, M. 2007. *Making Our Way Through the World: Human Reflexivity and Social Mobility*. Cambridge: Cambridge University Press.
Badat, S. 2009. "Theorising Institutional Change: Post 1994 South African Higher Education." *Studies in Higher Education* 34 (4): 455–467.
Boler, M., and M. Zembylas. 2003. "Discomforting Truths: The Emotional Terrain of Understanding Difference." In *Pedagogies of Difference: Rethinking Education for Social Change*, edited by P. Trifonas, 110–136. Falmer: Routledge.
Bosetti, L. 2015. "Academic Identity within Contested Spaces of a University within Transition." In *Contested Sites in Education: The Quest for the Public Intellectual Identity and Service*, edited by K. Ragoonaden, 107–112. New York: Peter Lang.
Boyer, E. 1990. *Scholarship Reconsidered: Priorities of the Professoriate*. Princeton, NJ: The Carnegie Foundation for the Advancement of Teaching.
Bozalek, V., and C. Boughey. 2012. "(Mis)Framing Higher Education in South Africa." *Social Policy & Administration* 46 (6): 688–703.
Bozalek, V., and R. Carolissen. 2012. "The Potential of Critical Feminist Citizenship Frameworks for Citizenship and Social Justice in Higher Education." *Perspectives in Education* 30 (4): 9–18.
Brew, A. 2007. "Approaches to the Scholarship of Teaching and Learning." In *Transforming a University: The Scholarship of Teaching and Learning in Practice*, edited by A. Brew and J. Sachs, 1–10. Sydney: Sydney University Press.
Brew, A., and E. Jewell 2012. "Enhancing Quality Learning Through Experiences of Research-based Learning: Implications for Academic Development." *International Journal for Academic Development* 17 (1): 47–58.
CHEC (Cape Higher Education Consortium). 2013. "Aspirations and Experiences of Emerging Scholars of Teaching and Learning in Higher Education." Annual Higher Education Learning

and Teaching Association of Southern Africa (HELTASA) Conference, Pretoria, November 22–24.
Clowes, L. 2013. "Teacher as Learner: A Personal Reflection on a Short Course for South African University Educators." *Teaching in Higher Education* 18 (7): 709–720.
Cooper, D. 2015. "Social Justice and South African University Student Enrolment Data by 'Race', 1998–2012: From 'Skewed Revolution' to 'Stalled Revolution.'" *Higher Education Quarterly* 69 (3): 237–262.
Costandius, E. 2012. "Teaching Citizenship in Visual Communication Design: Reflections of an Afrikaner." In *Higher Education for the Public Good: Views from the South*, edited by B. Leibowitz, 155–162. Stellenbosch: SunMedia/Trentham Books.
Department of Education. 2008. "Report of the Ministerial Committee on Transformation and Social Cohesion and the Elimination of Discrimination in Public Higher Education Institutions." Government Printers, Pretoria, November 30.
Donati, P. 2010. "Reflexivity After Modernity: From the Viewpoint of Relational Sociology." In *Conversations about Reflexivity*, edited by M. Archer, 144–164. Abingdon: Routledge.
Fraser, N. 2008. "Reframing Justice in a Globalizing World." In *Adding Insult to Injury: Nancy Fraser Debates her Critics*, edited by K. Olson, 273–291. London: Verso.
Fraser, N. 2009. *Scales of Justice: Reimagining Political Space in a Globalizing World*. New York: Columbia University Press.
Gale, R. 2009. "Asking Questions That Matter … Asking Questions of Value." *International Journal for the Scholarship of Teaching and Learning* 3 (2). http://digitalcommons.georgiasouthern.edu/ij-sotl/vol3/iss2/3
Gilpin, L., and D. Liston. 2009. "Transformative Education in the Scholarship of Teaching and Learning: An Analysis of SoTL Literature." 3 (2). http://digitalcommons.georgiasouthern.edu/ij-sotl/vol3/iss2/11
Griffiths, R. 2004. "Knowledge Production and the Research – Teaching Nexus: The Case of the Built Environment Disciplines." *Studies in Higher Education* 29 (6): 709–726.
Healey, M., and A. Jenkins. 2003. "Discipline-based Educational Development." In *The Scholarship of Academic Development*, edited by H. Eggins and R. MacDdonald, 47–57. Buckingham: SRHE and OUP.
Human Rights Watch. 2008. https://www.hrw.org/news/2008/05/22/south-africa-punish-attackers-xenophobic-violence
Hutchings, P., ed. 2000. *Opening Lines: Approaches to the Scholarship of Teaching and Learning*. Princeton: Carnegie Foundation for the Advancement of Teaching and Learning.
Hutchings, P., M. Huber, and T. Ciccone. 2011. *Scholarship of Teaching and Learning Reconsidered: Institutional Interaction and Impact*. San Francisco, CA: Carnegie Foundation for the Advancement of Teaching. Jossey Bass.
Jansen, J. 2009. *Knowledge in the Blood; Confronting Race and the Apartheid Past*. Cape Town: UCT Press.
Kreber, C. 2013a. *Authenticity In and Through Teaching in Higher Education*. Abingdon: Routledge.
Kreber, C. 2013b. "Empowering the Scholarship of Teaching: An Arendtian and Critical Perspective." *Studies in Higher Education* 38 (6): 857–869.
Leibowitz, B., and V. Bozalek. 2014. "Access to Higher Education in South Africa: A Social Realist Account." *Widening Participation and Lifelong Learning* 16 (1): 91–109.
Leibowitz, B., V. Bozalek, R. Carolissen, L. Nicholls, P. Rohleder, and L. Swartz. 2010. "Bringing the Social into Pedagogy; Unsafe Learning in an Uncertain World." *Teaching in Higher Education* 15 (2): 123–133.
Leibowitz, B., C. Ndebele, and C. Winberg. 2014. "The Role of Academic Identity in Collaborative Research." *Studies in Higher Education* 39 (7): 1256–1269.
Leibowitz, B., L. Swartz, V. Bozalek, R. Carolissen, L. Nichols, and P. Rohleder, eds. 2012. *Community, Self and Identity: Educating South African University Students for Citizenship*. Cape Town: HSRC Press.
Mabokela, R. 2000. "'We Cannot Find Qualified Blacks': Faculty Diversification Programs at South African Universities." *Comparative Education* 36 (1): 95–112.

Moje, E. 2007. "Chapter 1: Developing Socially Just Subject-Matter Instruction: A Review of the Literature on Disciplinary Literacy Teaching." *Review of Research in Education* 31: 1–44.

Ragoonaden, K. 2015. "Setting the Path Towards Emancipatory Practices." In *Contested Sites in Education: The Quest for the Public Intellectual, Identity and Service*, edited by K. Ragoonaden, 9–20. New York: Peter Lang.

Soudien, C. 2008. "'The Intersection of Race and Class in the South African University: Student Experiences." *South African Journal of Higher Education* 22 (3): 662–678.

Tabensky, P., and S. Matthews. 2015. *Being at Home: Race, Institutional Culture and Transformation at South African Higher Education Institutions*. Pietermaritzburg: University of Kwa-Zulu Natal Press.

Vice, S. 2015. "'Feeling at Home': The Idea of Institutional Culture and the Idea of a University." In *Being at Home: Race, Institutional Culture and Transformation at South African Higher Education Institutions*, edited by P. Tabensky and S. Matthews, 45–71. Pietermaritzburg: UKZN Press.

Beyond the binary: rethinking teachers' understandings of and engagement with inclusion

Stuart Woodcock and Ian Hardy

ABSTRACT
This article presents research into Canadian elementary and secondary teachers' understandings of inclusion. The research investigates how a sample of 120 teachers in the southern part of Ontario defined inclusion, and the extent to which they believed an inclusive classroom is an effective way to teach all students. The article draws upon literature into how inclusion is currently defined followed by research into the politics of diversity in inclusive education; the latter signals the socio-political aporia which attends many understandings of inclusion. The study employs Nancy Fraser's conception of justice as requiring redistribution, recognition, and representation; Fraser's approach also demands attention to issues of recognition as intimately connected with concerns about social status. The findings reveal teachers' relative lack of attention to issues of resourcing, but considerable emphasis upon issues of representation. While issues of recognition are largely valued, there is a tendency to reify categories of student identity, rather than challenging concerns about the lack of social status attending such foci. The research reveals a push 'beyond the binary' of considering teachers' practices as either inclusive or exclusive, and how teachers' engagement with resource provision, recognition of learners, and representation of student needs exists along contingent and intersecting spectra.

Introduction

Since the 1994 Salamanca Agreement (UNESCO 1994), there has been a strong international policy focus upon the right of all students to learn. This has spawned faith in inclusive practices as the best means of effecting learning for all students. However, this focus has also highlighted considerable challenges about the ways to achieve this end, including how to develop genuinely inclusive classrooms and schools. Attending this work has been a varied sense about what constitutes inclusion, and a tendency to reify binary notions of inclusion and exclusion. Such variability and reification is readily apparent internationally at the policy level, with incredibly diverse specific inclusive education policies within and across national jurisdictions (Hardy and Woodcock 2015).

However, perhaps too little attention is focused upon the actual point at which those responsible for enacting inclusive practices – teachers – make sense of notions of inclusion themselves, and the complexity and variability that attends such practices. This paper seeks to redress the relative lack of attention to the complexity of teachers' perspectives, including similarities and differences between Canadian elementary and secondary teachers at different stages of career development, revealing the often contradictory ways teachers engage with notions of inclusion.

To analyse these teachers' insights, the research draws upon political philosopher Nancy Fraser's conception of justice. For Fraser (1997, 2008), justice demands attention to redistributing resources where required, recognising difference, and ensuring adequate representation for all; this includes attention to issues of recognition as intimately connected with concerns about social status. This work is brought to bear in relation to a broader body of literature into the politics of diversity in schooling, which itself contrasts with how inclusion is defined in the literature more generally.

Defining inclusion in educational settings

While there is a wide range of literature which purports to define inclusion, an analysis of relevant reviews of literature, and a more focused analysis of the work of key internationally recognised and authoritative researchers within the field, reveals a relatively narrow focus, and reifying, of issues of inclusion more generally. There is also a tendency to privilege a conception of inclusion focused upon students with special educational needs, or disabilities, and a general conflation around these issues.

A considerable body of literature exists within the fields of special education and disabilities, but such foci are insufficiently inclusive of the needs of all students. Avramidis and Norwich's (2002) review of literature reveals elementary and secondary teachers' focus upon inclusion and integration as this pertains to students with special educational needs. de Boer, Jan Pijl, and Minnaert (2011) and Bossaert et al.'s (2013) literature reviews also focus upon students with special educational needs. De Vroey, Struyf, and Petry's (2016) literature review (2000–2012) shows how an emphasis upon students with special educational needs and/or disabilities permeates research into secondary schooling. Such attention to students with special educational needs and/or disabilities also seems to simply reinforce the experiences of many teachers during their initial teacher education and the early phases of continuing professional development (e.g. see Gargiulo and Metcalfe 2013; Mastropieri and Scruggs 2014).

These emphases upon students with special educational needs and students with disabilities are also evident in more specific studies within and across international settings (Agbenyega and Klibthong 2014; Bailey, Nomanbhoy, and Tubpun 2015; Burstein et al. 2004; Grenier 2010; McLeskey and Waldron 2007; Ross-Hill 2009; Strogilos 2012; Ypinazar and Pagliano's 2004). What is notable about this literature is the difficulty of actually focusing upon *all* students, of including *all* students in schooling settings.

Some of this international literature is more genuinely inclusive in its intent. Interestingly, Nusbaum's (2013) research in northern California, also claims to focus upon issues of inclusion in relation to students with disabilities, but is explicit in its critique of a segregated classroom for these students, and how such a stance is indicative of a lack of commitment to genuine inclusion. Greenstein (2014) explicitly critiques issues of 'engagement with issues of power' (379); drawing upon theorising from disability, feminist, and anti-capitalist standpoints, her focus is a single school's special education unit. Miles and Singal (2010) emphasise the importance of including all students within what they describe as the 'inclusive education debate' (1); importantly, inclusion is flagged as not simply about students with particular special educational needs and/or disabilities, but all students: 'Disability should be recognised as one of the many issues of difference and discrimination, rather than as an issue on its own, and broader developmental efforts should take account of the multidimensionality of such differences' (11). In broader policy studies, Engsig and Johnstone (2015) refer to the complex and contradictory discourses that surround inclusion in Denmark, with some policies advocating more genuinely wide-ranging, encompassing conceptions of inclusion, while others are focused upon more accountability-related issues. From an overtly critical position, and drawing upon Critical Race Theory, Disability Studies in Education and Cultural/Historical Activity Theory, Annamma et al. (2013) critique notions of normality and abnormality more broadly in US schooling settings.

This latter work flags the significance of issues of disputation and power – politics – in relation to conceptualising 'inclusion'. It is this concern with who is explicitly included and excluded, and how these processes are understood by elementary and secondary teachers at different stages in their careers, which is the focus of our attention.

An alternative approach: a politics of diversity

In a general text drawing upon relevant research and theory, Salend (2010) encourages a broader and more inclusive approach to schooling, explicitly referring to issues of disability, gender, race, ethnicity, language, socio-economic status, and family structure. Although limited to an Australian perspective, and largely oriented towards initial teacher education, Hyde, Carpenter, and Conway's (2010) volume on *Diversity and Inclusion in Australian Schools* takes a similarly broad-based approach to issues of inclusion and diversity.

In broad terms, Lingard (2007) refers to 'pedagogies of indifference' to bring to bear the relative lack of inclusive practices for students in schools. Drawing upon the Queensland School Reform Longitudinal Study, but resonating with other contexts more broadly, Lingard (2007) refers to how teachers failed to adequately account for students' individual needs in their teaching practices.

Sapon-Shevin (2001) takes a more overtly political stance in relation to issues of inclusion, arguing for a conception of inclusion based upon the valuing of difference and diversity. She argues that rather than 'labeling blindness and blackness as "differences"', which 'can result in racist conceptions of difference as deviance and something needing to be fixed' (35), it is more important to recognise the categorisation/labeling of such differences as social constructs, heavily influenced by the broader socio-political, cultural, and material-economic conditions within which such constructs become normalised. Such an approach then makes it possible to 'connect' specific issues of difference with a broader political project focused upon valuing diversity.

Such an ethos is in keeping with Arnesen, Mietola, and Lahelma's (2007) argument, drawing upon Slee and Weiner (2001), that we need to approach issues of inclusion in a much more radical way, reconceptualising what constitutes inclusion. Such a radical stance is similar to Annamma et al.'s (2013) critique of what constitutes 'normality' and 'abnormality'. This focus upon political inclusion is challenged institutionally by the ambivalent and ambiguous approach to inclusion in the political, legal, and administrative apparatus within and across national jurisdictions. Slee (2013) roundly criticises institutional biases in his critique of governments and international governance bodies, such as the United Nations, with their 'caveats, conditions and exemptions' (895) within their legal, administrative, and political architectures supposedly supportive of inclusion.

In their current and comprehensive review of relevant literature on professional development for inclusive education, Waitoller and Artiles (2013) argue for a much broader, genuinely inclusive approach to issues of difference and diversity. For Waitoller and Artiles (2013), inclusive education is intimately associated with issues of exclusion, based on particular categories/characteristics. Such constructions have important effects, significantly influencing the learning and lives of these students. Waitoller and Artiles (2013) draw upon Fraser's (1997, 2008) notion of social justice as necessitating attention to issues of redistribution, recognition, and representation. Such a multidimensional approach to redressing exclusion recognises the need to ensure adequate resourcing/funding to assist in cultivating more inclusive dispositions amongst teachers, valuing difference and diversity within schools and communities, and fostering a micro- and macro-political culture to achieve such ends. However, this research is also necessarily very broad in nature, and pertains to how inclusive education is defined in professional development literature, rather than in relation to how teachers themselves make sense of, and engage with, 'inclusion'; this research also does not capture the complexity and multiplicity of teachers' responses to inclusion.

Theorising inclusion: applying the work of Nancy Fraser

We argue that the reconceptualisation of inclusion advocated by the authors above can be usefully augmented by more detailed engagement with, and application of, the work of political philosopher Nancy Fraser to teachers' conceptions of inclusion. We draw upon Fraser's (1997, 2008) understanding of justice – specifically, the need for 'redistribution' to provide adequate resourcing for the benefit of all, the need for 'recognition' to validate and value the capacities and capabilities of all, and the need for 'representation' to ensure active participation of those most marginalised in society.

Such an approach also requires the need to 'rethink recognition' (Fraser 2008) away from a conception of 'identity' politics which displaces concerns about redistribution of resources ('the problem of displacement'), and which reifies group identities – thereby potentially 'freezing the very antagonisms it purports to mediate' (130) ('the problem of reification'). Instead, Fraser (2008) advocates emphasising issues of recognition as intimately connected with concerns about social status. For Fraser the emphasis needs to be upon:

> not group-specific identity but the status of individual group members as full partners in social interaction ... it means a politics aimed at overcoming subordination by establishing the misrecognized party as a full member of society. (134)

Such a positive and activist politics is a necessary corrective to the circumstances of exclusion which confront so many people's lives. This occurs when actors are construed as 'inferior, excluded, wholly other, or simply invisible – in other words, as less than full partners in social interaction' (135). In Fraser's words, such 'status subordination' is effectively 'an institutionalised relation of social subordination' (135). Going on, this status subordination leads to a form of misrecognition, which effectively disenfranchises through denying participation in social interaction. That is:

> To be misrecognized, accordingly, is not simply to be thought ill of, looked down upon or devalued in others' attitudes, beliefs or representations. It is rather to be denied the status of a full partner in social interaction, as a consequence of institutionalized patterns of cultural value that constitute one as comparatively unworthy of respect or esteem. (135)

The important point here is that such misrecognition is an actively constituted social practice, not some sort of 'ideal' to be cultivated or avoided. It is the 'workings of social institutions' which influence actual practices, contributing to, or challenging 'parity-impeding cultural norms' (135). It is these institutionalised patterns which need to be recognised for their effects, difficult though this may be. To do otherwise is to perpetuate a situation in which some are recognised as 'within the norm', 'normalised', indeed 'normal', whilst 'others' are pilloried as just that – 'other', and therefore somehow 'lesser'. For Fraser, 'redressing misrecognition' means replacing institutionalised value patterns that militate against full and equitable participation with ones that enable and foster it (136).

This focus upon recognition for social inclusion and participation also explicitly recognises the need to ensure adequate resourcing to enable this process. Some people simply 'lack the necessary resources to interact with others as peers' (137). To fail to address such issues of resourcing is to perpetuate the forms of misrecognition highlighted above. Consequently, the concerns about status to which Fraser refers entail a conception of social justice which values a dimension of recognition, as well as a dimension of redistribution to enable each to participate with all. Society comprises not only an important cultural dimension but significant economic assemblages which influence how social life is ordered.

In relation to inclusive schooling practices, this translates into ensuring adequate resourcing to provide for the needs of *all* students (redistribution), supporting social change which actively recognises and values the specific abilities and capacities of *all* students (recognition) and, providing opportunities for active and meaningful participation for *all* students (representation). In many ways, it is the professional practices which come to be normalised which are most difficult to recognise and challenge as discriminatory. While laws may be able to be changed, and seen to be changed, policies redrafted and administrative guidelines altered, the value of such changes is really only such if they help constitute changed practices on the part of those charged with enacting more inclusive schooling environments. Again, in Fraser's terms, working to 'deconstruct the very terms in which attributed differences are currently elaborated' (137) is an important part of this reculturing process, entailing 'changing the values that regulate interaction, entrenching new value patterns' which will enable 'parity of participation in social life' (137). The research presented in this paper makes use of Fraser's theoretical work, contributing to the relatively few recent contributions that draw on the detailed and complex insights of both elementary and secondary teachers, including across career stages, in national and international settings.

Critiquing disability studies in inclusion, and applications of Fraser's work

A review of relevant literature also reveals considerable application of Fraser's work in the area of disability studies, and particularly in relation to critical disability studies. However, while educators draw upon Fraser's work to critique the exclusive practices that occur within schooling settings, and in relation to social diversity more generally (cf. Keddie's (2012) work around the intersections of indigeneity, gender, ethnicity, and class), there is relatively little work that makes use of her political philosophical agenda for a more socially just society, focusing explicitly upon the complexity of teachers' understandings of inclusion. Interestingly, there is considerable work within the broader field of critical disability studies that draws upon her work. There are also alliances forged between these researchers, and researchers seeking to challenge entrenched social discrimination; a considerable body of work pertains to inclusion practices drawing upon critical disability studies and race studies (Jakubowicz and Meekosha 2002), and there are also critiques of this work (Anastasiou, Kauffman, and Michail 2016), and of critical disability studies more broadly (Vehmas and Watson 2014). However, such emphases in education are relatively rare.

While we advocate a broader conception of inclusion beyond disabilities studies alone, some literature exists that draws upon Fraser's work that can help inform discussions about inclusion more broadly. Knight (2015) refers to the conundrum of continued exclusion, and draws upon Fraser's notion of 'participatory parity' in an attempt to redress dilemmas of economic inequality and misrecognition in relation to people with disabilities. As with other researchers within the field, she also draws across multicultural and disabilities research and theorising in an effort to reconstitute notions of inclusion, and she makes reference to a small body of political philosophy that engages with issues of disability (including work by Berube 2009; Carey 2009; Clifford 2012; Nussbaum 2009). The social model of disability to which Fraser's work speaks is one in which 'a just theory of inclusion must preserve difference by securing external conditions and structures that will allow diverse citizens to participate on a relatively equal playing field' (Knight 2015, 101). It is through the valuing of difference that participatory parity might be more readily achieved. Soldatic and Grech (2014) also grapple with how to respond to what they describe as 'the contradictory politics of impairment', with their focus upon foregrounding issues of discrimination and inadequate resourcing with an affirmative politics of disability rights in the context of increasing circumstances of transnational claims for justice. At the same time as a politics of disability rights foregrounds the social constructedness of discrimination, transnational claims of abuse and discrimination are premised upon the recognition of conditions of impairment. As part of this grappling, they make brief mention of Fraser's critique of how governing practices seek to position some issues as 'political', while others are excluded; who is situated within the paradigm of disability rights, and who is excluded needs reconsidering. The solution, they argue is to advocate both an affirmative politics of disability rights, and what they describe as a transformative politics of impairment, which involves asserting and acknowledging impairment, as a means of redressing injustice at the global level.

In relation to education, Fitch (2002) provides a useful account of the social constructedness of notions of disability in education, and of the need to reconstitute the meaning of the term away from its use in a pejorative sense, to its deployment in a much more productive, transformative approach for the social valuing of all, and as a vehicle to critique practices of exclusion. He draws upon Fraser's (1997) identification of the 'redistribution-recognition dilemma' – the way in which there is an inherent tension between recognitive efforts to identify and foreground difference, at the same time as there are associated redistributive efforts that seek to undermine and overcome conceptions of difference. For example, (and paralleling Soldatic and Grech's (2014) work above), efforts to try to improve resourcing for students with disabilities more broadly have required the identification and 'labelling' of students in this way. At the same time, efforts to challenge such labelling, and to reconstitute how people see themselves and others in ways that challenge such 'norms', simultaneously serve to undercut efforts to ensure the adequate redistribution of resources to redress overt inequalities and injustices. In an effort to try to respond to this dilemma, Fitch (2002) argues for a transformative discourse of social valuing. More transformative approaches to affirmation involve challenging underlying social structures that foster normative, discriminatory conceptions of difference. This involves a reconstruction of special and general education, and that such differentiation no longer makes sense. Fitch (2002) argues that, given efforts to date have not been successful in this regard, there is a need to adopt a more overtly social justice position that involves a much closer engagement and interaction between inclusion practices around disability and critical multicultural education. For Fitch (2002) critical multicultural studies, in association with disability studies, hold the key for overcoming the tension highlighted by Fraser (1997) in the redistribution-recognition dilemma.

At the same time, there is also contestation about these associations between different identity positions, reflecting some of the complexity we seek to reveal here. Anastasiou and Kauffman (2012) argue against treating disabilities as forms of cultural difference from a more social theoretical perspective. By not differentiating disability from various forms of cultural difference, such as race and gender, and foregrounding a more positive identity positioning approach, Anastasiou and Kauffman (2012) argue that necessary adjustments are at danger of being denied to students, including, for example, for some students, dedicated classroom environments to 'better address' their specific needs. Our concern, however, with such a position, and the explicit concern of Fraser, is that the very social fabric that underpins current discriminatory practices is left entirely unchallenged by such an approach. While adequate resourcing for students with myriad needs is essential, *how* this resourcing is provisioned is of the utmost importance, and approaches that attempt to justify the 'norming' of some students as worthy of exclusion from educational settings, need to be challenged. Fraser's work is particularly helpful in this regard.

Methods and methodology

The research draws upon a sample of 120 Canadian teachers (78 elementary; 41 secondary teachers; and 1 non-identified) located within a large metropolitan region in southern Ontario. In keeping with the research focus upon inclusion, teachers were asked to define inclusion and whether they believed an inclusive classroom was an effective way to teach all students. Teachers' responses were then divided into those who *did* believe that an inclusive classroom is an effective way to teach all students, and those teachers who did *not* believe this. Reflecting how ambivalent responses to inclusion are actually occasions of exclusion, a discussion was had amongst the research team about the small number of teachers (four) who qualified their responses. In keeping with Fraser's (2008) call for full representation for all, and recognition of the diverse abilities of all, and reflecting a strong politics of advocacy for inclusion as inclusive educational researchers (challenging what Greenstein (2014) refers to as 'the exclusionary basis of mainstream schooling' (380)), we decided to include these teachers' responses in the category of teachers who did *not* believe an inclusive classroom is an effective way to teach all students. By flagging this process, and our own position as strong and active advocates of and for inclusive practices, we also seek to adopt a reflexive stance in relation to the research process itself; we do this even as we also acknowledge our own positionality as able bodied, white male middle-class researchers in relatively privileged positions (tenured academics). Through explicitly reflecting upon the knowledge production processes in which we have engaged, we also endeavour to be true to efforts to 'refract the research process and make new forms of research production possible' (Slee and Allan 2001, 186).

A random sample of schools was selected from local school boards whose senior personnel gave permission to conduct the research. Principals gave their informed consent for staff in their schools to participate, and teachers were subsequently informed about the research at their staff meetings. Again, in keeping with the need to ensure informed participation, teachers and school-based administrators volunteered to participate on the basis of information provided to them about the nature of the broader project. The research conforms with university and state/provincial/ school board educational authority ethical review processes, including explicitly acknowledging the importance of taking the needs of respondents into account. All responses were anonymous and confidential.

The research is part of a broader international study (Canada, England, and Australia) into teachers' understandings of and beliefs about the effectiveness of inclusion, including in relation to special education, and the nature of the teacher professional development practices which attend these foci. Again, foregrounding our own concerns as researchers for the cultivation of more inclusive practices in classrooms – as advocates for 'irregular' (inclusive) rather than 'regular' (exclusive) schooling (Slee 2011) – and seeking improved insights into the nature of teachers' perspectives on inclusive practices to better challenge prejudices, the research presented here focuses on initial questions, in a larger survey questionnaire, about teachers' understandings of inclusion, and their beliefs in the effectiveness of inclusion in the classroom for all students. The first question investigated here was originally Question 1, and was open-ended:

- How do you define an inclusive classroom?

The second question under analysis here was originally Question 2, and closed:

- Do you believe an inclusive classroom is an effective way to teach all students ['Yes'; 'No']

One of our principal contributions is that we are focusing on teachers' perceptions of inclusion for all, not just students with special educational needs and/or disabilities, which seem to have been key priorities in so much of the existing literature. Consequently, we deliberately ensured the question about defining inclusion was couched in broad terms to enable teachers to elaborate *their* understandings of inclusion, and do so in a way which did not flag issues of special educational needs and/or disabilities.

In this article, and reflecting our own predisposition for a more socially just world in which adequate material resources are provided to ensure the proper recognition, valuing and representation of diverse abilities, and status position of all with diverse abilities, we analyse teachers' responses to these questions in light of Fraser's political theory of justice to help ascertain the extent to which teachers seemed to be inclusive in their understandings of students' capabilities and capacities. To enable a comparative perspective across sector taught (elementary/secondary) and career stage (early; established; mid; and experienced), we also elaborated teachers' perspectives on inclusion vis-à-vis these categories, and in relation to Fraser's theory of justice. At all stages, this productive politics of advocacy for diversity informed the research process. Specifically, it was evident in the way we first separated teachers' responses to the second question according to whether teachers indicated 'yes' or 'no' to an inclusive classroom as an effective way to teach all students. (For the reasons noted earlier, including our own predisposition to unequivocally support inclusive practices, the four teachers who were ambivalent, were categorised under the 'no' column.) We then used Fraser's concepts of redistribution, recognition, and representation (and social status) to collate teachers' comments about their definition of inclusion according to whether they answered 'yes' or 'no'. Again reflecting our support for such a productive and rounded politics of inclusion, within each of these 'yes'/'no' categories, teachers' responses were further categorised according to whether they explicitly referred to issues of redistribution, recognition, and representation in largely positive or negative terms.

To help contextualise these more fine-grained analyses of teachers' conceptions of inclusion, and again in keeping with our own conviction in the importance of shedding light upon teachers' understandings of inclusion, the first part of the analysis/findings begins with an overview of the extent to which teachers' comments were primarily positive or negative in relation to whether they construed an inclusive classroom as an effective way to teach all students; this includes some indicative comments to exemplify teachers' responses. This is followed by more explicit reference to the nature of the extent to which teachers appeared to give adequate regard to issues of redistribution (resourcing) for inclusion; recognition (and social status) of all students; and, representation of all students as active learners.

Findings: teachers' perceptions of inclusion

Overall, the comments from participants reveal a predominantly positive attitude towards issues of inclusion in general. Eighty-five per cent of comments were positive, while only 15% of comments were negative; this includes comments about more limited conceptions of inclusion, such as inclusion as predominantly associated with disabilities – a situation reflected in so much of the broader literature (e.g. see Agbenyega and Klibthong 2014; Bailey, Nomanbhoy, and Tubpun 2015; Grenier 2010; Strogilos 2012). Of teachers who believed that inclusive classrooms were effective environments for all students to learn, 92% of comments were positive, while 8% were negative. For those teachers who claimed not to believe inclusive classrooms were an effective way to teach all students, 71% of comments were positive, while 29% of comments were negative. This indicates a level of understanding about what constitutes inclusive education, even as teachers claimed *not* to believe inclusive classrooms are an effective way to teach all students.

Of the positive comments that were made, 74% were made by teachers who believed inclusive classrooms were an effective way to teach all students. While there were some more incidental references to years of experience influencing teachers' conceptions of whether administrative support was provided, or whether there was adequate planning time and professional development (Blecker and Boakes 2010), much of the existing literature does not refer to the influence of teachers' experience/career stages. The research presented here presents some interesting insights into their conceptions of inclusion vis-a-vis these experiences.

Amongst elementary teachers, there was a tendency for less and more experienced teachers to believe an inclusive classroom is an effective way to teach all students; 78% of early career teachers believed this, compared with 56% of established teachers, 61% of mid-career teachers, and 67% of experienced teachers.[1] Amongst secondary teachers, there was a similar pattern at the beginning and later stages of the experience spectrum, but with secondary teachers tending to be less likely to believe an inclusive classroom is an effective way to teach all students in the middle stages of their career. However, they were more likely to believe in the value of inclusion further into the early stages of their career than their elementary colleagues; 75% of early career teachers believed this compared with 82% of established teachers, 53% of mid-career teachers, and 67% of experienced teachers. The proportion of elementary teachers (30%) who claimed that they did not believe an inclusive classroom is an effective way to teach all students was almost identical to the proportion of secondary teachers (34%) – that is, about one third of all teachers within the sample.

At the same time, 26% of positive comments were made by teachers who claimed not to believe inclusive classrooms were an effective way to teach all students. Perhaps most interestingly, of the negative comments that were made, 40% of those comments were made by teachers who claimed to believe that an inclusive classroom is an effective way to teach all students; this included a reasonably even spread of early career, established and mid-career teachers, but no experienced teachers. These teachers construed students' needs in myriad ways, all of them problematic. This included individualising students ('All learners can meet their definition of success provided the effort and opportunity is taken' (S35, Est^2)^3, 'All students can achieve their best results through using their strengths to overcome their needs' (E59, EC)); conflating issues of equity and equality ('treating everyone as an equal' (S33, Est)); equating inclusion with issues of disability ('Differentiation should occur for students who have learning and behavioral disabilities' (S9, Mid)); and inclusion as integration ('a classroom where all students are integrated' (E32, EC)). Teachers who made negative comments, and who also *did not* believe that inclusive classrooms were an effective way to teach all students, tended to emphasise inclusion as pertaining to students with special educational needs ('wide range of abilities, some students may have special needs' (E8, Mid), 'A classroom where students and teachers learn from each other regardless of abilities' (E37, Est), 'A classroom where students are placed with peers according to their age, including those with developmental delays' (E42, EC)).

Redistribution (resourcing) for inclusion

While issues of redistribution are recognised as important in other settings (e.g. Bourke's (2010) criticism of a lack of time and systemic support for teachers to understand what constitutes inclusion in Queensland), in relation to defining inclusion, across the sample as a whole, there was relatively little explicit focus upon issues of redistribution. That is, only 10 teachers out of 120 (8.3%) referred to issues of resourcing (the most common reference to distributive/redistributive matters); see Table 1. Of these 10 teachers, 9 worked in elementary schools. Half of all teachers referring to resourcing issues were at the early career stage, and most of these teachers referred to resourcing issues positively (four out of five teachers).

Generally, 'negative' responses related to funding issues/resourcing but in largely pejorative ways in relation to inclusion.

For one of the three teachers who did not believe in an inclusive classroom, inclusion was largely construed as synonymous with issues of funding in a negative way – that is, inclusive classrooms were seen as sites of deprivation, specifically in relation to perceptions of a lack of government support:

A classroom where the government doesn't give enough money for the proper resources to be available. (E4, EC)

For this teacher's colleague, a slightly more experienced teacher who also expressed concerns about resourcing, this related to access to support personnel, although again how these personnel were to be deployed was potentially very problematic for certain groups of what she referred to as 'these' students:

There may or may not be additional support from Educational Assistants to help with *these* students. (E61, Est; emphasis added)

Table 1. Teachers' perceptions of inclusive classrooms and redistribution (resourcing).

	Total number of teachers who mentioned resourcing	Proportion of teachers who believe in inclusive education	Proportion of teachers who do not believe in inclusive education
Positive comments	8	7	1
Negative comments	2	0	2
Total	10	7	3

For the third of these teachers, issues of resourcing were expressed more 'positively', and related to issues of equity, rather than equality:

> Fair in our classroom does not mean equal; it means everyone gets what they need. (E31, Mid)

At the same time, for teachers who did believe in inclusive classrooms, comments were very broad and provided little nuance about issues of redistribution. The secondary teacher, for example, took a very global approach, referring to the need to ensure students had access to the 'necessary tools' to enable their learning:

> An inclusive classroom is one where all students are given the tools necessary to learn, experiment and grow to the best of their ability. (S7, Est)

An elementary colleague referred to 'economic needs', alongside academic and social/emotions needs:

> One that meets the academic, social/emotional, economic needs in the classroom. (E3, EC)

Other teachers referred to 'a new and better space' (E39, Mid), and the need to ensure 'necessary assistance' (E53, EC). However, there was also some mention of issues of equity versus equality, and an understanding of the imperative to differentiate between the two:

> Being fair is valued and fair is not necessarily equal, as fairness isn't sameness. (E27, EC)

In this way, teachers exhibited varied responses to inclusion in relation to issues of redistribution, but overall, tended not to focus on these issues to any great extent. Such findings reflect not so much concerns about what Soldatic and Grech (2014) (in the domain of disability studies) refer to as tensions between 'a politics of impairment' (focused upon foregrounding issues of discrimination and inadequate resourcing) and an affirmative politics of disability rights, but a shallow conception of issues of resourcing more generally, and in relation to inclusion conceived more broadly. For those teachers who were genuinely more inclusive in their approach, their responses reflected concerns about the importance of adequate resourcing to assist them in their work, but little angst about the politics of representation that attended such work. In this way, arguably, these 'front-line' teachers may have appeared to elide these concerns, as they considered how to cater for students in their classroom. Either way, their responses indicate a mixed, and, arguably, contradictory understanding of inclusion.

Recognition (social status) of all students

In relation to defining inclusion, and unlike issues related to resourcing, there were many more responses and much more focus upon issues of recognition. As Table 2 summarises, 77 (64%) out of 120 teachers in the study referred to recognition-related issues within an inclusive context. Sixty-seven teachers referred to issues of recognition positively, while 10 teachers referred to issues of recognition negatively.

Forty-two per cent of early career secondary teachers were positive about issues of recognition in relation to inclusion, compared with 36% of more established teachers, 27% of mid-career teachers, and 50% of experienced teachers. One striking feature of these results is the significant gap between

Table 2. Teachers' perceptions of inclusive classrooms and recognition of students.

	Total number of teachers who mentioned recognition	Proportion of teachers who believe in inclusive education	Proportion of teachers who do not believe in inclusive education
Positive comments	67	50	17
Negative comments	10	6	4
Total	77	56	21

elementary and secondary mid-career teachers (81% versus 27%), but also how these figures 'balance out', relatively, towards the latter stages of teachers' careers (58% versus 50% respectively).

As indicated in Table 2, of the 56 teachers who claimed they believed in inclusive education, 6 made negative comments about inclusion, while the remaining 50 teachers were broadly positive. Of these 50 teachers, 47 teachers conceptualised recognition positively in broadly inclusive ways, while the remaining three teachers expressed a slightly more nuanced understanding, pertaining to issues of race, gender, socio-economic status, age, culture, language, creed, and learning needs; however, they seemed to exhibit a reified understanding of these 'categories'. That is, a strong identity politics persuasion was in evidence (Fraser 1997, 2008).

Of teachers who conceptualised issues of recognition positively (regardless of whether they believed an inclusive classroom is an effective way to teach all students, or not), 23 teachers (30%) referred to the need for learning environments which were 'safe'. Many of these teachers – both elementary and secondary – were within the first 10 years of their careers, but several were also mid-career teachers:

All students are engaged, feel safe; (E78, Est)

[An environment] where everyone feels safe and able to learn. (E1, Mid)

Eighteen teachers (23%) referred to the importance of learning environments in which students were 'valued'. Again, there was a spread of responses from teachers across career stages and sector (elementary/secondary):

All students are ... valued members of the community; (E38, EC)

A classroom where each student is valued. (S16, Est)

Fourteen teachers (18%) referred to the importance of learning environments in which students' 'needs' were addressed. These tended to be more established and mid-career teachers, with fewer early career and very experienced teachers represented; this was the case in both elementary and secondary sectors:

A classroom that aspires to meet the social and academic needs of all students within it; (E77, Mid)

Where the diverse needs and strengths of the students are assessed and programmed for. (S4, Exp)

Eight teachers (10%) referred to learning environments as needing to be places where students could 'succeed'; six teachers (8%) each referred to the need for learning environments which were 'welcoming', 'respected' students, and/or catered for varying 'ability levels'. There was considerable representation from more experienced teachers, in this category, even as there was a spread of responses across categories and sectors:

A place where all students have the opportunity to learn and succeed; (S26, Mid)

An inclusive classroom is open and welcoming to a diverse student population; (E63, Mid)

The environment is based on mutual respect and is fair; (Non-identified[4])

A classroom in which all students of varying ability levels are able to access curriculum. (S6, Exp)

The three teachers who conceptualised issues of recognition in slightly more nuanced ways still tended to reify issues of identity politics. They tended to cluster students according to specific categories – of age, gender, ethnicity/race, culture, creed, socio-economic background, and language – even as they also believed an inclusive classroom is an effective way to teach all students, and even as they conceptualised issues of recognition in broadly positive ways:

Consider[s] all aspects of the individuals involved, such as, age, gender, race, culture, languages spoken/read; (E11, EC)

Promotes the safety and well-being of students of all creeds, socio-economic backgrounds, cultures, gender identifications. (S39, Est)

Of the seven teachers who conceptualised issues of recognition negatively, and who did not believe an inclusive classroom is an effective way to teach all students, there was a bias towards less experienced teachers, and most placed considerable emphasis upon inclusion as dominated by special educational needs (cf. Avramidis and Norwich 2002; Scruggs and Mastropieri 1996) and disabilities (cf. Agbenyega and Klibthong 2014; Bailey, Nomanbhoy, and Tubpun 2015; Grenier 2010; Scruggs and Mastropieri 1996; Strogilos 2012):

> A classroom where students are placed with peers according to their age, including those with developmental delays (below 4th percentile) and gifted students (99th percentile); (E42, EC)

> An inclusive classroom has identified special needs students in it. (E61, Est)

Such responses are similarly reflected in Nusbaum's (2013) research highlighting teachers' emphasis upon students with disabilities, even as they espoused claims about addressing issues of inclusion more generally. These emphases upon disabilities are removed from Fitch's (2002) argument about the need to reconstitute the meaning of notions of disability away from its use in a pejorative sense, to its deployment in a much more productive, transformative way.

Interestingly, those teachers who did not believe an inclusive classroom is an effective way to teach all students and who made negative comments regarding recognition were all elementary teachers (albeit this was only 4 elementary teachers out of a total of 67 teachers, i.e., 6% of the elementary teacher cohort).

For one teacher who claimed to believe that an inclusive classroom is an effective way to teach all students, his comments reflected a much less inclusive stance than might be anticipated. For example, there was a privileging of issues pertaining to ability over other descriptors of difference: 'Where each child regardless of skill, ability, intelligence … feels welcome' (E76, Exp). Such a response suggests a need to interrogate the extent to which teachers genuinely understand inclusion.

Overall, issues of recognition were widely canvassed amongst teachers, generally positive in tone, but also tending to foreground more traditional conceptions of identity politics. The latter is in keeping with Fraser's (2008) concerns about the reification of particular groups of students, and the subordination of the status of members of these 'categories' within society more generally.

Representation of students as active learners

In relation to defining inclusion, and similar to issues pertaining to recognition, there was a significant number of responses, and focus upon, issues of representation. Eighty-three (69%) out of 120 teachers in the study referred to issues relating to representation within an inclusive context. Forty-five elementary teachers (88%) and 25 secondary teachers (83%) referred to issues of representation positively. In relation to issues of representation, and similar to issues of recognition, there was relatively little difference between elementary and secondary teachers. However, for secondary teachers, there was considerable balance across career stages even as a larger proportion of early career teachers (67%) were positive about issues of representation vis-à-vis their more experienced colleagues (45% of established teachers; 47% of mid-career teachers; and 42% for experienced teachers). For elementary teachers, 44% of early career teachers were positive about issues of representation in relation to inclusion, compared with a much larger proportion of established teachers (75%), mid-career teachers (48%), and experienced teachers (83%).

Fifty-one out of 55 teachers (93%) who believed an inclusive classroom is an effective way to teach all students conceptualised issues of representation positively. Forty-five elementary teachers (88%) and 25 secondary teachers (83%) referred to issues of representation positively (Table 3).

Nineteen out of 28 teachers (68%) who did not believe an inclusive classroom is an effective way to teach all students, also conceptualised issues of representation positively. In relation to issues of

Table 3. Teachers' perceptions of inclusive classrooms and the representation of students as active learners.

	Total number of teachers who mentioned representation	Proportion of teachers who believe in inclusive education	Proportion of teachers who do not believe in inclusive education
Positive comments	70	51	19
Negative comments	13	4	9
Total	83	55	28

representation, and similar to issues of recognition, there was relatively little difference between elementary and secondary teachers.

For those teachers who referred positively to issues relating to representation within an inclusive context – and reflecting calls for the inclusion of *all* students more broadly (Miles and Singal 2010) – 17 teachers focused upon the importance of the needs of all students being met. There was also a tendency for more experienced and mid-career teachers to be represented, with relatively fewer early career teachers; this was the case across both secondary and elementary cohorts:

> A classroom where all students get what they need. It is not necessarily equal for each student; (E23, Est)

> An inclusive classroom is one which tries to meet the needs of all learners as best as possible; (E30, Mid)

> A classroom where everyone's strengths and needs are identified and met. Where everyone respects each other's diverse needs and opinions. (E36, Mid)

Twelve teachers emphasised the importance of students sharing learning together. While elementary teachers tended to be more experienced, there was a proportionally larger representation of mid-career teachers amongst secondary cohort:

> An inclusive classroom is a classroom where all students are learning together; (S10, Mid)

> A community of learners where all gifts, abilities and challenges are shared; (E20, Exp)

Twelve teachers referred to the importance of students actively participating/being engaged/demonstrating their learning. While there was a considerable spread of responses amongst secondary teachers, there tended to be a bifurcation between early career and experienced teachers amongst their elementary colleagues:

> A space where students are engaged in their learning … and where there are varied opportunities for students to demonstrate their learning; (E12, EC)

> A place where every student has the opportunity to participate and learn. (S2, Est)

Of the 13 teachers who conceptualised issues of representation negatively, 12 teachers argued that an inclusive classroom is not an effective way to teach all students. Again reflecting broader foci upon issues of special educational needs (cf. Avramidis and Norwich 2002; Scruggs and Mastropieri 1996) and disabilities (cf. Agbenyega and Klibthong 2014; Bailey, Nomanbhoy, and Tubpun 2015; Grenier 2010; Scruggs and Mastropieri 1996; Strogilos 2012), most of these 12 teachers placed considerable emphasis upon issues of ability/level, special educational needs/disabilities, and integration/mainstreaming/'regular' classes. While the majority of these elementary teachers tended to be less experienced (early career and 'establishing'), the largest proportion of secondary teachers in this category were mid-career:

> Classes that are relevant to their life learning goals i.e. many global delayed students need to know how to do laundry and cook an egg and budget not about the history of the world; (E4, EC)

> A class that includes students with a wide range of abilities, some students may have special needs; (E8, Mid)

> Differentiation should occur for students who have learning and behavioral disabilities. (S9, Mid)

The one teacher who conceptualised issues of representation negatively, but who claimed to believe that an inclusive classroom is an effective way to teach all students, appeared to conflate inclusion with issues of ability, to the exclusion of other signifiers of difference:

> A classroom that provides appropriate instruction to students with a variety of needs and abilities. (S31, Mid)

Consequently, there was a relatively strong focus upon issues of representation amongst teachers, including meeting the needs of all students, sharing learning together and participating/being engaged/demonstrating learning, and cultivating a sense of belonging. However, there were also more concerning foci emphasising ability/level of students, special educational needs/disabilities, and integration/mainstreaming/'regular' classes. Again, these foci upon ability and disability were removed from broader discourses associated with critical disability studies with their emphasis upon challenging societal norms that discriminate against and therefore diminish these students as people (Knight 2015).

Discussion: beyond the 'binary'

One of the key findings of the research is that only a relatively small number of teachers expressed concerns about issues pertaining to resourcing (10 out of 120 teachers); these teachers worked mostly in the elementary sector, and tended to be in the earlier stages of their careers. Even as these teachers tended to mention issues of resourcing positively, overall this situation is problematic, because as Fraser (2008) argues, issues of resourcing are imperative to enable the sorts of reconstitution of institutional patterns of cultural value which marginalise so many students. Even as 'success of … inclusion is not only a matter of access to resources' (Agbenyega and Klibthong 2014, 1250), students cannot attain the forms of social status, which enable them to be full partners in their learning, and full members of school and wider social contexts more generally, if there is not adequate resource provision to bring to light, and redress, more problematic values and practices. The sorts of social constructions of difference, which are so consequential for mediating access and participation to learning in schools (Waitoller and Artiles 2013), cannot be challenged without adequate resourcing to enable those within and outside social institutions to critique problematic, actively constituted (albeit misrecognised) social practices, that marginalise the least advantaged.

The emphasis upon resourcing issues could be construed as in keeping with Anastasiou and Kauffman's (2012) argument that the identification of students as disabled focuses necessary attention to their particular needs, including resource-related needs. However, as critical disability studies more broadly argue, such a stance does not adequately address the more difficult and necessary need to challenge entrenched social practices that actively (and often overtly) discriminate against particular students and their families.

While issues of resourcing tended to be relatively marginalised amongst teachers, a small number of teachers *did* frame their understanding of issues of redistribution within an equity paradigm rather than simply in relation to equality. This explicit articulation of an equity principle – that equity is not about 'sameness' (equality of provision) but about redressing specific needs according to particular circumstances (equity) – is important, even as it is relatively rare.

While acknowledging that the total number of teachers who recognised issues of resourcing as important was low, the number of teachers who foregrounded issues of 'recognition' was relatively high. When issues of recognition were mentioned, they were mostly construed positively, and this 'positivity' tended to increase significantly for secondary teachers towards the latter stages of their careers, even as their elementary counterparts tended to be more erratic in the extent to which they recognised issues of difference. This is at least a starting point for developing the sorts of 'radical change in the ways of knowing' (Arnesen, Mietola, and Lahelma 2007, 99) supported by more politically informed theorists and researchers, including in the area of critical disability studies more generally. For those teachers who conceptualised issues of recognition positively (regardless of whether they believed inclusion is an effective way to teacher all students, or not) issues of student 'safety' were significant, as was ensuring that students' felt 'valued' within learning environments, and that their needs were addressed (social and academic, with strengths identified), that students could succeed, and that these environments were welcoming, respected students, and catered for students' varying ability levels. Such responses, whilst indicating at least some very broad understanding of inclusive practices and principles, also reveal the high level of abstraction and generality that characterises teachers' understandings of inclusion. That is, these teachers did not fit a simple binary of being either 'for' or 'against' inclusion, but instead reflected a varied understanding of what constituted inclusive practices. These responses resonate in part with the 'pedagogies of indifference' (Lingard 2007), even as teachers sought to redress these 'indifferences'.

Relatedly, the very point of signifying and foregrounding 'special needs students' by teachers is part of this story of not adequately recognising the variety of differences which characterise the student body. In keeping with critical disability studies more broadly, the use of the term 'special needs' (and its variations) diminishes concerns about Fraser's (2008) point about the need to challenge the reification of particular 'categories' ascribed to particular peoples, and the importance of the status of individuals as always deserving of full participation/ partnership with others, that is, 'status of individual group members *as full partners in social interaction*' (134; emphasis added). Furthermore, the foregrounding of 'special needs students' marginalises students' very sense of personhood – their importance as people first and foremost – and potentially foregrounds a deficit conception of these students' capabilities, thereby diminishing their intrinsic value as people (Slee 2013). A genuinely inclusive approach actively recognises and values *all* of the capacities of *all* students, enabling meaningful participation by *all* students.

To be truly inclusive, it is essential to foster diversity; this requires a strong stance and ideological commitment to genuine inclusion (Nusbaum 2013). Even the three elementary teachers who conceptualised issues of recognition in slightly more nuanced ways still struggled to move beyond a less reified conception of identity politics; students' needs were recognised as influenced by gender, ethnicity, socio-economic background, and language, but these 'categories' still tended to act as 'hold alls' for these teachers. Again, a simple binary distinction – as these teachers being either 'for' or 'against' inclusion – did not hold. Inclusion needs to be considered in a broad-ranging manner, not restricted to the needs of particular, reified 'groups' of students. In Fraser's (1997, 2008) terms, inclusion is a form of social justice which is actively and robustly responsive to the specificity of students' complex, inter-related, changing needs, over time. This resonates strongly with Sapon-Shevin's (2003) argument about going beyond issues of disability: 'inclusion is not about disability, nor is it only about schools. Inclusion is about social justice. Inclusion demands that we ask, "What kind of a world do we want to create and how should we educate students for that world?"' (26). An inclusive approach demands valuing multiple identities and avoiding the falsehoods of 'partial inclusion':

> Looking at all differences within this more inclusive framework can help us understand effective approaches to difference: valuing multiple identities and communities, involving families in children's lives and schooling, and avoiding the slippery slope of partial inclusion. (Sapon-Shevin, 2001, 35)

Such a stance is also reflected in Annamma et al.'s (2013) call for 'a fundamental societal shift', to challenge taken-for-granted practices, even as 'there is nothing trite about changing the way we speak, think and act as people and as a society' (1288). Arguably, such a stance also challenges more conservative approaches to particular identity categories, such as those associated with students identified as 'having a disability'; again, the tensions evident in Anastasiou and Kauffman's (2012) argument, that necessary adjustments are at danger of being denied to students without such signifiers, are apparent. However, such a stance is heavily contested in relation to disability studies more broadly (Knight 2015), and in relation to education in particular (Fitch 2002).

For those teachers who conceptualised issues of recognition negatively, there was a relatively strong emphasis upon inclusion as dominated by discourses of 'special educational needs' and/or 'disabilities'; this is entirely in keeping with more traditional conceptions of inclusion (cf. Avramidis and Norwich 2002; Burstein et al. 2004; de Boer, Jan Pijl, and Minnaert 2011; Gargiulo and Metcalfe 2013; McLeskey and Waldron 2007; Ross-Hill 2009; Scruggs and Mastropieri 1996; Ypinazar and Pagliano 2004). Most of these teachers construed inclusion as involving all students, even as they highlighted the category/ies of special educational needs and/or disabilities, but some teachers construed inclusion essentially as exclusion, that is, as entailing the provision of separate special education classrooms alongside 'mainstream' classrooms, and without taking into account the multidimensionality of differences (Miles and Singal 2010). Such an approach also sometimes reflected more traditional integration beliefs with students spending time in both 'special education' classrooms, and 'regular' classrooms. And such an approach also resonates with those less critical disability approaches that would frame students who need considerable interventions to assist them with their learning as having the 'right' to be able to access more 'specialised' services in separate, 'non-mainstream' settings (Anastasiou and Kauffman 2012). The problem with such perspectives, in terms of social justice, however, is that they ultimately seek to provide some sort of justification for what are essentially discriminatory practices (Ballard 2007).

In relation to teachers' understandings of representation, and amongst those teachers who identified as believing an inclusive classroom is an effective way to teach all students, there was a strong focus amongst teachers on: the importance of ensuring that all students' needs are met; challenging the conflation of issues of equity and equality; and, focusing upon and respecting students' strengths alongside their needs. However, again, teachers appeared to be at a variety of points along a spectrum of 'more' or 'less' inclusive practices in regard to representation, and this varied at different times during their careers. Secondary teachers tended to be more stable in their understandings of representation, even as they tended not to maintain the higher levels of enthusiasm that characterised earlier stages in their careers. Elementary teachers tended to be more erratic in their understandings of representation across the career, but ended up with improved understandings in the latter stages. Also, secondary teachers were more positive in their understandings of representation than their elementary colleagues at the earlier stages of their careers, but elementary teachers were more positive in this regard during the later stages of their careers.

There was also a strong emphasis amongst teachers upon the worth and value of sharing learning together. Significantly, this notion of sharing reflects Fraser's (2008) argument about the importance of all participants being able to engage as 'full partners in social interaction' (135); such social interaction is dependent upon sharing, acknowledging and valuing experiences, knowledges, and selves, going beyond conceptions of what constitutes 'normality' and 'abnormality' (Annamma et al. 2013). At the same time, there was also an explicit valuing of active participation on the part of students in their learning, and demonstrations of such learning, and acknowledgement of the importance of all students feeling a sense of belonging. This sense of belonging resonates with Fitch's (2002) push for educational settings to adopt a more overtly social justice position.

For those teachers who conceptualised issues of representation negatively, and who did not believe inclusive classrooms were an effective way to teach all students, there was a strong emphasis upon isolating and privileging students with special educational needs and/or disabilities. Some comments also reflected a deeply embedded deficit approach to students' capabilities and the potential to strongly limit students' experiences. There was a belief that certain students' learning should be confined to life-skills because of perceptions that these students would only ever operate within society at a very perfunctionary level. Again, this does not happen by chance, but through the active constitution of social practices (classroom 'norms'), resulting in the subordination of the social status of those affected (Fraser 2008) – in this case, those students most in need of a rich and engaging learning environment. To resist more discriminatory practices, such approaches could benefit from the sorts of boundary-crossing identity politics associated with efforts of those engaged in disability studies to learn from those working in multicultural politics and education (cf. Jakubowicz and Meekosha 2002).

Even as there were instances of more overt discrimination, a more complex, nuanced politics was also evident amongst those teachers who identified as believing that inclusive classrooms were an effective way to teach all students, but whose comments sometimes portrayed issues of recognition and representation negatively. Amongst these teachers, there was an important disjuncture between rhetorical support for inclusion ('believing' in inclusion), and actually understanding what constitutes inclusive practices. Such disjunctures were also evident amongst teachers who claimed not to believe in inclusion but whose comments actually indicated a more inclusive disposition (towards issues of resourcing, recognition, and/or representation). Again, it seems as if some teachers sought to be inclusive, even as they did not appear to succeed, while others were more successful in this regard, even as they claimed not to believe an inclusive classroom is an effective way to teach all students. Simply describing teachers as being 'against' or 'for' inclusion does not seem to capture the nuances that attended their understandings of inclusion more broadly.

From a policy perspective, this indicates a need to ensure that inclusion is defined more overtly, and that this then translates into substantive understandings on the part of teachers, rather than simply superficial compliance with the language of inclusion. As Greenstein's (2014) account of the effects of policy in the UK reveals, more oppressive neoliberal policy decisions exclude students from inclusive educational provision, and contribute to approaches that do not adequately take into account the power differentials at play in classroom settings. However, in relation to our argument at the start of this article about the incredible variability which attends national and international conceptions of inclusion in policy (Hardy and Woodcock 2015), it would be offering false hope to simply argue that policy (as currently construed) can proffer ready and consistent solutions to complex questions of practice. Again, we reinforce the need to interrogate teachers' beliefs about inclusion and whether they believe an inclusive classroom is an effective way to teach all students, even as we recognise the importance of policy in this work. A more overtly oriented social justice stance is imperative for cultivating more equitable stances in this regard.

Conclusion: cultivating a socially just approach to inclusion

Teachers' definitions of inclusion are generally focused around issues of recognition and representation. This is perhaps not surprising, given Fraser (2013) herself argues that 'centred on issues of membership and procedure, the political dimension of justice is concerned chiefly with *representation*' (193; emphasis original). Importantly, in relation to articulations of inclusion, issues of resourcing are almost completely ignored by teachers, particularly secondary teachers. The implications from this research are that there needs to be considerably more focus upon issues of resourcing. After all, as Fraser (2008) argues, it is necessary to consider issues of distribution alongside issues of recognition and representation if concerns about parity are to be challenged.

At the same time, there is also considerable evidence of more complex, sometimes contradictory, findings that reveal teachers as 'more' or 'less' inclusive in their approaches to engaging with students. For example, teachers' positive disposition towards issues of recognition tended to increase significantly for secondary teachers towards the latter stages of their careers, even as their elementary counterparts tended to be more erratic in the extent to which they recognised issues of difference across the career stages. Also, secondary teachers tended to be stable in their understandings of representation, even as they tended not to maintain higher levels of enthusiasm earlier in their career. And elementary teachers tended to be more erratic in their understandings of representation, even as they ended up with improved understandings of representation in the latter stages of their careers. That is, there was a varied array of positions, and position-taking, in relation to inclusion across a spectrum of beliefs, rather than simply outright rejection or acceptance of inclusion per se.

As part of this complexity, too many teachers construe inclusion in a negative light, and very few teachers define inclusion in ways that give *adequate* attention to resourcing, recognising, *and* representing the needs of all students. Consequently, there is a distinct need to cultivate a much more equitable and socially just approach to inclusion, to help teachers better understand what such practices might look like, and to challenge entrenched and embedded practices of discrimination. This emphasis upon social justice is also important because the more the scholarship in the field moves away from the divisive language of inclusion versus exclusion (binary arguments), the sooner will be the likelihood of shifts in policies and practices to support all learners.

Fraser's (1997, 2008) conception of social justice helps provide a robust analytical tool to explore the nuanced, complex, and sometimes contradictory ways in which teachers understand an inclusive classroom is an effective way to teach all students. Her focus upon challenging institutionalised patterns of cultural practice, and the deeply embedded values which guide such practice, and her emphasis upon bringing to light the status subordination which helps establish these institutionalised patterns, is particularly important for helping teachers to move closer to a more socially just conception of inclusion along the spectrum of positions that could be taken (see also Arnesen, Mietola, and Lahelma 2007; Nussbaum 2013; Slee and Weiner 2001). Establishing the circumstances for people to be adequately resourced, recognised, and represented in learning constitutes an alternative politics to such subordination, enabling the sorts of 'full partnership' in association with others which should characterise social relations – including schooling and classroom practices. Fraser's (2008) argument challenging status subordination is a call to reconstitute the social in ways that foster genuine and productive relations between people – a dialogic cohabitation. Such a stance helps to understand how people occupy positions beyond more binary understandings of justice, whilst simultaneously challenging more exclusive and derogatory 'categorisations' which diminish not only those to whom these insults are directed, but also those who believe they have the right to denigrate people in this way. We will know we have succeeded when the status ascribed to each is overtly positive and productive, and shared by all.

Notes

1. Teachers were asked to indicate the number of years they had been teaching: less than 3 years; 3–5 years; 6–10 years; 11–20 years; and greater than 20 years. We described teachers with up to 5 years' experience as 'early career', 6–10 years as 'established', 11–20 years as 'mid-career', and more than 20 years as 'experienced'.
2. 'S' refers to secondary teachers; 'E' refers to elementary teachers. EC = early career/up to 5 years' experience; Est = established/6–10 years' experience; Mid = mid-career/11–20 years' experience; Exp = experienced/more than 20 years' experience. The numbers are individual teacher codes allocated to each teacher in the full data set. For example, the first quote/indicative comment was from the 35th secondary teacher listed in the original data set.
3. Direct quotes have been presented verbatim; punctuation and other grammatical errors/inconsistencies have been retained, rather than corrected.
4. Participant did not identify as either an elementary or secondary teacher.

Disclosure statement

No potential conflict of interest was reported by the authors.

References

Agbenyega, J., and S. Klibthong. 2014. "Assessing Thai Early Childhood Teachers' Knowledge of Inclusive Education." *International Journal of Inclusive Education* 18 (12): 1247–1261.

Anastasiou, D., and J. Kauffman. 2012. "Disability as Cultural Difference: Implications for Special Education." *Remedial and Special Education* 33 (3): 139–149.

Anastasiou, D., J. Kauffman, and D. Michail. 2016. "Disability in Multicultural Theory: Conceptual and Social Justice Issues." *Journal of Disability Policy Studies* 27 (1): 3–12.
Annamma, S., A. Boelé, B. Moore, and J. Klingner. 2013. "Challenging the Ideology of Normal in Schools." *International Journal of Inclusive Education* 17 (12): 1278–1294.
Arnesen, A., R. Mietola, and E. Lahelma. 2007. "Language of Inclusion and Diversity: Policy Discourses and Social Practices in Finnish and Norwegian Schools." *International Journal of Inclusive Education* 11 (1): 97–110.
Avramidis, E., and B. Norwich. 2002. "Teachers' Attitudes towards Integration/Inclusion: A Review of the Literature." *European Journal of Special Needs Education* 17 (2): 129–147.
Bailey, L., A. Nomanbhoy, and T. Tubpun. 2015. "Inclusive Education: Teacher Perspectives from Malaysia." *International Journal of Inclusive Education* 19 (5): 547–559.
Ballard, K. 2007. "Education and Imagination: Strategies for Social Justice." The Herbison Lecture presented to the national conference of the New Zealand association for research in education, University of Canterbury, December 4–7. Accessed July 16, 2016. http://www.nzare.org.nz/portals/306/images/Files/keith_ballard_herbison2007.pdf.
Berube, M. 2009. "Equality, Freedom, and/or Justice for All: A Response to Martha Nussbaum." *Metaphilosophy* 40 (3–4): 352–365.
Blecker, N., and N. Boakes. 2010. "Creating a Learning Environment for All Children: Are Teachers Able and Willing?" *International Journal of Inclusive Education* 14 (5): 435–447.
de Boer, A., S. Jan Pijl, and A. Minnaert. 2011. "Regular Primary Schoolteachers' Attitudes towards Inclusive Education: A Review of the Literature." *International Journal of Inclusive Education* 15 (3): 331–353.
Bossaert, G., H. Colpin, S. Jan Pijl, and K. Petry. 2013. "Truly Included? A Literature Study Focusing on the Social Dimension of Inclusion in Education." *International Journal of Inclusive Education* 17 (1): 60–79.
Bourke, P. 2010. "Inclusive Education Reform in Queensland: Implications for Policy and Practice." *International Journal of Inclusive Education* 14 (2): 183–193.
Burstein, N., S. Sears, A. Wilcoxen, B. Cabello, and M. Spagna. 2004. "Moving toward Inclusive Practices." *Remedial and Special Education* 25 (2): 104–116.
Carey, A. 2009. *On the Margins of Citizenship: Intellectual Disability and Civil Rights in Twentieth-Century America*. Philadelphia, PA: Temple University Press.
Clifford, S. 2012. "Making Disability Public in Deliberative Democracy." *Contemporary Political Theory* 11 (2): 211–228.
De Vroey, A., E. Struyf, and K. Petry. 2016. "Secondary Schools Included: A Literature Review." *International Journal of Inclusive Education* 20 (2): 109–135.
Engsig, T., and C. Johnstone. 2015. "Is There Something Rotten in the State of Denmark? The Paradoxical Policies of Inclusive Education – Lessons from Denmark." *International Journal of Inclusive Education* 19 (5): 469–486.
Fitch, F. 2002. "Disability and Inclusion: From Labeling Deviance to Social Valuing." *Educational Theory* 52 (4): 463–477.
Fraser, N. 1997. *Justice Interruptus: Critical Reflections on the Post-Socialist Condition*. New York: Routledge.
Fraser, N. 2008. "Rethinking Recognition: Overcoming Displacement and Reification in Cultural Politics." In *Adding Insult to Injury: Nancy Fraser Debates her Critics*, edited by N. Fraser and K. Olsen, 129–141. London: Verso.
Fraser, N. 2013. *Fortunes of Feminism: From State Managed Capitalism to Neoliberal Crisis*. London: Verso.
Gargiulo, R., and D. Metcalfe. 2013. *Teaching in Today's Inclusive Classrooms: A Universal Design for Learning Approach*. 2nd ed. Belmont, NC: Wadsworth, Cengage Learning.
Greenstein, A. 2014. "Is This Inclusion? Lessons from a Very 'Special' Unit." *International Journal of Inclusive Education* 18 (4): 379–391.
Grenier, M. 2010. "Moving to Inclusion: A Socio-Cultural Analysis of Practice." *International Journal of Inclusive Education* 14 (4): 387–400.
Hardy, I., and S. Woodcock. 2015. ""Inclusive Education Policies: Discourses of Difference, Diversity and Deficit." *International Journal of Inclusive Education* 19 (2): 141–164.
Hyde, M., L. Carpenter, and R. Conway. 2010. *Diversity and Inclusion in Australian Schools*. South Melbourne: Oxford University Press.
Jakubowicz, A., and H. Meekosha. 2002. "Bodies in Motion: Critical Issues Between Disability Studies and Multicultural Studies." *Journal of Intercultural Studies* 23 (3): 237–252.
Keddie, A. 2012. *Educating for Diversity and Social Justice*. London: Routledge.
Knight, A. 2015. "Democratizing Disability: Achieving Inclusion (without Assimilation) Through "Participatory Parity"." *Hypatia* 30 (1): 97–114.
Lingard, B. 2007. "Pedagogies of Indifference." *International Journal of Inclusive Education* 11 (3): 245–266.
Mastropieri, M., and T. Scruggs. 2014. *The Inclusive Classroom: Strategies for Effective Differentiated Instruction*. Upper Saddle River, NJ: Pearson.
McLeskey, J., and N. Waldron. 2007. "Making Differences Ordinary in Inclusive Classrooms." *Intervention in School and Clinic* 42 (3): 162–168.

Miles, S., and N. Singal. 2010. "The Education for All and Inclusive Education Debate: Conflict, Contradiction or Opportunity?" *International Journal of Inclusive Education* 14 (1): 1–15.

Nusbaum, E. 2013. "Vulnerable to Exclusion: The Place for Segregated Education within Conceptions of Inclusion." *International Journal of Inclusive Education* 17 (12): 1295–1311.

Nussbaum, M. 2009. "The Capabilities of People with Cognitive Disabilities." *Metaphilosophy* 40 (3–4): 331–351.

Ross-Hill, R. 2009. "Teacher Attitude towards Inclusion Practices and Special Needs Students." *Journal of Research in Special Educational Needs* 9 (3): 188–198.

Salend, S. 2010. *Creating Inclusive Classrooms: Effective and Reflective Practices.* 7th ed. Upper Saddle River, NJ: Pearson.

Sapon-Shevin, M. 2001. "Schools fit for all." *Educational Leadership* 58 (4): 34–39.

Sapon-Shevin, M. 2003. "Inclusion – A Matter of Social Justice: How can We Create Schools that Will Help Students Thrive in a Diverse Society?" *Educational Leadership* 61 (2): 25–28.

Scruggs, T., and M. Mastropieri. 1996. "Teacher Perceptions of Mainstreaming/Inclusion, 1958–1995: A Research Synthesis." *Exceptional Children* 63 (1): 59–74.

Slee, R. 2011. *The Irregular School: Exclusion, Schooling and Inclusive Education.* Abingdon: Routledge.

Slee, R. 2013. "How do We Make Inclusive Education Happen When Exclusion Is a Political Predisposition?" *International Journal of Inclusive Education* 17 (8): 895–907.

Slee, R., and J. Allan. 2001. "Excluding the Included: A Reconsideration of Inclusive Education." *International Studies in Sociology of Education* 11 (1): 173–192.

Slee, R., and G. Weiner. 2001. "Education Reform and Reconstruction as a Challenge to Research Genres: Reconsidering School Effectiveness Research and Inclusive Schooling." *School Effectiveness & School Improvement* 12 (1): 83–98.

Soldatic, K., and S. Grech. 2014. "Transnationalising Disability Studies: Rights, Justice and Impairment." *Disabilities Studies Quarterly* 34 (2). http://dsq-sds.org/article/view/4249.

Strogilos, V. 2012. "The Cultural Understanding of Inclusion and its Development within a Centralised System." *International Journal of Inclusive Education* 16 (12): 1241–1258.

UNESCO. 1994. *Salamanca Statement and Framework for Action on Special Needs Education.* Paris: UNESCO-Special Education, Division of Basic Education.

Vehmas, S., and N. Watson. 2014. "Moral Wrongs, Disadvantages, and Disability: A Critique of Critical Disability Studies." *Disability and Society* 29 (4): 638–650.

Waitoller, F., and A. Artiles. 2013. "A Decade of Professional Development Research for Inclusive Education: A Critical Review and Notes for a Research Programme." *Review of Educational Research* 83 (3): 319–356.

Ypinazar, Y., and P. Pagliano. 2004. "Seeking Inclusive Education: Disrupting Boundaries of 'Special' and 'Regular' Education." *International Journal of Inclusive Education* 8 (4): 423–442.

Education markets, the new politics of recognition and the increasing fatalism towards inequality

Sally Power and Daniel Frandji

> This paper explores the complex ways in which the marketisation of education and the associated publication of performance data have contributed to the emergence of a new politics of recognition which has paradoxically served further to naturalise educational inequalities. Of all the reforms associated with subjecting education to market forces, it is the publication of 'league tables' of raw performance data which has sparked the most controversy. These tables have provoked a range of criticisms from educational professionals and practitioners concerning their reductionist nature, their misleading attribution of outcomes to institutional processes rather than intake variables and their potentially damaging side-effects. These league tables can be said to constitute a form of cultural injustice. In order to counter this injustice, a new politics of recognition has emerged which seeks to valorise the performance of disadvantaged schools and which can be seen in the development of alternative and 'value-added' league tables. This paper argues that there are a number of difficulties and dangers inherent within this new politics of recognition. These relate to the impossibility of separating a school from its context, the displacement of a politics of redistribution and the increasing naturalisation of inequalities.

Introduction

This paper analyses the dilemmas and dangers posed by the publication and interpretation of school performance data associated with the marketisation of education. To some extent, the underlying issues relating to how we present and explain educational inequalities are not new. Nor are many of the processes which underpin the production of these inequalities, particularly those associated with socio-economic background. Educational inequalities have been an enduring feature of all education systems, and, because education is a positional good, there have always been elements of competition for educational opportunities which have unevenly privileged different social groups.

However, neoliberal-inspired policies have brought about an intensification of these processes. Since the 1980s, many countries have sought to regulate education provision though the operation of market forces. Attempts to stimulate market forces have involved making schools behave more like businesses (e.g., through giving them greater autonomy over finances and admissions arrangements) and encouraging parents to behave more like consumers (e.g., through relaxing admissions policies and diversifying types of school). The introduction of these kinds of policies has always been accompanied by fierce debate. However, it is perhaps the publication of educational 'league tables' which has sparked the most controversy. This is because these tables expose the uneven distribution of educational attainment and bring to public attention the extent to which schools are differentially able to gain 'market' advantage and parents are differentially able to secure places for their children at the 'best' schools.

In this paper, we begin by exploring the controversy surrounding 'league tables' and, in particular, criticisms that they misrepresent educational processes and actually compound educational inequalities associated with socio-economic disadvantage. Drawing on examples from France and England, which have seen similar trends despite very different national and political starting points, we then show how these critiques have led to support from educational professionals and researchers for alternative ways of comparing school performance which seek to valorise the achievements of disadvantaged schools. These new mechanisms can be interpreted as comprising a new politics of recognition. Drawing on Fraser's (1997, 2000) framework for unravelling the complex relationships between social injustices and political responses, we argue that attempting to redress the cultural injustice of crude league tables through alternative evaluations may only displace the problem. It may even serve to naturalise unequal educational outcomes and neutralise the injustices experienced by disadvantaged schools, their teachers and students.

Markets and the publication of attainment data

There is now an extensive literature on the emergence of market forces in education and the extent to which these are associated with the rise of neo-liberalism in the 1970s and 1980s. While some studies have focused on international comparisons of policies and their constituent elements (e.g., Whitty, Power, and Halpin 1998; Apple 2001), other research works have explored the impact of reforms on local networks of 'choice' and school cultures (e.g., Gewirtz, Ball, and Bowe 1995; Bagley, Glatter, and Woods 1998) and patterns of parental choice (Lauder et al. 1999; Gorard, Taylor, and Fitz 2003). Although there is disagreement within this body of literature about the scale and impact of the reforms, there is little disagreement amongst researchers that they have heightened awareness of the differences between school outcomes. This is because, in many countries, making different school outcomes visible through the publication of school attainment data has been seen as an integral part of stimulating market forces in education.[1] Advocates argue that it is an essential element in 'empowering' parents to make 'informed' school choices for their children. Although these data are not necessarily ranked, it is commonplace for the media to reproduce such data as 'league tables' of educational success and failure. In England, where the publication of attainment data has been a legal requirement for over 20 years, every summer sees the national and local newspapers fill their pages with tables and commentary 'raising the stakes with each round of reporting' (Warmington and Murphy 2004). Even in countries such as France, where the moves towards the marketisation of education are more recent and much weaker, the press regularly construct league tables, or 'palmarès' (e.g., Pech 2009).

Wherever the publication of school performance data has been proposed or introduced, the reaction from the education profession has been overwhelmingly negative. Teachers' trade unions in particular have lobbied vociferously against them. In some places, union resistance has managed to forestall their introduction – even if only for a short time. For example, in many Australian states, teachers' unions agreed to the introduction of testing in basic skills only on the condition that the results would neither be published nor used for comparative purposes (Gannicott 1998). And even where league tables have become an established feature of the education landscape, there continue to be ongoing demands for their abolition. For example, only last year the two largest teaching unions in England called on the government to 'scrap' them on the grounds that they were 'unnecessary and unhelpful' (cited in Lipsett 2009).

Commentators from the right argue that this continuing hostility towards the publication of league tables is little more than a desire for professional closure from teachers who fear the exposure of incompetency (e.g., Woodhead 2005). However, many education researchers argue that their publication is not only flawed but dangerous.

Critiques of league tables

There is an extensive academic literature which discusses the problems of educational league tables. The literature revolves around three main critiques relating to reductionism, misleading attribution of outcomes and collateral damage.

Critiques from a humanist perspective hold that the league tables reduce education from what is essentially a qualitative and holistic developmental process to a technical accounting exercise. In so doing, it is argued, they effectively devalue the many other purposes of education and provide little information on those things that matter. For example, research into the changing values of primary schools shows how professional discourse which, until recently, had been based largely on a 'set of values centred around holism, person-centredness, and warm and caring relationships' (Woods and Jeffrey 2002, 91), has become 'less personal, less emotional, less sensitive, less warm and less empathetic' (Jeffrey 2002, 544).

While accusations of reductionism tend to come from a qualitative and interpretative research tradition, powerful critiques of league tables have also been articulated by quantitative researchers. School effectiveness researchers, for example, have long argued that league tables based on 'raw' performance data are misleading (e.g., Mortimore and Stone 1991; Sammons, Nuttall, and Cuttance 1993; Goldstein and Myers 1996; Herbert and Coe 1998; Plewis and Goldstein 1998). Far from measuring institutional performance, these critics claim that league tables largely reflect external attributes, particularly those associated with the social background of the pupil intake.

Certainly this is a conclusion which is hard to avoid after even the most cursory glance at league tables. In both England and France, expensive fee-paying and academically selective schools, lycées and colleges dominate the top ranks. State-maintained comprehensive schools located in, or serving, disadvantaged communities languish at the bottom of the league tables.

Two of the UK's leading educational statisticians, with extensive expertise of trying to evaluate institutional effectiveness, have argued that if the English government continues to publish these crude performance tables (as indeed it has done) it not only will be 'inconsistent' but will 'fall short of the standards which a democratic society has a right to expect' (Plewis and Goldstein 1998, 20).

The third kind of critique focuses less on the reductive or misleading nature of the data presented and draws attention to the damaging side-effects that the publication of attainment data will have (e.g., Karsten, Visscher, and De Jong 2001). This collateral damage, it is argued, is particularly acute when a school either becomes officially labelled as 'failing' (as happens in England as a result of external inspection) or simply finds itself at or near the bottom of the league table. For example, Woods and Levačić's quantitative (Levačić and Woods 2002) and qualitative (Woods and Levačić 2002) analyses of schools' capacity to improve their performance in attainment tables show that in localities where there was strong competition between schools, 'failing' schools suffered what they refer to as a 'malign, dyadic relationship in which school character and performance (within the school), and perceptions of that character and performance (within the school and beyond it as part of the contextual factors), exacerbate each other' (Woods and Levačić 2002, 245). Nicolaidou and Ainscow's (2005) analysis of internal school processes found that being designated a 'failing' school led teaching staff to think of themselves as failures contributing to professional demotivation and discontent.

The cultural injustice of league tables

Taken together, these critiques provide a powerful indictment of league tables. It is possible to argue that they compound the social injustices already experienced by disadvantaged communities, and in particular the cultural injustice of misrecognition.

Nancy Fraser makes a compelling argument that not all injustices are the same. In particular, she shows that there is an important analytical distinction to be made between economic and social injustices. Although, as Fraser herself acknowledges, these different injustices rarely exist in their 'pure' forms, there are important insights to be gained from disentangling them.

The economic injustices derive from maldistribution, and include exploitation (having the fruits of one's labour appropriated for the benefit of others); economic marginalisation (being confined to undesirable poorly paid work – or having access to none); and deprivation (being denied an adequate material support). The cultural injustices of misrecognition, on the other hand, have been characterised by Fraser (1997) as including: cultural domination (being subjected to patterns of interpretation and communication that are associated with another culture and are alien and/or hostile to one's own); non-recognition (being rendered invisible by means of authoritative representational, communicative and interpretative practices); and disrespect (being routinely maligned or disparaged in stereotypic public cultural representations and/or in everyday life situations).[2]

It could be claimed that schools which do badly in league tables suffer from all three dimensions of misrecognition. They operate in a dominant culture where educational success is narrowly defined and on terms on which they can never hope to succeed relative to other schools. Such successes as they do achieve – which might be very substantial relative to their pupil intake – are rendered invisible in the crude rankings. Moreover, these very rankings themselves constitute a form of disrespect. Schools which become labelled as failures are routinely disparaged in the media.

It is possible to go further and argue that these cultural injustices compound social and educational inequalities. If one belongs to a school – as a member of staff, a pupil or even a parent – that is visibly devalued by the education market – and particularly and most visibly through the publication of league tables – this misrecognition may become internalised. Staff, pupils and parents may come to believe their market value to be justified. While some may be able to leave the 'sinking ship', the most disadvantaged will rarely have that option. They may find themselves trapped in a spiral of institutional and aspirational decline.

The development of a new politics of recognition in education

Partially in order to counter the misrecognition created by school league tables, we are seeing the emergence of what we believe is a *new* politics of recognition. This new politics seeks to rescue schools from the injustice of crude comparison by creating alternative evaluations which are sensitive to the contexts in which schools work. In particular, through using a variety of indicators and statistical techniques, educational researchers and analysts can acknowledge and celebrate the achievements of teachers and pupils working in *relatively* successful schools in disadvantaged areas and reduce the collateral of unadjusted league tables.[3]

One method of going beyond the crude comparisons of academic performance is to acknowledge officially the broader range of educational qualifications which pupils can achieve. For example, in 2005, the English government published league tables which included performance in vocational subjects which had not previously been 'counted'. The School Standards Minister argued that this new kind of table marked 'a significant step forward in *recognising* the achievements of all pupils and of the importance of flexible and vocational routes of learning' (our emphasis) (cited in Halpin 2005). This broadening of the range of subjects meant that, for the first time, two non-selective state-maintained schools outperformed selective private schools in the national rankings.

Another approach has involved measuring and ranking schools in terms of institutional improvement. Shortly after New Labour came to power in 1997, they developed an 'Improving Schools' league table. Within these tables, the 'successful' schools are those which have seen the largest increase in attainments compared with their previous year's performance. The recognition of improvement rather than performance means that schools with very high levels of attainment cannot appear at the top of the table because they have less scope for improvement. Indeed, these tables are in many ways a reversal of conventional league tables in as much as it is *only* those schools that are consigned to the bottom of the league that have the possibility of appearing at the top of this table.

By far the most common strategy, though, for redressing the injustice of crude league tables is the development of 'value-added' tables which measure relative performance of schools once the characteristics of the pupil intake have been taken into account.

Pupil intake characteristics are usually measured in terms of a range of variables relating to socio-economic factors and/or prior attainment. In France, for example, there is a system called IPES (Indicateurs de Performance des Établissements Scolaires) established by the Direction de l'Evaluation et de la Prospective (DEP) of the Ministère de l'Education nationale (Emin and Sauvageot 1995). IPES are generally based on age and social background and are used to predict the likely future performance of a cohort on entry to a lycée. Discrepancies between the predicted results (based on statistical analysis of past performance) and the actual results are then used to evaluate the effectiveness of the institution. Thus, if the baccalaureate results are higher than forecast, the lycée will be considered effective. If lower, and even if the raw scores are excellent, the lycée will be considered ineffective (Derouet 2006, 15). Institutions can then be compared in terms of their relative effectiveness rather than their unadjusted examination results, and the search for internal causal factors can begin.

There are debates about the methodological validity of this approach. Felouzis (2005), for example, has argued that, while age and social background provide some approximation of opportunity, the most important predictor of academic success (and therefore the necessary measure of institutional effectiveness) is prior attainment. As a result of criticisms such as these, the Ministère is in the process of introducing a baseline achievement level to future evaluations (Ministère de l'Éducation nationale 2009). However, while this may promise a more sophisticated basis for comparing institutions in France, it does not avoid the dangers we believe are inherent in this kind of approach – as can be seen when we look at countries, such as England, where it is possible to make value-added adjustments on the basis of prior attainment.

In England, the introduction of a national system of standard assessment tasks for pupils aged seven, 11 and 14 has made it possible to measure how much progress has been made by pupils as they move from one stage to another. There has been considerable debate about what adjustments need to be made to allow for intake variables and other contextual factors outside the school's control (see, e.g., Goldstein 2003). However, once these variables have been built into the model and the average pupil progress calculated, these value-added tables can reveal a different picture of school performance. Schools towards the top of unadjusted tables can appear towards the bottom once the necessary adjustments have been made, and vice versa. Thus, for example, there have been a number of criticisms levelled at 'coasting' schools – schools such as grammar schools whose results are 'respectable' but not as good as one might expect given their selective intake (e.g., Cassidy 2002).

These value-added tables can be used to valorise the achievements of disadvantaged schools. The following extract, called 'Hidden Triumphs' (Crace 2006), is taken from a *Guardian* newspaper report on a school which does badly in a conventional performance league table, but well in a value-added league table:

> You wouldn't know the corridors were painted only a few months ago. Damp stains have already appeared on the ceilings and the walls are peeling … King Richard secondary school in Portsmouth is falling apart. Literally. It was built in the late 1940s and should have been knocked down 10 years ago …. There again, the school blends in with its surroundings. King Richard is in the heart of Paulsgrove, a run-down working-class estate on the northern edge of the city …. Everything about Paulsgrove screams low expectations. Check out the government's GCSE school league tables and King Richard seems to fall in line with the neighbourhood. In 2005, 46% of its pupils achieved five or more passes at A*–C, bang on the average pass rate for Portsmouth … but 10% down on the rest of England. Yet research published today … shows that King Richard is doing a great deal better than these figures suggest. … and has thus significantly outperformed expectations.

The transformation of this school from a struggling comprehensive to a 'hidden triumph' can be seen as a manifestation of this new politics of recognition. Despite the run down buildings and the impoverished locality, the teachers and pupils at King Richard's are now presented as doing well and achieving public acknowledgement of their hard work.

These attempts to find alternative ways of valuing the achievements of some disadvantaged schools can be interpreted as an understandable response to the cultural injustices inflicted on schools through the publication of league tables and the marketisation of education. However, the development of these counter-evaluations is highly problematic and potentially perilous.

The perils of the new politics of recognition

There are, we believe, a number of difficulties and dangers inherent in countering the education inequalities exposed and compounded within the education market through this new politics of recognition. These relate to: the impossibility of separating a school from its context; the displacement of a politics of redistribution; and the naturalisation of inequalities.

Separating a school from its context

The development of value-added assessments of institutional effectiveness is a complex and difficult business, as is evident in the ongoing debates between researchers about what variables should be included in order to 'rule out' the intake characteristics and isolate the school effect. These debates reveal just how nebulous the concept of institutional effectiveness is. This nebulousness, we believe, arises because the concept is premised on the need to distinguish 'external' and 'internal' variables – a distinction which is ontologically confused and empirically elusive.

In terms of ontology, value-added calculations constitute, as Derouet (2006) argues, an institutional retranslation of debates within the sociology of education between approaches which privilege structure or agency. But these different approaches cannot be easily reconciled. Moreover, the separation of 'external' factors and 'internal' processes that are involved when assessing 'value-added' measures creates a false impression that schools can somehow be disconnected from the contexts in which they operate. As Angus (1993) has argued, the point of value-added research is to eliminate the 'noise' of external variables to focus on internal ones. The impossibility of eliminating this 'noise' is evident in Thrupp's (2001) research on school mix, which he argues is constantly undervalued in school effectiveness research. He claims (2001, 27–8) that his research on school mix suggests:

> That school effectiveness researchers may not have been able to 'control' for student social class as well as they have thought. So that many school processes considered to contribute to student achievement may be less independent of school mix than typically allowed. It also suggests that many effectiveness factors will be hard to replicate because while they may be *school-based*, they may nevertheless not be *school-caused* (emphases in original).

The artificial bracketing off of the 'outside' in order to measure the 'inside' makes it difficult to develop any relational analysis of the interplay between a school and its social context. It is an approach which is trapped within what Crahay (2006) terms the 'process–product' paradigm, which, he argues, erroneously presumes that it is possible to attribute particular outcomes to processes independently of the context in which they were realised. It evades the kind of praxeological understanding supported by Habermas (1973[1968]) which would expose how inequalities are *constituted* through the interactions between school and society.

The elusiveness of identifying any internal 'school effect' is also evident in empirical explorations. As Gorard (2006, 237) argues:

> The larger the study, the more variables available for each student, the more reliable the measures are, and the better conducted the study, the stronger is the link between school intake and outcomes.

As he goes on to argue, the undisputed fact that the majority of attainment outcomes can be explained in terms of the characteristics of a school's intake can lead one to two very different conclusions. One conclusion is to believe that such variation, albeit small, as cannot be explained by intake characteristics must be attributed to school effectiveness. The other, and to our minds the most convincing conclusion, is to accept that internal school processes have only a very limited impact on achievement. Thus, if we are interested in equalising achievement gaps, political solutions will need to be focused on what is going on *outside* the school. This brings us on to what we see as the second major problem with this new politics of recognition – the way in which it displaces a politics of redistribution.

The displacement of a politics of redistribution

The importance of attempting to distinguish different kinds of injustice is that they need to be challenged through different kinds of strategies. While cultural injustices can be addressed through a politics of recognition, economic injustices need to be addressed through a politics of redistribution. If an injustice is misdiagnosed it can lead to strategies which may not only be ineffective, but potentially create further injustices.

In general, Fraser (2000, 107) claims that in recent decades we have seen an increase in struggles based around the politics of recognition, and a relative decline in claims for egalitarian redistribution. These struggles, she goes on to argue (2000, 108), 'are serving less to supplement, complicate and enrich redistributive struggles than to marginalize, eclipse and displace them'. And, when a politics of recognition displaces a politics of redistribution, it may actually *promote* inequality.

In relation to education, for example, the argument that the exacerbation of educational inequalities *arises* from the misrecognition associated with marketisation and the publication of league tables obscures the fact that these schools belong to a political economy of failure. It proposes, in our view mistakenly, that the economic inequalities which result from educational failure are a *secondary* effect. Although we acknowledge that, as Gewirtz (1998) points out, working class pupils do suffer cultural injustices, we would argue that *these* are a secondary effect. Clearly, the separation of these different causes of injustice is always, to some extent, artificial. Nevertheless, the importance of the separation and the need to identify whether we are talking about a politics of recognition or a politics of redistribution is evident if we push the argument to the extreme. Aspects of working class culture and knowledge may well be devalued, but the close and persistent correlation between low socioeconomic status and low educational attainment is more adequately accounted for (like the relationship between poverty and poor health) by material disadvantage. To celebrate the relative educational successes of poor schools is, ultimately, to divert attention away from the relative poverty they experience.

Recognising that schools have to educate children in difficult conditions, and that some schools are better at it than others, may make the teachers working in them feel less stigmatised. But it will do nothing to tackle the underlying causes of educational failure. Indeed, far from protecting the disadvantaged from the inequities of the education market-place, we argue that it also serves to 'naturalise' the failure of the disadvantaged.

The naturalisation of educational failure

To some extent, the attempt to valorise the relative successes of disadvantaged schools and disadvantaged children is to accept their educational inferiority as inevitable and insurmountable. It accepts, as Thrupp points out, that the overwhelming proportion of school achievement that cannot be attributed to schools is 'outside their remit'. The low attainment of these schools and students is simply a 'fact of life'. Rather than insist on the need to level the playing field, we change the definition of success. And setting different criteria of success for different kinds of pupils inscribes their failure as 'normal' and 'natural'. Through 'correcting' schools' unequal attainments in this way, the new politics of recognition introduces a disempowering fatalism into the education system.

There are interesting parallels here with many of the debates which have surrounded disability, special educational needs and inclusion. In both cases, separate criteria of 'success' are built into evaluations of attainment. In both cases, the contrast between 'external' (i.e., social factors) and 'internal' (e.g., individual attributes) has led to a pathological view of difference which has been severely critiqued (see Armstrong 2000). Just as the medical model of special need locates the source of the problem and the solution within the individual, the value-added adjustments draw attention away from the systemic and structural determinants of educational success and failure through measuring and 'neutralising' the deficits of the pupils.

Over 30 years ago, Ford argued that the medical model of diagnosing and 'treating' special educational need served to maintain the ecology of the education system. It is possible to argue that the new politics of recognition may serve a similar function within a marketised education system. To promote value-added judgements of success as more equitable than the hierarchies of crude league tables is to accept rather than contest structural inequalities in education systems. Despite the good intentions of the opponents of league tables, this new politics may reduce the disquiet and disillusionment created by the visible display of educational inequality.

Taking things forward

We are not suggesting that the publication of unadjusted 'league tables' is a 'good thing'. While there is little evidence to suggest that their publication is having some of the systemic problems that were predicted (Gorard, Taylor, and Fitz 2002), there is also little doubt that the publication of crude performance indicators *does* contribute to the stigmatisation of schools and negatively impact on the self-esteem of teachers working in these schools. It can also distort practice (McNess, Broadfoot, and Osborn 2003) and perceptions (Wiggins and Timms 2002) and increase exclusions (West and Pennell 2000). To put it simply, league tables *do* contribute to the injustices of misrecognition and intensify processes of marketisation. However, we want to argue that responding to this injustice with a *new* politics of recognition which simply absorbs and neutralises institutional differences is highly problematic. This new politics of recognition simply displaces the underlying injustices that arise from the injustices of economic maldistribution.

As Fraser (2000) argues, the problem of displacement which occurs when attempts are made to redress an economic injustice with a politics of recognition cannot easily be resolved. It is, she claims, no longer possible simply to return to an unreconstructed politics of redistribution. It is not an 'either'/'or' situation. What is needed is a way of ascertaining the extent to which the cultural injustice of misrecognition is linked to an economic injustice of maldistribution. For our part, we do not accept that unequal educational outcomes can be explained only in terms of the misrecognition. What is needed, therefore, is an explanation of uneven educational outcomes that is related to maldistribution. As Nash (2001) has argued, despite the huge volume of research on the relationship between home and school, sociologists of education have tended to avoid tackling the difficult issue of accounting for educational outcomes as being more than a reflection of a cultural injustice. However, until we have a stronger explanatory understanding of the problem of unequal attainment, our interpretations and attempts to redress the stigma of failure at institutional and individual levels will rest on shaky foundations.

Notes
1. It is worth noting that since democratic devolution in Scotland and Wales, both countries have distanced themselves from English neo-liberalism through not publishing lists of school performance data.
2. In her elucidation of the distinction, Fraser contrasts the different injustices faced by 'exploited classes' and 'despised sexualities'. She argues that the working class suffers the economic injustices of exploitation, marginalisation and deprivation, and that their disadvantaged position is determined by, indeed is defined by, the political and economic structure of society. Although members of the working class may also suffer cultural injustices, Fraser suggests that these usually arise from the material hardships they experience. Gay and lesbian people, Fraser contends, largely suffer cultural injustices in that they live in a largely heterosexist society in which their own sexuality is either rendered invisible or routinely maligned.
3. The emergence of the techniques and approaches which lie behind these alternative evaluations arises not only from their appeal to many researchers and educationists, but also because of their potential usefulness for holding schools to account. Indeed, some have argued that the rise in school effectiveness research is based on its utility for neoliberal reforms (see, e.g., Angus 1993; Gibson and Asthana 1998; Hatcher 1998; and Thrupp 2001). The proliferation of this new regime of statistical evaluations can similarly be seen as part of a new regime of educational governance (Ozga 2009).

References

Angus, L. 1993. The sociology of school effectiveness. *British Journal of Sociology of Education* 14, no. 4: 333–45.

Apple, M.W. 2001. Comparing neo-liberal projects and inequality in education. *Comparative Education* 37, no. 4: 409–23.

Armstrong, F. 2000. Les paradoxes de l'éducation inclusive en Angleterre. In *L'école face aux handicaps. Éducation spéciale ou éducation intégrative?* [The paradoxes of inclusive education in England. In *Schools coping with disability: Special or integrated provision?*] ed. M. Chauvière and E. Plaisance, 117–32. Paris: PUF.

Bagley, C., R. Glatter, and P. Woods. 1998. *School choice and competition: Markets in the public interest?* London: Routledge.

Cassidy, S. 2002. Grammar schools underperform, says top academic. *The Independent,* July 1.

Crace, J. 2006. Hidden triumphs. *The Guardian,* November 7. http://www.guardian.co.uk/education/2006/nov/07/schools.gcses (accessed March 3, 2009).

Crahay, M. 2006. *Un bilan des recherches processus-produit. L'enseignement peut-il contribuer à l'apprentissage des élèves et, si oui, comment?* [A review of process-product research: Does teaching promote learning and, if so, how?] Geneva: Carnet des sciences de l'éducation.

Derouet, J.-L. 2006. Entre la récupération des savoirs critiques et la construction des standards du management libéral. Recherche, administration et politique en France de 1975 à 2005 [Between the recovery of critical knowledge and the construction of liberal management standards: Research, administration and policy in France 1975–2005]. *Revue des sciences de l'éducation* 32, no. 1: 7–30.

Emin, J.-C., and C. Sauvageot. 1995. Trois indicateurs de performance des lycées [Three indicators of school performance]. *Administration et éducation* 68: 41–57.

Felouzis, G. 2005. Performances et 'valeur ajoutée' des lycées: le marché scolaire fait des différences [School performance and 'value added': the education market makes a difference]. *Revue Française de sociologie* 46, no. 1: 3–36.

Fraser, N. 1997. From redistribution to recognition? Dilemmas of justice in a 'Postsocialist' age. In *Justice interruptus: Critical reflections on the 'Postsocialist' condition,* ed. N. Fraser, 11–39. New York: Routledge.

Fraser, N. 2000. Rethinking recognition. *New Left Review* 3, May–June: 107–20.

Gannicott, K. 1998. League tables of school performance. *Policy* 14, no. 3: 17–22.

Gewirtz, S. 1998. Conceptualizing social justice in education: Mapping the territory. *Journal of Education Policy* 13, no. 4: 469–84.

Gewirtz, S., S.J. Ball, and R. Bowe. 1995. *Markets, choice and equity.* Milton Keynes: Open University Press.

Gibson, A., and S. Asthana. 1998. School performance, school effectiveness and the 1997 White Paper. *Oxford Review of Education* 24, no. 2: 195–210.

Goldstein, H. 2003. A commentary on the secondary school value added performance tables for 2002. http://www.cmm.bristol.ac.uk/team/H6_Personal/value-added-commentary-jan03.htm (accessed March 19, 2010).

Goldstein, H., and K. Myers. 1996. Freedom of information: Towards a code of ethics for performance indicators. *Research Intelligence* 57: 12–6.

Gorard, S. 2006. Value-added is of little value. *Journal of Education Policy* 21, no. 2: 235–43.

Gorard, S., C. Taylor, and J. Fitz. 2002. Does school choice lead to 'spirals of decline'? *Journal of Education Policy* 17, no. 3: 367–84.

Gorard, S., C. Taylor, and J. Fitz. 2003. *Schools, markets and choice policies.* London: Routledge.

Habermas, J. 1973[1968]. *La technique et la science comme 'idéologie',* [Technology and Science as Ideology]. Paris: tel Gallimard.

Halpin, T. 2005. State schools top the table but private rivals cry foul. *The Times,* January 13. http://www.timesonline.co.uk/tol/life_and_style/education/article411813.ece (accessed March 4, 2009).

Hatcher, R. 1998. Social justice and the politics of school effectiveness and school improvement. *Race, Ethnicity and Education* 1, no. 2: 267–89.

Herbert, D.T., and C.J. Coe. 1998. School performance, league tables and social geography. *Applied Geography* 18, no. 3: 199–223.

Jeffrey, B. 2002. Performativity and primary teacher relations. *Journal of Education Policy* 17, no. 5: 531–46.

Karsten, S., A. Visscher, and T. De Jong. 2001. Another side to the coin: The unintended effects of the publication of school performance data in England and France. *Comparative Education* 37, no. 2: 231–42.

Lauder, H., S. Hughes, S. Watson, and M. Waslander. 1999. *Trading in futures: Why markets in education don't work.* Buckingham: Open University Press.

Levačić, R., and P.A. Woods. 2002. Raising school performance in the league tables (Part 1): Disentangling the effects of social disadvantage. *British Educational Research Journal* 28, no. 2: 207–26.

Lipsett, A. 2009. Scrap Sats and league tables, say teaching unions. *The Guardian,* February 11.

McNess, E., P. Broadfoot, and M. Osborn. 2003. Is the effective compromising the affective. *British Educational Research Journal* 29, no. 2: 243–57.

Ministère de l'Éducation nationale. 2009. *Trois indicateurs de résultats des lycées publics et privés sous contrat* [Three performance indicators for public and grant-aided secondary schools]. http://indicateurs.education.gouv.fr/brochure.html (accessed April 24, 2009).

Mortimore, P., and C. Stone. 1991. Measuring educational quality. *British Journal of Educational Studies* 39, no. 1: 69–82.

Nash, R. 2001. Class, 'ability' and attainment: A problem for the sociology of education. *British Journal of Sociology of Education* 22, no. 2: 189–202.

Nicolaidou, M., and M. Ainscow. 2005. Understanding failing schools: Perspectives from the inside. *School Effectiveness and School Improvement* 16, no. 3: 229–48.

Ozga, J. 2009. Governing education through data in England: From regulation to self-evaluation. *Journal of Education Policy* 24, no. 2: 149–62.

Pech, M.-E. 2009. Palmarès des lycées: l'engouement pour le privé [School league tables: the craze for private schools]. *Le Figaro* 8, avril. http://www.lefigaro.fr/actualite-france/2009/04/08/01016-20090408ARTFIG00044-palmares-des-lycees-l-engouement-pour-le-prive-.php (accessed March 19 2010).

Plewis, I., and H. Goldstein. 1998. Excellence in schools: A failure of standards. *British Journal of Curriculum and Assessment* 8: 17–20.

Sammons, P., D. Nuttall, and P. Cuttance. 1993. Differential school effectiveness: Results from a reanalysis of the Inner London Education Authority's Junior School Project Data. *British Educational Research Journal* 19, no. 4: 381–405.

Thrupp, M. 2001. Sociological and political concerns about school effectiveness research: Time for a new research agenda. *School Effectiveness and School Improvement* 12, no. 1: 7–40.

Warmington, P., and R. Murphy. 2004. Could do better? Media depictions of UK educational assessment results. *Journal of Education Policy* 19, no. 3: 285–99.

West, A., and H. Pennell. 2000. Publishing school exam results in England: Incentives and consequences. *Educational Studies* 26, no. 4: 423–36.

Whitty, G., S. Power, and D. Halpin. 1998. *Devolution and choice in education: The school, the state and the market.* Buckingham: Open University Press.

Wiggins, A., and P. Tymms. 2002. Dysfunctional effects of league tables: A comparison between English and Scottish primary schools. *Public Money and Management* January–March: 43–8.

Woodhead, C. 2005. Turn the tables to your advantage. *Times Online,* November 20.

Woods, P., and B. Jeffrey. 2002. The reconstruction of primary teachers' identities. *British Journal of Sociology of Education* 23, no. 1: 89–106.

Woods, P.A., and R. Levačić. 2002. Raising school performance in the league tables (Part 2): Barriers to responsiveness in three disadvantaged schools. *British Educational Research Journal* 28, no. 2: 227–47.

Alternative education and social justice: considering issues of affective and contributive justice

Martin Mills, Glenda McGregor, Aspa Baroutsis, Kitty Te Riele and Debra Hayes

This article considers the ways in which three alternative education sites in Australia support socially just education for their students and how injustice is addressed within these schools. The article begins with recognition of the importance of Nancy Fraser's work to understandings of social justice. It then goes on to argue that her framework is insufficient for understanding the particularly complex set of injustices that are faced by many highly marginalised young people who have rejected or been rejected by mainstream education systems. We argue here for the need to consider the importance of 'affective' and 'contributive' aspects of justice in schools. Using interview data from the alternative schools, we highlight issues of affective justice raised by students in relation to their educational journeys, as well as foregrounding teachers' affective work in schools. We also consider curricular choices and pedagogical practices in respect of matters of contributive justice. Our contention is that the affective and contributive fields are central to the achievement of social justice for the young people attending these sites. Whilst mainstream schools are not the focus of this article, we suggest that the lessons here have salience for all forms of schooling.

Introduction

This article has evolved from a project exploring the types of learning occurring in flexible learning sites/alternative[1] education in Australia during the period 2012–2014. The project was concerned with the ways in which such sites supported a socially just education for their students. Our concerns were framed around Nancy Fraser's (1997, 2009) conceptions of social justice in that we were interested in the ways in which such schools took account of: issues of distribution, or the economic injustices faced by the young people attending the schools; issues of recognition, that is, the cultural injustices faced by these young people; and issues of representation, with regard to the political injustices experienced by young people.

In the main, we have been impressed by what these schools do in relation to addressing all of these forms of injustice (see for example, McGregor, Mills, Te Riele, & Hayes, 2015; Mills, McGregor, Hayes, & Te Riele, 2015). However, to us there was something missing in the analysis when it came to describing the types of relationships

---

This article was originally published with errors. This version has been corrected. Please see Erratum (http://dx.doi.org/10.1080/17508487.2016.1123079).

that support young people's engagement in schooling, as well as those that disrupt this engagement. We have come to the conclusion that social justice is a complex and multifaceted concept that is inadequately explained by Nancy Fraser's framework and we suggest here that there are other elements that need to be considered when addressing issues to do with socially just education. In so doing, we are drawn to the work of both Kathleen Lynch (2012) and Andrew Sayer (2009, 2011). Lynch (2012) in her critique of Fraser's theory suggests that 'it does not recognize the affective domain of life as a discrete site of social practice' (p. 49). In terms of schooling, the affective sphere is concerned with the quality of relationships, care and support available to students. Interrelated with this is Sayer's qualitative understanding of 'contributive justice' and its relationship to meaningful work. Based on our own observations of multiple alternative schooling sites in Australia and England (see for example, Baroutsis, McGregor, & Mills, 2015; Hayes, 2013; McGregor et al., 2015; Mills & McGregor, 2010, 2014; Mills, McGregor, & Muspratt, 2013; Mills, McGregor, Martin, Tomaszewski, & Waters, 2014; Te Riele, 2012, 2014; Te Riele, Davies, & Baker, 2015), and drawing on notions of contributive justice we suggest that 'care' needs to be taken in the provision of flexible education to ensure that students do not receive a watered down curriculum that fails to engage them intellectually and that damages their sense of self-respect.

This article begins with an outline of the research project and its relationship to the work of Nancy Fraser; we then move on to discuss concepts of affective justice and contributive justice and their relevance to schooling, contextualising our theories with interview data collected from teachers and students in flexible learning sites situated in three different Australian jurisdictions. We highlight those issues of affective justice raised by students both in relation to their former and current schools, and we foreground teachers' affective work in schools. A consideration of the types of curricula and pedagogical practices present in these schools and their relationship to contributive justice supports our contention that such approaches are central to the achievement of social justice for the young people attending these sites. Whilst our focus is on young people in alternative forms of education, we suggest that the lessons here have salience for all forms of schooling.

Flexible learning and social justice

We, like others (see for example, Cribb & Gewirtz, 2003; Keddie, 2012a, 2012b; Lipman, 2008; Power & Frandji, 2010), have found the work of Nancy Fraser useful in considering what a socially just school might look like. Her work has focussed on considering how the sometimes competing demands of economic justice and cultural justice can be worked together to provide a comprehensive theory of justice. In more recent times, she has embedded a concern with political justice into her theoretical framework.

Within Fraser's framework, economic injustice refers to an inequitable distribution of resources and the damaging effects of this 'maldistribution'. Cultural injustice refers to the ways in which various groups have become 'despised', for example, on the grounds of sexuality, gender, or race/ethnicity. This 'misrecognition' occurs when people are forced to suppress their own cultural ways of being and communicating to the (often hostile) norms of the dominant culture, are rendered invisible or are disrespected as a result of belonging to a particular cultural group. Political injustice, which Fraser refers to as 'misrepresentation', occurs in those instances when people are denied an opportunity to make justice claims when they are experiencing economic or cultural injustice or when they are unable to contribute to the decisions that have an impact on their lives. She contends that misrepresentation can occur (although unlikely) in the absence of economic and cultural injustices. Fraser argues that all such aspects of injustice have to be attended to in order to achieve a socially just society where there is 'parity of participation'. Her work has not been without its critics (see for example, Olsen, 2008). However, we have found this framework a useful device for considering how economic, cultural and political injustices, and their respective solutions of distribution, recognition and representation, relate to contemporary schooling, both in the mainstream and alternative sectors (see for example, McGregor et al., 2015; Mills et al., 2015).

Mainstream schools have a long history of not serving particular groups of young people well. Students who come from low socioeconomic backgrounds are disproportionately represented in the lower bands of achievement and attendance data and in the upper bands of data on exclusion, suspension and 'special needs'(see for example, Abrams, 2010; Evans, Meyer, Pinney, & Robinson, 2009; Gale & Densmore, 2000; Kane, 2011; Mills & Gale, 2010; Mosen-Lowe, Vidovich, & Chapman, 2009). Multiple reasons for this have been suggested to us by participants in our study. These include, students' access to particular forms of cultural capital, lack of fit between the middle class expectations of schooling and (non)working class culture, teacher prejudices, lack of resources and even diet. Whilst we have very definite understandings of our own as to why this is the case, we would also suggest that whatever the reason, there is no doubt that an injustice is being perpetrated against the children of the poor. This economic injustice works to ensure that the benefits of schooling are unfairly distributed amongst young people according to their family's economic circumstances, and given the strong relationship between educational success and social mobility (OECD, 2012) reproduces the existing patterns of wealth and poverty. In many of the schools we have visited, this injustice has been addressed through, for example, the provision of food, accommodation support for homeless young people, transportation, basic services (for example, showers) and free excursions (see for example, Mills & McGregor, 2014).

Defining 'culture' in its broadest sense to include gender, sexuality, race/ethnicity, religion, language background and so on, it is clear that young people who belong to marginalised 'cultures' often encounter schooling as a less than positive experience. This 'cultural injustice' can be shaped by a lack of academic reward, but also by harassment and violence, by being ignored, silenced or having one's existence denied, by active and hidden discrimination at multiple levels, and it can be perpetrated by teachers and students alike (Smyth, 2006). In many of the flexible schools we have visited, this injustice has been addressed by a strong commitment to recognising and valuing difference. This has been demonstrated through, for example, seeking input from local Indigenous Elders into organisational and curriculum content, the provision of crèches for those students who have children, ensuring that homophobia or racism is never ignored and providing support around domestic violence issues.

It is also apparent that many young people experience schooling as oppressive because they have no forum in which to express their opinions or challenge the injustices they have experienced (Black, 2011). The importance of student voice in schools has been well documented (see Beane & Apple, 1999; Dewey, 1916; Fielding & Moss, 2011), however its presence is often lacking. The absence of voice, or political injustice, may be apparent in the ways in which students, especially those from marginalised backgrounds, can be summarily suspended from school, given detentions and other forms of punishment without options to challenge those decisions. It is apparent in dress codes, in timetabling restrictions, in the appointment of teachers and in curriculum decisions. It is perhaps not surprising, as Teese and Polesel (2003) indicated, that for many young people who are not achieving well at school, their most common descriptor of school is as a prison. In the schools that we have visited as part of this project, we have seen attempts to give students a voice through regular community meetings (Baroutsis et al., 2015), through consultations on renovations, even in one case working closely with architects to design new premises, and by including them on teacher interview panels.

Whilst in the main, we have been highly supportive of these alternative schools and the various ways in which they have worked to challenge injustice (see for example, Hayes, 2012; Mills & McGregor, 2014; Te Riele, 2006, 2007, 2011), we are of the view that as a matter of social justice these schools also have to consider the types of learning that students do in the classroom. It has been noted in many studies, and compounded by an era of high stakes testing (Darling-Hammond, 2010; Hardy, 2013; Lingard, Martino, & Rezai-Rashti, 2013; Lingard & Sellar, 2013), that many classrooms in mainstream schools are devoid of curriculum, pedagogy and assessment that inspire, challenge and provoke all students (Hayes, Mills, Christie, & Lingard, 2006; Smyth, McInerney, & Fish, 2013). However, whilst concerned about this current state of affairs, we are of the view that such an absence in flexible learning centres is particularly damaging to those students who have already been disenfranchised from learning. We are not alone here.

There have been some concerns raised about the alternative education sector being constructed as a dumping ground for students 'unwanted' by the education system where there is then little academic challenge (Kim, 2011; Kim & Taylor, 2008; Mills, Renshaw, & Zipin, 2013; Smyth et al., 2013). de Jong and Griffiths (2006), for instance, have expressed concerns that the increased use of alternative education programmes for younger and younger students can lead to them being separated from the mainstream and its benefits, and that 'poorly constructed and resourced' programmes will reinforce students' poor outcomes from schooling (p. 37). Thus, in highlighting the necessity for elements of affective justice and contributive justice to be significant considerations when working with disenfranchised young people, we are not suggesting that 'care' *by itself* is sufficient to address all their needs. Our intention is to tease out the complexity inherent in notions of a 'socially just' education as explained in the following sections.

Multi-sited ethnography

This study represents a 'multi-sited ethnography' of alternative schools (Falzon, 2009; Kraftl, 2013; Marcus, 1995; Pierides, 2010). Marcus (1995) explained that this mode of ethnographic research 'moves out from the single sites and local situations of conventional ethnographic research designs to examine the circulation of cultural meanings, objects, and identities in diffuse time-space' (p. 96). The strength of multi-sited ethnography is that it enables the researchers to 'make connections between sites' (Pierides, 2010, p. 186) in a 'spatially dispersed field through which the ethnographer moves' (Falzon, 2009, p. 2). In this research project, we used ethnographic observations and semi-structured interviews with students, teachers and other workers in three flexible learning schools across three Australian states and one territory during multiple visits over a period of 18 months in 2013 and 2014. We sought to explore a range of themes that included the following broad areas, as relevant to teachers, workers and students: previous experiences; a pathway into the alternative site; reasons for staying; what works (relational, material, pedagogical and curricular elements) and why; and, resourcing and sustainability issues. In this article, we draw upon data from three of these sites, identified using the pseudonyms: Elkhorn Community College in Queensland; Banksia College in the Australian Capital Territory (ACT) and Boronia Flexi School in Victoria, in order to explore concepts of affective and contributive justice that emerged as significant concerns within these schools.

Elkhorn Community College is a non-government and non-fee paying school providing educational programmes for young people in years 10, 11 and 12, the final 3 years of secondary education in Australia. At the time when the researchers were at the College, there was an enrolment of approximately 60 young people and 5 staff, comprising a principal, 2 teachers and 2 youth and community development workers (one of whom was completing teaching qualifications). Banksia College is a mainstream government senior high school in a major Australian city that runs two alternative programmes (now both operating out of the main campus) for students who have difficulties fitting into the mainstream and usually come from very difficult personal circumstances: one is a flexible learning centre for approximately 100 pregnant girls and young parents (mostly mothers) who attended both part and full-time; the other is a 'Big Picture'[2] inspired offering with a focus on flexibility of delivery and project-work for approximately 35 students. Staffed by small teams of dedicated teachers, both programmes provide significant levels of material and personal support to the young people in their care. Boronia Flexi School is a metropolitan year 7–12 alternative school and is part of the Edmund Rice Education Australia (EREA) Youth + network, which 'seeks to respond to the needs of young people disenfranchised and disengaged from education. This non-fee paying school caters to approximately 130 students, and as with Elkhorn and Banksia, their life experiences have been challenging – including poverty, mental illness, out-of-home care, drug dependency, juvenile justice and settlement as recent migrants. Boronia Flexi School offers year 7–12 formal junior and senior secondary credentials.

In the following sections of this article, we consider affective and contributive injustice. Affective justice relates very much to the relationship and supportive structures that are in place within a school, which indicate to young people that they are cared about. We would suggest that learning approaches which appear to have no purpose to the student and provide little by way of satisfaction and serve to demoralise them, not only represent an affective injustice, a lack of care, but also constitute a contributive injustice. Such learning would include, for example, routinised test skilling, worksheets and form filling with an emphasis on basic skills. This does not mean that some rote learning or developing of skills has no place in the delivery of meaningful learning, but that they need to be part of a broader approach to learning and not an end in themselves. We then provide examples of affective and contributive justice, where all students are engaged in meaningful work in a caring and supportive environment. This has particular salience given the context of where these justice acts are taking place. The schools that form the basis of our case study sites are those whose students, in the most part, have not been previously engaged in learning, have been labelled as academically and socially deficit and yet are now willing to come to school. We would suggest that this emphasises the importance of all schools demonstrating a commitment to affective and contributive justice.

Affective justice and learning environments

The relational and caring dimensions of schooling have been widely recognised (Bingham & Sidorkin, 2004; Noddings, 1988) and these are arguably particularly important when working with students who have experienced marginalisation in school and society (Beck & Cassidy, 2009; Smyth, Angus, Down, & McInerney, 2008; Te Riele, 2006). Additionally, many feminist writers have stressed the political importance of emotions and understandings of 'affective justice' (Blackmore, 1999, 2006; Boler, 1999; Hochschild, 1983). As Lynch (2012) has indicated it is often feminist scholars who 'have drawn attention to the salience of care and love as goods of public significance' (p. 47). Her work informs our concern with social justice and alternative education. Those schools deemed alternative, as all schools, are communities where their success, in terms of being a place where both workers and students want to attend, is dependent upon the quality of relationships for all. As with Lynch, we recognise that the care provided by members of that community to each other is a matter of social justice both in relation to who gives it and who receives it (Lynch, 2012, p. 49). She argues that what she refers to as 'affective equality' is focussed on two issues: 'securing equality in the distribution of the nurturing through love, care and solidarity relationships and securing equality in the doing of emotional and other work involved in creating love, care and solidarity relations' (p. 50).

Whilst we are concerned with the issue of who is responsible for 'caring', and recognise the mutuality of such caring, our focus here is on who gets the 'caring'. Many of the young people in our study, when asked to outline the strengths of their current schools suggested that it was the relationships that mattered, that they felt that the teachers and other workers cared for them. This was often contrasted with previous experiences of schooling, for example Audrey, a Boronia Flexi School student, said the following about her current school:

> They care, they care a lot about the students. No matter who you are they care … Because they're so sweet, they do so much for the students here and more than what other schools would do because the way I've seen in other mainstream schools is you're a teacher, you teach, that's it. They're more caring. Like I say, it's like a community, it's like a family. So the teachers really care about the students and they're also youth workers as well so they deal with the children. If you have something on your mind you talk to a teacher and they're full open with you and they're so nice, they're just the most nicest people here.

Lynch outlines three sets of relations that constitute affective justice: love, care and solidarity. In the first instance, love is said to be related to relationships of high interdependency and intense engagement; she suggests that even when such relationships are absent they often have great significance (for example the parent–child relationship even in abusive situations). Care relations are viewed as having a lower order of dependency and obligations, but are significant nonetheless; she suggested that friends, work colleagues and some distant relations fall into this category. Solidarity relations do not involve intimacy, but are, Lynch (2012) suggested 'the more political or public face of affective relations' (p. 52). Here, we can think of advocate groups (for example, refugee support groups), unions and government departments. Lynch suggested that these three categories are not mutually exclusive and that they are interdependent. She also argued that these systems of 'affective equality' are all interrelated with Fraser's framework. She argues that 'it is not possible to address problems of inequality or social justice in one social system therefore without addressing those in related social systems' (p. 53). We contend that it is the relational sets of 'care' and 'solidarity' that construct the affective domain within schools and that these elements are especially important for achieving socially just outcomes for marginalised young people.

Applying Lynch's (2012) conceptualisation of 'relational care work' (p. 56) in alternative settings suggests that teachers play an important mediating role in the nexus of these relationships: supporting and working with students and their families or caregivers; developing flexible structures and processes that provide a caring schooling environment and working in solidarity with students to resist their continued marginalisation in schooling and beyond. For example, Faye, who attended Banksia College, commented:

> I got kicked out of home and I came in and saw the counsellor and straight away she got me straight onto housing. They do that little bit extra all the teachers here. It's more than just what a normal teacher does at a school. They look out for you in your entire life, not for just the 6 hours that I'm here for.

Additionally, many of the students we interviewed talked about how their prior schooling experiences contributed to the complexity of their lives, rather than providing a place of care and support. Drew, a student from Elkhorn Community College, provided us with an example:

> I was always 'your bad student'. I wasn't bad. Like, I was respectful in some ways but I couldn't concentrate on work and it was, like, hard, just coming from my old life ... drugs, drinking and wrong people and violence and – yeah.

Leanne, a student at Banksia College, contrasted her experiences with her former and current school. She said about the programme at Banksia:

> We get to come into school and you are not stressed. Like, when you have got family issues and that, you can sit down and, like, talk to Leigh and Stuart (teacher and deputy principal) and they will, like, help you through the day and that. And then you can go and make yourself a cup of tea. It's more relaxed and chilled. Like, you are not stressed about going into class and that. You are running a bit late on an assignments – they do help you out.

Irrespective of social class background, complex home environments can disrupt young people's engagement with schooling because they may be called upon, as we have observed, to exercise independence at an early age, to care of younger siblings and disabled parents, to manage relationships with neighbours and service providers and so on. While it is not the role of teachers to replace or substitute these primary relationships, even when complex, they can provide care and support that enhances young people's capacity to sustain their engagement in schooling. At Banksia College, for example, a teacher named Leigh came up constantly in our interviews with young people. We heard numerous stories of how she went beyond the role of 'teacher' in the ways she cared for her students. In one discussion with students Callum and Leanne, they joked: 'Leigh needs to clone herself!' and Leanne added 'Yeah – we need more Leighs!' Evidence of her high level of care was threaded through all the data from Banksia College. For example, in a discussion about the food available at the site, the conversation indicated that packs of noodles were once provided for students but this is no longer the case. Darren commented: 'Don't have them lately. If it was really bad, Leigh would probably just give you some money to go to the canteen or something'. And Robbie,

> I missed out on a lot of schoolwork because I was really sick, that was due last semester – not last semester, last term. And I have been allowed to catch up pretty much nearly all of it. In the last few days, I was supposed to get some other work done, but my mother is in hospital now. So Leigh is supporting me and making sure that I can get to places easily ... Pretty much anything that she can do, like, transport – I believe she's done it for other people.

It appeared that Leigh's approach was to develop modes of caring, which were appropriate for the needs of individual students as summed up here by Leanne:

> Yes, she works – she has a different relationship – she has a relationship with everyone but it's different, which is really good. She sits there and knows everyone but she will have to change her, like, talking and that. She's like, 'Alright, I am talking to this student now, so I have got to talk to her in this way', you know what I mean. Yeah, she's really good.

In the case of marginalised students, care and support are likely to involve solidarity expressed through curriculum and pedagogy that values, respects and builds upon the knowledge and cultural backgrounds of students, while also supporting their capacity to engage with the kinds of knowledge that contribute to success at school and beyond. This is a challenge faced by teachers in both alternative and mainstream settings. However, for the former, it requires finding ways to engage young people in learning that do not involve repeating or reinforcing students' prior experiences of failure (Hayes, 2012).

We contend that a concern with 'affective equality' is critical to the success of alternative schooling. This is achieved relationally and academically. We suggest that, as with the dimensions of justice outlined in Fraser's work, both types of affective equality are necessary, and neither is sufficient on its own for considering what makes up a socially just school. Kim and Taylor (2008), for example, examined one alternative school in the mid-west of the United States, attended by many young people who have not been served well by current educational practices, to explore the benefits or otherwise of this school for its students. Their view was that the school was, indeed, a caring place; however, they were also of the view that it did little to break 'the cycle of educational inequality' (Kim & Taylor, 2008, p. 208). In this school, many of the students indicated that they wanted to go to college; however, the school's focus on 'credit recovery', where students who have fallen behind on their grades or school work attempt to catch up with their peers in the mainstream school, did not facilitate this goal. However, as Kim and Taylor (2008) go on to say: 'Their dreams required a more rigorous college-bound curriculum and career counselling' (p. 213). Echoing De Jong and Griffiths (2006), Kim and Taylor (2008) claimed that:

> A school program is beneficial to students when it provides content, processes, rigor, and concepts that they need to develop and realize their future career goals. A school program that is beneficial to students engages them and leads them through varying processes to critical thinking and synthesis of the concepts and content. Conversely, a school program that is not beneficial to students is behavioristic, positivistic, and reductive. That is, the focus of the program is primarily on an either–or dichotomy: It addresses only lower order thinking and processing skills and does not move students toward their future career goals. (p. 208)

Others to critique the types of learning taking place in such settings include Thomson and Russell (2007) in the UK who suggested that there was a tendency to assume that all young people in alternative learning environments need and want is vocational options, which limits scope of provision (p. viii). Similarly, Dovemark and Beach (2014) in Sweden demonstrated some of the ways in which deficit understandings of students in a programme for non-academic, non-vocational students contributed to their already precarious existence. In such instances, it is imperative that teachers and workers in alternative schools become advocates for young people, enacting Lynch's notion of 'solidarity' in caring for the long-term prospects of their students. We have also witnessed the absence of engaging, intellectually challenging and meaningful classroom practice in the alternative schools that formed part of our study, as illustrated here by Anthony, a student at Boronia Flexi School, who commented about his English studies:

> The quality of work – for instance, if I was still going to [name of previous school] I'd be expected to do, in English say, a 3,000-word essay. You're not expected to do that in English here.

Both Anthony and another student, Colin, agreed that classes at the Flexi school were 'a lot easier'. When asked if they liked their current situation, Anthony replied:

> Yeah, it's good because it's a lot less workload, but bad because … I honestly don't feel like I learn anything, like what I haven't already learned. It just feels like I'm just repeating.

The development of an appropriate and challenging curriculum for their students was clearly of great concern to the teachers in our case study schools. This kind of curriculum work is made even more complex in these settings because the students come from a variety of background learning experiences. Teachers are required to assess each student's learning needs and preferences, and map these to appropriate curriculum pathways. Maddy, a teacher at Elkhorn Community College, for example, explained how she got to know her student as learners:

> I have just recently started trying to do, 'what kind of learner am I?' That starts with a worksheet thing where they grade – put a scale, you know. They answer questions and then we have conversations, 'Why do you learn best in this way? What can we do in this setting to make it most beneficial for you, and the best way that I can support you in your learning?'

We acknowledge that many of the students who attend alternative schools have significant educational gaps that need to be addressed. Our concern is that rather than bridging the gaps and moving the learning forward, the 'gaps' will remain if learning is restricted to basic skills such as literacy and numeracy and 'job readiness'.

Branson from Elkhorn Community College spoke about a class that is offered at his college called employment, education and training:

> We have got a class that we can go to, if we want to do our job searches, résumés, certificates, get work experience. Yeah, I have got a couple so far. Heaps of stuff. It's pretty good here. TAFE is just down the road, so they take us down there in the bus, or they will come here; instead of finding your own way to TAFE.

In our experience, this state of affairs, as in lower streamed classes in mainstream schools, and lower expectations across whole schools located in low socioeconomic and marginalised communities, is justified often on the grounds of deficit understandings of students' abilities and dispositions. The absence of student work premised on high expectations and engaging activities, and the justifications for this absence would not be present in classrooms for 'gifted and talented' students or in schools proud of their academic reputations. Such attitudes may signify a lack of intellectual care and respect for the young people, their current abilities and their future potential. In recognising that there is a need to go beyond care, and indeed solidarity, as with Lynch, we have engaged with the work of Sayer and the notion of contributive justice. We argue here that this understanding of justice is crucial in ensuring that alternative schools consolidate their ethos of care as a basis for ensuring that their students have access to meaningful learning.

Contributive justice and meaningful learning

Whilst affective justice has a focus upon care of and respect for the individual in terms of the material, relational and intellectual supports and opportunities provided, contributive justice (Gomberg, 2007; Sayer, 2009, 2011) is overtly concerned with what a person actually gets *to do*. Sayer (2011) stated that: 'contributive justice concerns what people are allowed, expected or required to do or contribute' (p. 9). As such, it contrasts with, but complements justices concerned with what a person gets (economic), who a person is (cultural), how a person is heard (political) and how a person is cared for (affective). He goes on to argue that:

> What people are allowed to contribute, particularly in terms of work, is at least as important as what they get in terms of resources, because the type of work that they do has far-reaching effects on the kinds of people they become, on how they view themselves and are viewed by others, and hence on the quality of their lives. (Sayer, 2011, p. 9)

This is an echo of his distinction between contributive justice and economic justice, when he argued that: 'what we *do* in life has at least as much influence on who we become and the quality of our lives, as does what we *get*' (Sayer, 2009, p. 2). For Sayer, there are two aspects to contributive justice. The first has a quantitative element to it and is concerned with doing a 'fair share' of the workload. Teachers, and indeed university academics, who set project work and group tasks are familiar with the complaints that others are not pulling their weight or are taking over – both relate to the notion of contributive justice. However, whilst important, we are more concerned here with the qualitative element of contributive justice. This relates to the type of work being done and the intrinsic and extrinsic rewards associated with this work. It also relates to the opportunities that people have to make a contribution to the conception and execution, and all stages in between, of a shared project. This form of injustice is also linked and works closely with those frames identified by Fraser. For example, there are times when boring, repetitive, low skilled tasks are necessary to complete a project. However, how those tasks are distributed and rewarded is a matter of social justice. The unfair distribution of work occurs in both the formal economy and in domestic life. In the formal economy, contributive injustice, according to Sayer, occurs both within and between occupations and workplaces.

Sayer provided a set of arguments from Murphy (1994) and Gomberg (2007), to indicate why this state of affairs is unjust. These all relate to a person's quality of life. The kind of work that a person does has an impact on who they become and on their emotional, physical and intellectual well-being. People experience enjoyment in doing complex tasks that enable them to employ and extend their capacities (see Griffiths, 2012, for a discussion of social justice and 'joy'). For example, Lilly from Banksia College who, after fleeing there from an abusive family relationship in another major city, had been homeless in the ACT, before finding her way to the College, excitedly told us about how she wanted to build her own computer and noted: 'At the moment I am working towards getting an IT apprenticeship – I would never been able to finish Year 12 without [this program]'.

Dignity is also enhanced when people have control over their labour in that they are trusted, understand their contribution to the larger project and have an opportunity to question their and others' roles throughout the process of conception and execution of a project. Understanding the various links in a project and reasons for embarking on a particular task also ensures that even mundane tasks when shared around are meaningful. There is great resonance here with schooling and classroom work. This was evident when

Stuart, the teacher in charge of the alternative programme at Banksia College, was describing the types of projects they undertook in their programme. A key aspect of their work involved students working on a range of tasks, including some menial ones, to develop a product that had real world impacts. Stuart told us:

> [For our next project] we are going to aim to make some swags[3] with an industrial sewing machine, roll them with toothpaste, toothbrushes, towel, whatever we find, soap, and then we will give them to one of our local homeless shelters for the winter because it's pretty harsh in [the city] – well, you know, it is not pleasant anyway. So wherever possible we take a leadership or a community service thing in addition.... We don't have too many students who wallow and they have – pretty much all have had difficult circumstances.

In this case, it was indicated that the students were proud of their achievements and developed a sense of contributing to their community.

Students who are deemed to be the most competent are often those most likely to be provided with opportunities to extend themselves and to receive diverse learning experiences (see for example, Charlton, Mills, Martino, & Beckett, 2007). Similar parallels can be found with a differentiated schooling system where certain schools specialise in academic learning and others have a more technical focus. The growing presence of flexible learning options points to a schooling system that is increasingly diversifying in ways that have the potential to exacerbate this situation (Hayes, 2013; Slee, 2011). The defence of such arrangements include arguments to the case that it is more efficient to have specialised or differentiated schools and classrooms that cater to differences in abilities, interests and behaviours. This, it is sometimes argued, helps to ensure that the schooling system is efficient, that it is stabilised in that disruptions and poor behaviours are minimised (at least to the extent that 'good students' do not have their work interfered with) and that this situation caters to different abilities, potential and dispositions. However, Bardsley (2007) has argued that:

> Where social stability and economic efficiency are valued above all else, the aim of education becomes the provision of basic skills to train citizens amongst the socioeconomically deprived classes to perform the menial tasks essential to keep society functioning, without disrupting established power structures (Laberee, 1997; Lynch & Lodge, 2002). Justice within education systems should be committed to the premise that all children must be adequately prepared for effective societal roles of their own choosing. (p.496)

Bardsley's (2007) work also suggests that a socially just education has to provide young people with the skills and knowledge to engage with 'emerging societal contexts'. This will entail school work engaging with technology, developing critical citizenship skills and understandings of contemporary society.

It is our contention that contributive justice is present in a classroom when students are presented with learning opportunities that enable them to develop a sense of pride in the outcomes of that learning – in much the same way as a craftsperson feels pride in the construction of a product (Sennett, 2009). This recount from Stuart, a deputy and head of the alternative programme at Banksia College, exemplifies this contention:

> We have Miriam who all of last year spent 6 months making polymers with one of our chemistry teachers and she explained it to me ... And she's a pretty eclectic little thinker. ... I missed the exhibition where her family came to the exhibition... And the family sees something that the kid is proud of and there is a moment where they do a little bit of readjustment. Yeah, they settle back – there is that moment when the kid goes, 'Oh, you

do actually see something good about me. I am making progress', and that's transformative for both sides. We have got parents that were reviewed as part of that review process. They are some of our biggest fans. As I said, they have enrolled second kids in it. I think that what they like about it is the concept that the kid has to do something fairly rigorous.

At Boronia Flexi School, the music teacher provided a similar example:

The staff and the students see people walking out of this room with such big chests, you know. The pride is just visibly obvious to see when they have just had some success. That I think is, I am not saying it is all about music, but some sort of high level professional product that is in the digital domain I think every school would benefit from.

What the data from our research indicate is that such learning occurs when it has a purpose (whether personal or instrumental) and that purpose is evident to the student. Julian (a teacher at Boronia Flexi School) linked this to 'a sense of empowerment for the young people to be who they feel as though they want to be'. It also has some connection to the world beyond the classroom and stretches and challenges all young people, not just those deemed to be of 'high ability'.

Conclusion

Our concern with what a socially just schooling system might look like and, in particular, how schools can meet the needs of the most marginalised students, led us to explore 'what works' in those schools catering to students who have been excluded from mainstream schools or have themselves rejected what the mainstream has to offer. In many instances, we have been impressed by these schools' efforts to address economic, cultural and political injustices. In this article, we have thus contended that a socially just education for students attends to Fraser's (1997, 2009) dimensions of social justice in respect of economic, cultural and political inequities. However, drawing upon the work of Lynch (2012) and Sayer (2009, 2011), we have also argued that these dimensions are enhanced by the inclusion of affective and contributive forms of justice, which pay attention to inequities in relational care and individual potential for meaningful participation.

The teacher participants in our study expressed a strong commitment to the social and emotional well-being of their students. Affective justice (in the forms of significant support structures and respectful, caring relationships) was of primary concern to them. Many of the students we interviewed indicated that its absence in their former school(s) had been a key factor in their departure from the mainstream sector. This concern with affective justice was thus critical to the success of such schools. However, we suggest that if it exists in isolation from other necessary elements, care is insufficient for ensuring the provision of socially just schooling. The quality of curriculum and pedagogy, which varied in some instances across the sites, is also of critical concern, and hence why we also argue that contributive justice needs to be incorporated into concerns about affective justice.

In this article, we have indicated examples of where we have come across flexible learning arrangements that facilitated students' engagement in meaningful learning, demonstrating a commitment to contributive justice; however, there were sometimes reservations expressed. In some instances, teachers indicated that in their alternative setting some students were not able to tackle challenging work and that this was why they were in the alternative school in the first place. Because of the patchy nature of the educational backgrounds of young people in alternative education, there was often a focus on literacy, numeracy and vocational options. Clearly, these skills are necessary for economic participation in society; however, if such competencies and training are considered sufficient education for these, usually marginalised and disadvantaged, young people it could be argued that this may also condemn them to a lifetime of political and social marginalisation despite their ability to obtain employment. We thus argue that the quality of curricular choices and pedagogical approaches made available to young people in alternative education sites is fundamental to the achievement of contributive justice, and hence social justice. We are also of the view that concerns with affective justice and contributive justice should have occurred long before students such as those interviewed for this project found themselves in alternative education provision.

Acknowledgements

Martin would like to thank Kathleen Lynch for her comments at the Vere Foster Trust and the Institute of Educational Research in Ireland Lecture, 2013.

Funding

This work was supported by the Australian Research Council under Grant DP120100620

Notes

1. In this article, we have used the terms flexible learning centre and alternative school somewhat interchangeably. We note, as do Mills and McGregor (2014) that there is no agreed-upon definition and much contestation regarding what constitutes 'alternative education'. The schools involved here are those that cater to marginalised young people and are also often referred to as 'second chance' schools.
2. The Big Picture model of schooling has its origins in the USA. Its basic principles articulated on its Australian website state: 'highly personalised approach to education combines academic work with real world learning. It places the student, their passions and their interests, at the centre of the learning process' (See http://www.bigpicture.org.au/).
3. An Australian colloquial term for a bedroll containing all one's personal belongings.

References

Abrams, F. (2010). *Learning to fail: How society lets young people down*. London: Routledge.
Bardsley, K. (2007). Education for all in a global era? The social justice of Australian secondary school education in a risk society. *Journal of Education Policy, 22*(5), 493–508. doi:10.1080/02680930701541691
Baroutsis, A., McGregor, G., & Mills, M. (2015). Pedagogic voice: Student voice in teaching and engagement pedagogies. *Pedagogy, Culture and Society*. Advance online publication. doi:10.1080/14681366.2015.1087044
Beane, J. A., & Apple, M. W. (1999). The case for democratic schools. In M. W. Apple & J. A. Beane (Eds.), *Democratic schools: Lessons from the chalk face*. Buckingham: Open University Press.
Beck, K., & Cassidy, W. (2009). Embedding the ethics of care in school policies and practices. In K. Te Riele (Ed.), *Making schools different: Alternative approaches to educating young people* (pp. 55–64). London: SAGE.
Bingham, C. (2004). *No education without relation*. (A. Sidorkin, Eds.). New York, NY: Peter Lang Publishing.
Black, R. (2011). Student participation and disadvantage: Limitations in policy and practice. *Journal of Youth Studies, 14*(4), 463–474. doi:10.1080/13676261.2010.533756
Blackmore, J. (1999). *Troubling women: Feminism, leadership and educational change*. Buckingham: Open University Press.
Blackmore, J. (2006). Social justice and the study and practice of leadership in education: A feminist history. *Journal of Educational Administration and History, 38*(2), 185–200. doi:10.1080/00220620600554876
Boler, M. (1999). *Feeling power: Emotions and education*. New York, NY: Routledge.
Charlton, E., Mills, M., Martino, W., & Beckett, L. (2007). Sacrificial girls: A case study of the impact of streaming and setting on gender reform. *British Educational Research Journal, 33*(4), 459–478. doi:10.1080/01411920701434011
Cribb, A., & Gewirtz, S. (2003). Towards a sociology of just practices. In C. Vincent (Ed.), *Social justice education and identity* (pp. 15–29). London: Routledge.
Darling-Hammond, L. (2010). *The flat world and education: How America's commitment to equity will determine our future*. New York, NY: Teachers College Press.
De Jong, T., & Griffiths, C. (2006). The role of alternative education programs in meeting the needs of adolescent students with challenging behaviour: Characteristics of best practice. *Australian Journal of Guidance & Counselling, 16*(1), 29–40. doi:10.1375/ajgc.16.1.29
Dewey, J. (1916). *Democracy and education: An introduction to the philosophy of education*. New York, NY: Macmillan.
Dovemark, M., & Beach, D. (2014). Academic work on a back-burner: Habituating students in the upper-secondary school towards marginality and a life in the precariat. *International Journal of Inclusive Education*. doi:10.1080/13603116.2014.961676
Evans, J., Meyer, D., Pinney, A., & Robinson, B. (2009). *Second chances: Re-engaging young people in education and training*. Essex: Barnardo's.
Falzon, M.-A. (2009). Introduction. In M.-A. Falzon (Ed.), *Multi-sited ethnography: Theory, praxis and locality in contemporary research* (pp. 1–23). Surrey: Ashgate.
Fielding, M., & Moss, P. (2011). *Radical education and the common school: A democratic alternative*. London: Routledge.
Fraser, N. (1997). *Justice interruptus: Critical reflections on the 'postsocialist' condition*. New York, NY: Routledge.
Fraser, N. (2009). *Scales of justice: Reimagining political space in a globalizing world*. New York, NY: Columbia University Press.
Gale, T., & Densmore, K. (2000). *Engaging teachers: Towards a radical democratic agenda for schooling*. Buckingham: Open University Press.
Gomberg, P. (2007). *How to make opportunity equal: Race and contributive justice*. Malden, MA: Blackwell Publishing.
Griffiths, M. (2012). Why joy in education is an issue for socially just policies. *Journal of Education Policy, 27*(5), 655–670. doi:10.1080/02680939.2012.710019
Hardy, I. (2013). A logic of appropriation: Enacting national testing (NAPLAN) in Australia. *Journal of Education Policy, 29*(1), 1–18. doi:10.1080/02680939.2013.782425

Hayes, D. (2012). Re-engaging marginalised young people in learning: The contribution of informal learning and community-based collaborations. *Journal of Education Policy, 27*(5), 641–653. doi:10.1080/02680939.2012.710018

Hayes, D. (2013). Customization in schooling markets: The relationship between curriculum and pedagogy in a 'pop-up' learning project, and the epistemic opportunities afforded by students' interests and backgrounds. *International Journal of School Disaffection, 10*(2), 3–22.

Hayes, D., Mills, M., Christie, P., & Lingard, B. (2006). *Teachers and schooling making a difference: Productive pedagogies, assessment and performance.* Crows Nest: Allen & Unwin.

Hochschild, A. (1983). *The managed heart.* Berkeley, CA: University of California Press.

Kane, J. (2011). *Social class, gender and exclusion from schools.* London: Routledge.

Keddie, A. (2012a). Schooling and social justice through the lenses of Nancy Fraser. *Critical Studies in Education, 53*(3), 263–279. doi:10.1080/17508487.2012.709185

Keddie, A. (2012b). *Educating for diversity and social justice.* New York, NY: Routledge.

Kim, J.-H. (2011). Narrative inquiry into (re)imagining alternative schools: A case study of Kevin Gonzales. *International Journal of Qualitative Studies in Education, 24*(1), 77–96. doi:10.1080/09518390903468321

Kim, J.-H., & Taylor, K. A. (2008). Rethinking alternative education to break the cycle of educational inequality and inequity. *The Journal of Educational Research, 101*(4), 207–219. doi:10.3200/JOER.101.4.207-219

Kraftl, P. (2013). *Geographies of alternative education: Diverse learning spaces for children and young people.* Bristol: Policy Press.

Labaree, D. F. (1997). Public goods, private goods: The American struggle over educational goals. *American Educational Research Journal, 34,* 39–81.

Lingard, B., Martino, W., & Rezai-Rashti, G. (2013). Testing regimes, accountabilities and education policy: Commensurate global and national developments. *Journal of Education Policy, 28*(5), 539–556. doi:10.1080/02680939.2013.820042

Lingard, B., & Sellar, S. (2013). 'Catalyst data': Perverse systemic effects of audit and accountability in Australian schooling. *Journal of Education Policy, 28*(5), 634–656. doi:10.1080/02680939.2012.758815

Lipman, P. (2008). Mixed-income schools and housing: Advancing the neoliberal urban agenda. *Journal of Education Policy, 23*(2), 119–134. doi:10.1080/02680930701853021

Lynch, K. (2012). Affective equality as a key issue of justice: A comment on Fraser's 3-dimensiponal framework. *Social Justice Series, 12*(3), 45–64.

Lynch, K., & Lodge, A. (2002). *Equality and power in schools: Redistribution, recognition and representation.* London: RoutledgeFalmer.

Marcus, G. E. (1995). Ethnography in/of the world system: The emergence of multi-sited ethnography. *Annual Review of Anthropology, 24,* 95–117. doi:10.1146/annurev.an.24.100195.000523

McGregor, G., Mills, M., Te Riele, K., & Hayes, D. (2015). Excluded from school: Getting a second chance at a 'meaningful' education. *International Journal of Inclusive Education, 19*(6), 608–625. doi:10.1080/13603116.2014.961684

Mills, C., & Gale, T. (2010). *Schooling in disadvantaged communities: Playing the game from the back of the field.* Dordrecht: Springer.

Mills, M., & McGregor, G. (2010). *Re-engaging students in education: Success factors in alternative schools.* Brisbane: Youth Affairs Network Queensland.

Mills, M., & McGregor, G. (2014). *Re-engaging young people in education: Learning from alternative schools.* London: Routledge.

Mills, M., McGregor, G., Hayes, D., & Te Riele, K. (2015). 'Schools are for us': The importance of distribution, recognition and representation to creating socially just schools. In K. Trimmer, A. Black, & S. Riddle (Eds.), *Researching mainstreams, margins and the spaces in-between* (pp. 150–167). London: Routledge.

Mills, M., McGregor, G., Martin, B., Tomaszewski, W., & Waters, R. (2014). *Engaging young people in education.* Brisbane: Department of Education, Training and Education.

Mills, M., McGregor, G., & Muspratt, S. (2013). *Flexible learning options/centres in the Australian Capital Territory (ACT).* Canberra: ACT Education and Training Directorate.

Mills, M., Renshaw, P., & Zipin, L. (2013). Alternative education provision: A dumping ground for 'wasted lives' or a challenge to the mainstream? *Social Alternatives, 32*(2), 13–18.

Mosen-Lowe, L. A. J., Vidovich, L., & Chapman, A. (2009). Students 'at-risk' policy: Competing social and economic discourses. *Journal of Education Policy*, *24*(4), 461–476. doi:10.1080/02680930902759712

Murphy, J. B. (1994). *The moral economy of labor*. New Haven, CT: Yale.

Noddings, N. (1988). An ethic of caring and its implications for instructional arrangements. *American Journal of Education*, *96*(2), 215–230. doi:10.1086/aje.1988.96.issue-2

OECD. (2012). *Equity and quality in education: Supporting disadvantaged students and schools*. Paris: OECD Publishing. doi:10.1787/9789264130852-en

Olsen, K. (Ed.). (2008). *Adding insult to injury: Nancy Fraser debates her critics*. London: Verso.

Pierides, D. (2010). Multi-sited ethnography and the field of educational research. *Critical Studies in Education*, *51*(2), 179–195. doi:10.1080/17508481003731059

Power, S., & Frandji, D. (2010). Education markets, the new politics of recognition and the increasing fatalism towards inequality. *Journal of Education Policy*, *25*(3), 385–396. doi:10.1080/02680930903576404

Sayer, A. (2009). Contributive justice and meaningful work. *Res Publica*, *15*, 1–16. doi:10.1007/s11158-008-9077-8

Sayer, A. (2011). Habitus, work and contributive justice. *Sociology*, *45*(1), 7–21. doi:10.1177/0038038510387188

Sennett, R. (2009). *The craftsman*. London: Penguin Books.

Slee, R. (2011). *The irregular school: Exclusion, schooling and inclusive education*. London: Routledge.

Smyth, J. (2006). Educational leadership that fosters 'student voice'. *International Journal of Leadership in Education: Theory and Practice*, *9*(4), 279–284. doi:10.1080/13603120600894216

Smyth, J., Angus, L., Down, B., & McInerney, P. (2008). *Critically engaged learning: Connecting to young lives*. New York, NY: Peter Lang Publishers.

Smyth, J., McInerney, P., & Fish, T. (2013). Re-engagement to where? Low SES students in alternative-education programmes on the path to low-status destinations? *Research in Post-Compulsory Education*, *18*(1–2), 194–207. doi:10.1080/13596748.2013.755862

Te Riele, K. (2006). Schooling practices for marginalized students – practice-with-hope. *International Journal of Inclusive Education*, *10*(1), 59–74. doi:10.1080/13603110500221750

Te Riele, K. (2007). Educational alternatives for marginalised youth. *The Australian Educational Researcher*, *34*(3), 53–68. doi:10.1007/BF03216865

Te Riele, K. (2011). Raising educational attainment: How young people's experiences speak back to the compact with young Australians. *Critical Studies in Education*, *52*(1), 93–107. doi:10.1080/17508487.2011.536515

Te Riele, K. (2012). Negotiating risk and hope: A case study of alternative education for marginalized youth in Australia. In W. Pink (Ed.), *Schools and marginalized youth: An international perspective* (pp. 31–79). Cresskill, NJ: Hampton Press.

Te Riele, K. (2014). *Putting the jigsaw together: Flexible learning programs in Australia. Final report*. Melbourne: The Victoria Institute for Education, Diversity and Lifelong Learning. Retrieved from: http://dusseldorp.org.au/priorities/alternative-learning/jigsaw/

Te Riele, K., Davies, M., & Baker, A. (2015). *Passport to a positive future. Evaluation of the Melbourne Academy*. Melbourne: The Victoria Institute for Education, Diversity and Lifelong Learning. Retrieved from http://www.vu.edu.au/sites/default/files/victoria-institute/pdfs/Passport-to-a-Positive-Future-%28web%29.pdf

Teese, R., & Polesel, J. (2003). *Undemocratic schooling: Equity and quality in mass secondary schooling in Australia*. Melbourne: Melbourne University Press.

Thomson, P., & Russell, L. (2007). *Mapping the alternatives to permanent exclusion*. New York, NY: Joseph Rowntree Foundation.

The political economy of language education research (or the lack thereof): Nancy Fraser and the case of translanguaging

David Block

ABSTRACT
This article problematizes the politics of language education research with regard to social injustice, which is not only cultural, but also material. Its starting position is that most language education research today is, following Nancy Fraser, recognition oriented, in that it takes on culture- and identity-based injustices such as racism, gender bias, religious bias, and LGBTQ-phobia. It does not, however, have much to say about more economic and class-based injustices—redistribution issues—and it does not draw on the political economy literature essential to any attempt to explore such issues. The author develops these arguments and then applies them to a specific area of language education research that has become popular in recent years, translanguaging. It concludes that while translanguaging research may deal with recognition issues, in particular ethnolinguistic racism, it is not likely to alter in any way the underlying the current capitalist order that is causing deep and profound damage to the social fabric of societies worldwide and surely is the most likely cause of the poverty in which many translanguagers live. Language education research thus needs to work at the level of recognition, as it already does, while also taking on redistribution issues.

What remains of the radical left now operates largely outside of any institutional or organized oppositional channels, in the hope that small-scale actions and local activism can ultimately add up to some kind of satisfactory macro alternative. This left, which strangely echoes a libertarian and even neoliberal ethic of anti-statism, is nurtured intellectually by thinkers such as Michel Foucault and all those who have reassembled postmodern fragmentations under the banner of a largely incomprehensible poststructuralism that favors identity politics and eschews class analysis. Autonomist, anarchist and localist perspectives are everywhere in evidence. But to the degree that this left seeks to change the world without taking power, so an increasingly consolidated plutocratic capitalist class remains unchallenged in its ability to dominate the world without constraint. (Harvey, 2014, p. xii–xiii)

> Above all in the US, but also elsewhere throughout the world, there was a paradigm shift toward the dimension of recognition, and it arose exactly at the moment—it's quite ironic—when the Keynesian social-democratic formation was beginning to unravel. We got the astonishing resurrection of liberal free-market ideas that everyone had assumed were in the dustbin of history forever. The rise of neoliberalism at the same time as left movements for emancipation were focused overwhelmingly on culture and recognition is a very dangerous mix: in effect the critique of political economy dropped out at exactly the moment where it was most necessary. (Fraser, 2015, p. 23)

In the first quote reproduced here, David Harvey assesses the state of what he calls "the radical left" at a time when its members are most needed, or may be deemed to find themselves in a highly propitious moment as regards their prospects for helping to bring about changes in the way that contemporary societies are organized. This, given the rising indignation among large sectors of the population in countries affected by the 2007 economic crisis. However, notwithstanding the symbolic value of Bernie Sanders's ultimately doomed presidential bid in the United States, Jeremy Corbyn's precarious leadership of the British Labour Party from 2015 to the present, and the relative success of new left political parties such as Podemos in Spain and Syriza in Greece (the latter generally deemed to have sold out its principles upon winning the general election in Greece in January 2015), the radical left cannot be said to have made its presence felt that much more since the crisis began over a decade ago. Indeed, the political left, radical or more mainstream, has for some time now been drifting in a direction that perhaps defies left-right distinctions, toward a liberal multiculturalism, both celebratory and militant, in which battles—sometimes superficial, sometimes more profound—are fought out and victories sometimes won. Harvey is not against multicultural battles—far from it. However, he does suggest that by only fighting such battles, the left has abandoned the very important struggle over who controls the means of production and the financial system that undergird much of the current economy worldwide, and how this control is made effective.

The second quote shows a similar vein of thought as Nancy Fraser takes on what she sees as a near-total abandonment of political economy in both the academic analysis and social activism carried out by left-leaning Americans (and indeed, left-leaning academics, activists, and politicians worldwide) over the past several decades. Fraser has for some time argued that those who support and campaign for the rights of women, ethnic, and racial minorities and members of LGBTQ communities all too often have little or nothing to say about the current dominant form of capitalism (what many call neoliberalism). Thus, inadvertently, and surely unintentionally, they enter into an unacknowledged, though significant, collusion with the current economic status quo. The later, both ideologically and in practice, can and does accommodate the social liberalism that undergirds "movements for emancipation ... focused overwhelmingly on culture and recognition" (Fraser, 2015, p. 23). Similar to Harvey, Fraser is not against the cultural turn made by the left worldwide from the 1970s onward, as human rights and social issues writ large came to prominence in debates taking place in both private and public spheres. Rather, her point is that those on the left need to work a little harder, moving toward activity that is transformative and not just affirmative, and multivalent and not just one-dimensional (more on this below).

In my own work over the past several years (e.g. Block, 2014), I have similarly noted how in language educations studies, researchers have tended to follow more general trends in evidence in the social sciences and humanities. In this sense, they have adopted a broadly poststructuralist approach that frames reality as socially constructed and that situates said social construction in cultural terms, excluding for the most part concerns related to political economy. And in the midst of framing reality in this way, there has been a tendency to marginalise and even erase social class as a key way to capture a great deal of what constitutes being in the world (Block, 2014). This "culturalist" approach has become dominant in particular in the Anglophone world, but as scholars working in countries such as the United States and the United Kingdom tend to shape research agendas worldwide, it has become very common in many other parts of the world.

Bearing such developments in mind, and following the overall aim of this special issue, in this article I problematize the politics of language education research with regard to its positionality in the face of social injustice that is not only cultural, but also material. My starting position is that most critical language education research done today is recognition oriented, with a firm base in poststructuralist thought, and that there is a general lack of attention to redistribution issues and the political economy literature which would undergird any attempt to explore such issues. I develop these arguments and then apply them to a specific area of language education research that has become popular in recent years, translanguaging. I should add here that I base the previous assertion about critical language education research on my reading of articles published in refereed journals, edited collections, and monographs in which authors self-position as critical but do so with little or no attention to political economic-based inequalities and injustices (for a justification of my position, see Block, 2014, 2015, 2017).

To carry out such a discussion I first deal with the larger theoretical issue, which I derive from Nancy Fraser's discussions of recognition and redistribution over the years. Starting with her landmark article on the topic, which appeared in the *New Left Review* in 1995, she has repeatedly addressed Harvey's lament that many on the political left "have reassembled postmodern fragmentations under the banner of a largely incomprehensible poststructuralism that favors identity politics and eschews class analysis" (Harvey,

2014, p. xiii). And she has grasped the sensitive nettle of what would constitute radical transformative political activity and research and scholarship in 21st century societies. Her work has not passed without criticism, so this will necessitate some attention to such criticism before moving to the second half of the article, where, as explained previously, I discuss translanguaging as an example area of language education research from a Fraser-inspired perspective.

Nancy Fraser on recognition and redistribution

Over two decades ago, Charles Taylor (1994) wrote about the state of individual and collective identity in late 20th century societies and how injustices committed in the name of cultural prejudice against "minority or "subaltern" groups," what he termed "misrecognition," may be seen as "a form of oppression, imprisoning someone in a false, distorted, and reduced mode of being" (Taylor, 1994, p. 25). He further argued that such cultural or symbolic violence can cause "real damage, real distortion" to members of minority or subaltern groups "if the people or society around them mirror back to them a confining or demeaning or contemptible picture of themselves" (Taylor, 1994, p. 25). As a remedy to this misrecognition, Taylor proposed "recognition." Recognition is about respect for others and "an ideal reciprocal relationship between subjects in which each sees the other as an equal and also separate from it" (Fraser & Honneth, 2003, p. 10). It is about acknowledging difference, but further to this accepting it, understanding it, and even valuing it positively.

In 1995, Nancy Fraser published an article entitled "From redistribution to recognition? Dilemmas in justice in a "postsocialist" age" in the political journal *New Left Review*. Her article proved to be both ground-breaking and controversial, leading to a series of rebuttals and counter rebuttals (see Fraser, 2008). Writing in the context of debates about the future of left-wing political activity in the United States (and beyond) in what some scholars were calling the "postsocialist age," Fraser contrasted recognition, understood more or less in Taylor's terms, with what she called "redistribution," understood as a concern with how material resources are produced, distributed, acquired, and used in society. She argued that recognition had supplanted redistribution as the primary concern of those on the political left concerned with social justice. Fraser was writing about the United States above all, but there is little doubt that what she had to say about the United States was also applicable to political developments in Europe and beyond from the 1990s onward. And although the article was written and published over two decades ago, its main points and arguments have proven to be enduring, as Fraser's preoccupations and proposed solutions are as relevant today as they were in the 1990s. Indeed, in her writing from 1995 onwards (e.g., Fraser, 2005, 2008, 2015; Fraser & Honneth, 2003, 2013), Fraser has maintained the basic premises that she first developed in this article, even if, she has added a third form of injustice, the "political," to her framework.[1] The moral and intellectual force with which Fraser wrote her article is clear from the opening paragraph in which she states her main point both boldly and clearly:

> The "struggle for recognition" is fast becoming the paradigmatic form of political conflict in the late twentieth century. Demands for "recognition of difference" fuel struggles of groups mobilized under the banners of nationality, ethnicity, "race," gender, and sexuality. In these "post-socialist" conflicts, group identity supplants class interest as the chief medium of political mobilization. Cultural domination supplants exploitation as the fundamental injustice. And cultural recognition displaces socioeconomic redistribution as the remedy for injustice and the goal of political struggle. (Fraser, 1995, p. 68)

In proposing redistribution as the remedy to "maldistribution," Fraser is describing solutions to what she sees as "socioeconomic injustice ... rooted in the political-economic structure of society" (Fraser, 1995, p. 70). This socioeconomic injustice includes phenomena such as "exploitation (having the fruits of one's labour appropriated for the benefit of others); economic marginalization (being confined to undesirable or poorly paid work or being denied access to income-generating labour altogether); and deprivation (being denied an adequate material standard of living)" (Fraser, 1995, pp. 70–71). Fraser's way through the potential conflict between recognition claims and redistribution claims, and indeed the notion (which she rejects) that one must choose to focus on one or the other, is "perspectival dualism." Perspectival dualism means an exploration of how the recognition claims, which derive from social liberalism, interrelate with redistribution claims, which derive from a Marxist view of the world, focusing, as they do, on inequalities arising from the material bases of society and the need for social change and revolution.

Perspectival dualism and bivalency

One key element in attempts to establish the intersectionality of recognition and redistribution dimensions of being is the extent to which they exhibit what she calls "bivalency." For Fraser, "[a]t one extreme are modes of collectivity that fit the redistribution model of justice ... [while a]t the other extreme are modes of collectivity that fit the recognition model ... [and i]n between are cases that prove difficult because they fit both models of justice simultaneously" (Fraser, 1995, p. 74). To exemplify this point, Fraser discusses four forms of injustice—those relating to class, gender, race, and sexuality, using the heuristic of idealized forms at the extremes (recognition and redistribution) and valenced forms along the extremes-mediating scale. She defines the first of these four forms of injustice, class, as follows:

> ...class is a mode of social differentiation that is rooted in the political-economic structure of society. A class only exists as a collectivity by virtue of its position in that structure and of its relation to other classes. Thus, the Marxian working class is the body of persons in a capitalist society who must sell their labour-power under arrangements that authorize the capitalist class to appropriate surplus productivity for its private benefit. (Fraser, 1995, p. 75)

For Fraser class is as close as we come to an "ideal-typical mode of collectivity ... rooted in political economy" (Fraser, 1995, p. 75), given that both individual and collective class positions exist in direct relation to where individuals and collectives are situated with regard to property, the ownership and control over the productive forces in an economy, the division of labor and access to the wealth created in said economy. In simple terms the capitalist class owns, controls, and profits on the back of the exploitation of workers, extracting their surplus labor time and value. Injustice, in this case, is primarily about the maldistribution of resources and it is remediable via a change in the way that the economy is organized. This is not to say that there are no cultural consequences in such material injustice. Indeed, Fraser is careful to note how "ideologies of class inferiority proliferate to justify exploitation" (Fraser, 1995, p. 75). However, it is important to retain the key idea that the realm of the political economic very often (though not always) wags the tail constituted by the social, cultural and symbolic. Or, in Marxist terms, problems of recognition associated with class arise from the material realities of class.

Meanwhile, for Fraser, sexuality stands as an example of an "ideal-typical mode of collectivity ... rooted wholly in culture as opposed to political economy" (Fraser, 1995, p. 76). Any type of injustice which targets individual and collective sexualities is primarily a recognition issue, and any economic consequences of such injustice are derivative but not integral to the existence of said injustice. Thus, as Fraser explains, lesbians may be negatively evaluated and despised by certain individuals and collectives in society. And they may suffer harassment, shaming and discrimination as regards entry to and participation in certain social environments or job markets. They may also be subjected to discriminatory practices institutionalized in and sanctioned by the legal system, as when in contexts where marriage is the exclusive domain of heterosexuals, the partners in an unmarried lesbian couple do not have the same common law guarantees as the partners in an unmarried heterosexual couple. However, as Fraser notes, all of this amounts to misrecognition as lesbians do not occupy any single position in the division of labour and they therefore are not exploited for their surplus labor as members of the social, cultural, and symbolic category called "lesbians." In this sense, "the injustice they suffer is quintessentially a matter of recognition [as they] suffer from heterosexism: the authoritative construction of norms that privilege heterosexuality ... [and] homophobia: the cultural devaluation of homosexuality" (Fraser, 1995, p. 77). In contrast to class, sexuality is a deeply cultural matter and injustices that apply to it do not have their roots in political economy, even if, as noted previously, some maldistribution can be associated with them as when a lesbian is fired from a job simply because her boss has discovered that she is a lesbian.

Situating class and sexuality as ideal polar extremes, Fraser writes about fundamental differences between recognition claims and redistribution claims as regards how they embody clearly contrasted views of individual and group identity in societies at large. As Fraser explains:

> Recognition claims often take the form of calling attention to, if not performatively creating, the putative specificity of some group, and then of affirming the value of that specificity. Thus they tend to promote group differentiation. Redistribution claims, in contrast, often call for abolishing economic arrangements that underpin group specificity. (An example would be feminist demands to abolish the gender division of labour.) Thus they tend to promote group de-differentiation. The upshot is that the politics of recognition and the politics of redistribution appear to have mutually contradictory aims. Whereas the first tends to promote group differentiation, the second tends to undermine it. The two kinds of claim thus stand in tension with each other; they can interfere with, or even work against, one another. (Fraser, 1995, p. 74)

Race and gender stand in contrast to class and sexuality in that they are subject to both misrecognition and maldistribution and elicit both recognition and redistribution claims as routes to remedy injustice. They are, in Fraser's words, bivalent. Thus, while both race and gender are about "the putative specificity" of a group identity, differentiable from other group identities, they are also profoundly intersected with the maldistribution of economic resources in societies around the world. Gender is thus seen as "a basic structuring principle of the political economy" (Fraser, 1995, p. 78) in the sense that all capitalist societies are organized (to varying degrees to be sure) around the fundamental difference between "paid productive labour," traditionally the domain of men, and "unpaid reproductive and domestic labour," traditionally the domain of women. And when women enter the job market in significant numbers they tend to occupy the worst paid sectors of the economy. In some cases, the massive feminization of a profession such as medicine may lead to less financial remuneration and worsening work conditions, as has been the case in Spain over the past decade. Such a development over time, in effect "constitutes gender as a political-economic differentiation endowed with certain class like characteristics" (Fraser, 1995, p. 78). This means further that "gender injustice appears as a species of distributive injustice that cries out for redistributive redress ...[as m]uch like class, gender justice requires transforming the political economy so as to eliminate its gender structuring" (Fraser, 1995, p. 78)

Meanwhile, race equally shows recognition/redistribution bivalency. As Fraser explains, it is not unlike class in that it can serve to structure economic activity, in particular in socio-political contexts which resemble caste-like divisions of groups identified as different according to racial phenotype. In this sense, racialized groups in the United States, in particular African Americans and dark-skinned Latinos, have historically been subjected to institutionalized and systemic racism. And they have, on the whole, been relegated to particular job sectors. As Fraser explains, "low-paid, low-status, menial, dirty, and domestic occupations … [are] held disproportionately by people of colour, and higher-paid, higher-status, [while] white-collar, professional, technical and managerial occupations … [are] held disproportionately by "whites" (Fraser, 1995, p. 80). In 21st century Europe, one sees a similar trend as Black migrants from Sub-Saharan Africa tend to be employed at the lower end of the occupational scale, doing work that autochthonous and more established groups in these societies will not do. In such circumstances, as Fraser explains, "'race' … structures access to official labour markets, constituting large segments of the population of colour as a 'superfluous', degraded sub proletariat or underclass, unworthy even of exploitation and excluded from the productive system altogether" (Fraser, 1995, p. 80).

In her 1995 article and indeed to this day, Fraser has maintained that recognition and redistribution claims meant to combat misrecognition and maldistribution, respectively or in combined form, may be satisfied in very different ways. On the one hand, action taken can be "affirmative," providing "remedies aimed at inequitable outcomes of social arrangements without disturbing the underlying framework that generates them" (Fraser, 2008, p. 28). This is what happens when in response to recognition claims, diversity and difference are supported and even promoted in multicultural societies as a general defense against xenophobic, racist, sexist, homophobic, and religion-based attacks (anti-Semitic, Islamophobic, anti-Christian, etc.). In response to redistribution claims, affirmative actions include measures such as progressive tax regimes, which exact higher rates of tax from high earners and corporations, thus providing the means to fund the provision of resources to those who, for whatever the reason, cannot obtain or access them and therefore are most in need of them. In both of these examples of affirmative action, little or nothing is done to deal with underlying conditions that lead to the inequalities emerging from misrecognition and maldistribution.

The question that arises here is whether or not affirmative action is enough if we wish to get to the roots of inequality and injustice in societies with a view to eliminating them. In Fraser's view, it cannot and does not, and she proposes instead that actions taken in favor of recognition and redistribution need to be "transformative," providing "remedies aimed at correcting inequitable outcomes precisely by restructuring the underlying generative framework" (Fraser, 2008, p. 28). Transformative recognition means problematizing and deconstructing group differentiations, such as black versus white, or male versus female, or straight versus gay or lesbian, and so on. As Fraser explains, "transformative remedies … would redress disrespect by transforming the underlying cultural-valuational structure. By destabilizing existing group identities and differentiations, these remedies would not only raise the self-esteem of members of currently disrespected groups … [but also] change *everyone's* sense of belonging, affiliation, and self" (Fraser, 1995, pp. 82–83). Meanwhile, transformative redistribution means dealing with the class relations (and class struggle and warfare) deriving from material inequality. It therefore requires a deep restructuring of the political economy of a nation-state, in short, an economic and social revolution. Fraser illustrates the differences between the two forms of recognition-oriented political action by examining "the case of the despised sexuality" as follows:

> Affirmative remedies for homophobia and hetero-sexism are currently associated with gay-identity politics, which aims to revalue gay and lesbian Identity. Transformative remedies, in contrast, include the approach of "queer theory," which would deconstruct the homo–hetero dichotomy. Gay-identity politics treats homosexuality as a substantive, cultural, identificatory positivity, much like an ethnicity. This positivity is assumed to subsist in and of itself and to need only additional recognition. "Queer theory," in contrast, treats homosexuality as the constructed and devalued correlate of heterosexuality; both are reifications of sexual ambiguity and are co-defined only in virtue of one another. The transformative aim is not to solidify a gay identity, but to deconstruct the homo–hetero dichotomy so as to destabilize all fixed sexual identities. The point is not to dissolve all sexual difference in a single, universal human identity; it is rather to sustain a sexual field of multiple, debinarized, fluid, ever-shifting differences. (Fraser, 1995, p. 83).

Responses to Fraser, moving matters on

Fraser's 1995 article, along with subsequent publications appearing up to the time of writing, have provoked strong responses from scholars who see in her work a veiled critique of recognition politics and a reversion into determinist, mechanistic, economist positions that these scholars see as relics of the epistemological past in the social sciences and humanities. For example, Judith Butler (1997) has criticized Fraser for treating recognition battles as "merely cultural" and of premising her arguments on the notion that "the distinction between material and cultural life is a stable one." As observed previously, Fraser does see scope for distinguishing between Weber's "status" sphere and "social class sphere," the former being in the realm of the social and the cultural, while the latter is more grounded in political economy. However, she has over the years distanced herself from strict and clear divisions between these and other worlds, as she has demonstrated a clear understanding of the kind of cultural Marxism that arose in Britain from the 1980s onward (Fraser, 2015). But more to the point, she has never proposed the "ontological distinction between the material and the cultural," arguing that "injustices of misrecognition are … just as material as injustices of maldistribution" (Fraser, 2008, p. 66). In a sense, she wishes to combine the fundamentals of Butler's and other scholars' work on gender and sexual politics with a stronger political economic dimension that she sees as lacking in this work.

More recently, Johanna Brenner (2017) has taken Fraser to task for suggesting that in many societies, we have witnessed the rise of a "progressive neoliberalism" organized around "a new alliance of entrepreneurs, suburbanites, new social movements, and youth, all proclaiming their modern, progressive bona fides by embracing diversity, multiculturalism, and women's rights" (Fraser, 2017a). Accepting that the term "progressive neoliberalism" is something of an oxymoron, Fraser nonetheless points out how being antiracist and LGBTQ-friendly is simply not enough, given the by-now demonstrable permanence and endurance of neoliberalism, which despite the economic crisis provoked by its policies and practices, remains, it seems, the only alternative as a driver of worldwide political economy (Crouch, 2011; Streeck, 2016). Thus, while Brenner accuses Fraser of "attacking 'identity politics'" in favor of "class politics" and being "clearly suspicious of multiculturalism and diversity" (Brenner, 2017), Fraser remains firm in her resolve, arguing that "[n]eoliberals gained power by draping their project in a new cosmopolitan ethos, centered on diversity, women's empowerment, and LGBTQ rights … [and d]rawing in supporters of such ideals, they forged a new hegemonic bloc, … progressive neoliberalism" (Fraser, 2017b). It is hard for me to understand why so many social sciences and humanities researchers fail to see political developments in this way, although in language education, scholars such as Nelson Flores (2013) and Ryuko Kubota (2016) have made the point that neoliberalism is in no way incompatible with contemporary cultural and identity politics.

My aim in this article is not to go on endlessly about the ideas of Nancy Fraser and the academic debate that these ideas have generated. Rather, my intention thus far has been to lay out in more detail than I have done in previous publications the basics of Fraser's thinking about battles for social justice around key issues related to recognition and redistribution. And as I have made clear elsewhere (Block, 2014), I think that Fraser points to gaps in thinking and scholarship, not only in the social sciences and humanities in general, but also more specifically in language education research. In the remainder of this paper, I examine language education research organized around the notion of translanguaging, doing so with a view to showing how such research has generally been far more concerned with recognition issues than redistribution issues. This bias has meant a certain marginalization of maldistribution, which in turn has meant that there is insufficient attention to the how key political economic phenomena play out in societies, for example, "exploitation (having the fruits of one's labour appropriated for the benefit of others); economic marginalization (being confined to undesirable or poorly paid work or being denied access to income-generating labour altogether); and deprivation (being denied an adequate material standard of living)" (Fraser, 1995, pp. 70–71). To be sure there is a concern with exploitation, economic marginalization, and deprivation motivating many researchers. The problem is that when intentions turn to actions the result is far more recognition-oriented research than redistribution-oriented research, and there is, therefore a lack of the "perspectival dualism" and attention to "bivalency" that Fraser argues for.

An example to examine: Translanguaging research

To insert this discussion of Fraser's thinking into language education research, it is necessary to find an example area of research. After careful consideration, I have decided to focus on research carried out under the heading of translanguaging. However, before beginning my examination of this research, three caveats are in order. First, what follows will necessarily be a very partial representation of translanguaging research even if I have made every effort to make it a fair one. In effect, one cannot possibly cover the entirety of a field of research that has expanded rapidly over the past decade, but one can try to be fair in one's portrayal of it. Second, and related to the first point, I need to explain that I am primarily interested in translanguaging research that is embedded in ongoing education practices (what we may call the sociolinguistics of education). There are many other ambits in which translanguaging may figure prominently, some of which I will mention in their course of this article. However, my main concern is education. The third caveat is to make clear that I have nothing against translanguaging research, although it is true that I see some problems and gaps in the conceptual edifice that undergirds it, not least the wholesale jettisoning of many of the traditional staples of multilingualism research such as codeswitching, as too beholding to the "antiquated" notion that discrete languages exist (for an interesting critique of translanguaging, see MacSwan, 2017).

Above all, I have chosen translanguaging because there is by now a rich and varied literature that is becoming progressively more influential every day in sociolinguistics of education circles.

In a survey article on translanguaging, Creese and Blackledge (2015, p. 21) noted how in recent years "a number of terms have emerged, as scholars have sought to describe and analyse linguistic practices in which meaning is made using signs flexibly." They go on to cite some of these terms, such as Canagarajah's (2011) translingual practice and Otsuji and Pennycook's (2011) metrolingualism, before centering their discussion on translanguaging. It is the latter term that is of concern here, as it is the one that has garnered the most attention, used as a new way to frame communication practices in a range of social contexts, including communication in bi/multilingual educational settings. In the latter, it can, in addition be framed as a teaching/learning strategy. As has been noted by many authors (e.g. García & Wei, 2014), the term originates in English-Welsh bilingual education as Cen Williams (1994) first used it to capture how students in Wales worked back and forth using English and Welsh while reading and writing. However, in more recent times, translanguaging has been defined in more detail, with different contexts and intentions in mind. For example, in his work on transnational identities, Suresh Canagarajah (2011) defines translanguaging as "the ability of multilingual speakers to shuttle between languages, treating the diverse languages that form their repertoire as an integrated system" (p. 401). This definition is very much in line with Vivian Cook's classic work on multicompetence (e.g. Cook, 1996). However, García and Wei (2014) suggest that there is far more to translanguaging than multicompetence. And indeed, there is far more to translanguaging than what has traditionally fallen under the umbrella term of "code switching." Thus, as García and Kleyn (2016a) note, while translanguaging may be seen as "the deployment of a speaker's full linguistic repertoire," this repertoire "does not in any way correspond to the socially and politically defined boundaries of named languages" (p. 14).

In addition, García and Wei (2014) frame translanguaging in terms of dynamic systems theory (Herdina & Jessner, 2002), which explores links between language and the environment. They therefore see translanguaging as "a creative process that is the property of the agent's ways of acting in interactions, rather than belonging to the language system itself" (García & Wei, 2014, p. 25). They also see connections with the work of scholars such as Larsen-Freeman and Cameron (2008), who have examined language and language use from a complexity theory perspective, taking the view that "the individual's cognitive processes as inextricably interwoven with their experiences in the physical and social world" (Larsen-Freeman & Cameron, 2008, p. 155).

Further to this interest in dynamism and complexity, translanguaging specialists have also made clear that the "language" in translanguaging is not just about language as a set of linguistic features; rather, it acts as something of a holding term for multimodal communication in which the deployment of multiple linguistic codes is deemed to be significant. Ultimately, it is very much in line with the turn to repertoire as a key central construct in sociolinguistics research (for a discussion, see Snell, 2013), where repertoire refers to the entirety of an individual's semiotic resource which may at any given time be drawn on in communication. In addition, it fits into the broad frame of "superdiversity" that has been promoted by Jan Blommaert, Ben Rampton, and other scholars in recent years (see Arnaut, Blommaert, Rampton, & Spotti, 2016). In broad terms, superdiversity is about the diversity of diversity in complex 21st century societies (for the original formulation of the term, see Vertovec, 2007) and relevant to trans-languaging, in its sociolinguistic version, it is about the

> ongoing revision of fundamental ideas (a) about languages, (b) about language groups and speakers, and (c) about communication. Rather than working with homogeneity, stability and boundedness as the starting assumptions, mobility, mixing, political dynamics and historical embedding are now central concerns in the study of languages, language groups and communication. (Blommaert & Rampton, 2011, p. 3)

Elsewhere, García and Wei (2015) return to language education as they outline what they see as the seven pedagogical purposes of translanguaging as follows:

(1) To differentiate amongst students' levels and adapt instruction to different types of students in multilingual classrooms ...
(2) To build background knowledge so that students can make meaning of the content being taught and the ways of language in the lesson.
(3) To deepen understanding, develop and cognitive engagement, develop and extend new knowledge, and develop critical thinking.
(4) For cross-linguistic transfer and metalinguistic awareness so as to strengthen the students' ability to translanguage in order to meet the communicative exigencies of the socioeducational situation.
(5) Cross-linguistic flexibility so as to translanguage competently.
(6) For identity investment and positionality, to engage learners.
(7) To interrogate linguistic inequality and disrupt sociopolitical structures so as to engage in social justice. (p. 235)

The authors go on to summarize their view that translanguaging is valuable for at least four general reasons in educational contexts. First, it is consistent with theories of language and cognition whereby individuals use an array of semiotic resources as they make their way through a variety of practices, activities and events. In addition, translanguaging, as a teaching strategy, may lead to more learning. There is no hard evidence that this is indeed the case, but judging by the number of publications coming out on the topic in 2016 and 2017 (see García, Ibarra Johnson, & Seltzer, 2016; García & Kleyn, 2016b; Lublinmer & Grisham, 2017; Mazak & Carroll, 2017; Paulsrud, Rosén, Straszer, & Weden, 2017), it is safe to say that a research agenda focusing specifically on translanguaging and learning is well underway.

A third beneficial aspect of translanguaging is that it provides respect for individual and collectives whose multilingual communicative practices have historically been denigrated by educational institutions and society at large. The case of Spanish-speaking Latinos in the United States is a good example, as they have found themselves caught within a three-way pincer movement involving (a) those who push them toward competence in standard American English, (b) those who push them toward competence in a standard Spanish, and (c) those who push them toward competence in both. And through all of this, they are told by far too many individuals and collectives in American society that they are "semilingual" speakers of "Spanglish." In addition, the majority of children who can trace their roots to countries such as Puerto Rico are also *racialized* users of language, suffering multiple discriminations (Flores, 2016; Urciuoli, 1996). As García and Wei (2015) explained, "[b]y exposing alternative histories, representations, and knowledge, translanguaging has the potential to crack the "standard language" bubble in education that continues to ostracize many bilingual students, and most especially immigrant and other minoritized students" (p. 236).

Finally, as translanguaging has become a key prism through which researchers view multilingual practices in and around education, many scholars have begun to argue that it has transformative potential, that is, that the promotion of translanguaging may be key element in ongoing battles against inequality and injustice in contemporary multilingual and multicultural societies. The following two quotes capture this line of reasoning:

> Translanguaging theory has the potential to transform speakers and listeners, as privilege is taken away from "native speakers" and appropriated by all. By focusing on language features of the speaker's repertoire, and not on named autonomous languages per se, translanguaging has the potential … to provide all learners with equal educational opportunity and build a more just society. (García & Seltzer, 2016, p. 21)

> The advantage of educating adult migrants with translanguaging theory and pedagogy in mind is that in focusing on the practices of people, it gives agency to minoritized

speakers, decolonizes linguistic knowledge, and engages all of us in the social transformations that the world so sorely needs today. (García, 2017, p. 24)

This may be seen as a case of claiming quite a lot for a change in pedagogical practice.[2] I say this because phrases such as "provide all learners with equal educational opportunity and build a more just society" and "engages all of us in the social transformations that the world so sorely needs today" point me in the direction of the kind of transformative action that Fraser calls for in her work. At a minimum, the proposals of translanguaging scholars are in the realm of affirmative, recognition-based action, in that they are about a surface level-change in practices to redress an injustice based on what is, in effect, ethnolinguistic racism situated more broadly in what has come to be known as raciolinguistics (Alim, Rickford, & Ball, 2016). As for whether the widespread adoption of translanguaging theory in language education might constitute a case of recognition-based transformation, I am not convinced. That is, I am not convinced that such a move would somehow filter upward into the ideological realm, and to the roots of the discrimination that it aims to combat and/or eliminate, having a positive impact on how both translanguaging practices—and translanguagers—are positioned and treated by power structures. As García and other translanguaging scholars have acknowledged, such a turn of events seems difficult in the current political/educational climate in the United States, which has surely been made worse by the neo-jingoist and blatantly racist campaign for the presidency conducted by Donald Trump in 2016, along with his equally neo-jingoist and blatantly racist behavior as president.

In my view, what is missing here is a bivalent (or even multivalent) approach to inequality, one that would examine the intersection of what, in effect, is ethnolinguistic racism, with a particular class position in society. This has been done before, as when Bonnie Urciuoli (1996) focused on the intersection of racism, ethnolinguistic prejudice and class bias that Puerto Ricans have traditionally faced in the United States (for a recent attempt to work in a similarly intersectional manner, see Flores, 2017). Such an approach challenges not only the discriminatory policies and practices that often (though crucially, not always) position bi/multilingualism and bi/multilinguals in a negative way, but also the capitalist system that condemns so many children to lives of poverty or relative poverty, as class hierarchies are continually reproduced across a range of institutions and day-to-day practices. Along with scholars ranging from bell hooks (2000) to Erik Olin Wright (2015), I align with the view that class matters in the United States, as it does everywhere else in the world (see Block, 2014), and that it intersects with identity dimensions such as race, ethnicity and gender in ways which are both complex and clear (Block & Corona, 2014). Thus, the children of Spanish-speaking migrants in the United States who are university-educated professionals with a White European phenotype, are surely not in the same economic, social, cultural, and political situation as the racialized, minorities, and denigrated individuals we see in much translanguaging research. In effect, for the children who are the focus of García and Seltzer's very useful research, there is much work to do because there is double the injustice: a strong load of ethnolinguistic racism added to, and intertwined with, the class politics of American society.

Indeed, in the United States and worldwide, we need to be wary of lumping all forms of translanguaging together. Sandhu and Higgins (2016) discuss research in India, where translanguaging is a strategy in the advertising of upmarket products directed at those who can afford such products. The focus here is thus on a middle/upper class–inflected translanguaging that has certain prestige in society. By contrast, translanguaging from below in India, that is translanguaging at the lower end of the class hierarchy in India, may be seen by local elites as case of not having a sufficient command of English. Elsewhere, Wei and Hua (2013) examined the translanguaging practices of highly privileged university students in London, who claim a common Chinese identity despite coming from different countries and speaking different varieties of English and Chinese. These students show a high degree of ambivalence: they seem to want to claim an individual identity and not a Chinese identity, while wanting to claim a Chinese identity as opposed, for example, a British identity. Highly educated, and highly empowered, they translanguage as a ludic activity which contributes to their ongoing construction of what may be termed identities of affinity and identities of difference. As the authors explain, their "examples show that the Chinese university students feel that they are not Chinese from a specific place; neither are they Chinese in Britain in general. They are Chinese students at universities in London" (Wei & Hua, 2013, p. 532). Nevertheless, this identity ambivalence, and the translanguaging practices that these students engage in, are not likely to have negative consequences in their lives, as they already are a part of, and in all likelihood will remain a part of, the cosmopolitan (upper) middle class that lives in isolation from the kinds of issues faced by the students that García and others (e.g. Sayer, 2013) are concerned with.

Conclusion

> The transgressive translanguaging practices between French and English teachers ... demonstrate new pedagogical possibilities and ideological spaces ... to prepare students to become critical bilingual users to enact social change. (Lau, Juby-Smith, & Desbiens, 2017, p. 121)

Lau et al. (2017) made this observation after discussing the introduction of translanguaging as a teaching strategy in French-English bilingual education in Quebec. In this context, they frame translanguaging as "transgressive" for several reasons. First, it overcomes "traditional boundaries that confine students to assembly-line rote passive learning and compartmentalized bits of knowledge that bear little impact on their lives"(Lau et al., 2017, p. -100). Second, it involves the "intermingling [of] both languages [English and French] to challenge the traditional monolingual-biased bilingual education"(Lau et al., 2017, p. 100. Third, and last, it shows a "commitment to the Freirean view of literacy as reading (and writing) the word and the world ..." (Lau et al., 2017, p. 100). As was argued previously, this type of approach is fine as far as it goes. It is transgressive in that it does take on the misrecognition (Taylor, 1994) of bi/multilingual students who translanguage, drawing on the entirety of their semiotic resources in their attempts to make sense of and make sense in the world around them. And it is affirmative in that it provides "remedies aimed at inequitable outcomes of social arrangements without disturbing the underlying framework that generates them" (Fraser, 2008, p. 28).

Reading Lau et al. and many other publications focusing on translanguaging, there remains a question posed elsewhere in response to sociolinguistic research that defends the English of working class youth in the North of English and positions it as no better or worse than middle-class varieties imposed in formal education (Snell, 2010, 2013):

> a question arises as to what would happen if we could convince the dominant class to respect working class dialects and not vilify and denigrate them. ... What would this achieve as regards the material-based deprivation and poverty which serves as the base-level shaper, not only of ways of speaking and communicating in general, but also of every other index of social class in socioeconomically stratified societies? (Block, 2014, p. 104)

Translanguaging research, as it is currently framed and executed, is not likely to provide an answer to this question, which is about transformative redistribution. But then again, when translanguaging researchers use the term *transformative*, they quite likely are not doing so with Fraser's meaning in mind and therefore the overall aim and purpose is altogether more modest (and perhaps even more realistic). When these researchers focus on injustice and inequality, they are not doing so from a political economy perspective; rather they are concerned with political activity in the social and cultural realm. In this sense, my reading of translanguaging research is very similar to my reading of most language in education research, in that I think that it provides much needed palliatives to social injustices based on race, ethnicity, gender, and other social dimensions of identity, but that it has little to say about redistribution and even less to say about transformative redistribution. Identifying that one way of speaking is (unfairly) considered superior to another and then setting out to remedy this situation by teaching that all ways of speaking are equal and therefore should be equally respected, may go some distance toward increasing the self-esteem of (and even empowering) those who are most denigrated in society. This is important and it is a way forward that I agree with. However, at the same time, I believe that it is not likely to take us very much closer to overturning the current capitalist order that is causing deep and profound (and even irreversible) damage to the social fabric of societies worldwide. Language education research thus needs to work at the level of recognition, as it already does in most cases. But it also needs to pay more attention to redistribution issues rooted in political economy. And beyond all of this, it needs to combine the two strands, adopting perspectival dualism in the examination of, for example, the bivalency of class and ethnolinguistic identity. Nevertheless, the hard-core reality is that if we wish to effect profound change in society with regard to redistribution, working through education exclusively is never going to be enough. This is the weak pillar on which most critical education stands. Transformative redistributive change can only come, as I have just suggested, through a fundamental and wholesale change in how the economy is organized. And that type of change cannot be brought about solely through pedagogy.

Notes

1. Fraser explains what she means by the political as a third kind of justice as follows: "I mean political in a more specific, constitutive sense, which concerns the scope of the state's jurisdiction and decision rules by which it structures contestation. Then political in this sense furnishes the stage on which struggles over distribution and recognition are played out. Establishing criteria of social belonging, and thus determining who counts as a member, the political dimension of justice specifies the reach of these other dimensions: it tells us whom is included in, and who excluded from, the circle of those entitled to a just distribution and reciprocal recognition" (Fraser, 2010, p. 17).
2. Although it is by no means uncommon. See Davis and Phyak (2017), who wrote about translanguaging in a similar way from a language policy perspective.

Acknowledgments

The author thanks Adriana Patiño, John Gray, and two anonymous reviewers for helpful comments on an earlier version of this paper.

References

Alim, S., Rickford, J., & Ball, A. (Eds.). (2016). *Raciolinguistics: How language shapes our ideas about race.* Oxford, UK: Oxford University Press.

Arnaut, K., Blommaert, J., Rampton, B., & Spotti, M. (Eds.). (2016). *Language and superdiversity.* London, UK: Routledge.

Block, D. (2014). *Social class in applied linguistics.* London, UK: Routledge.

Block, D. (2015). Social class in applied linguistics. *Annual Review of Applied Linguistics, 35,* 1–19. doi:10.1017/S0267190514000221

Block, D. (2017). Researching language and social class in education. In K. King & Y.-J. Lai (Eds.), *Research methods. Encyclopedia of language and education* (Vol. 10, 3rd ed., pp. 159–169). New York, NY: Springer.

Block, D., & Corona, V. (2014). Exploring class-based intersectionality. *Language, Culture and Curriculum, 27*(1), 27–42. doi:10.1080/07908318.2014.894053

Blommaert, J., & Rampton, B. (2011). Language and superdiversity. *Diversities, 13*(2), 1–22.

Brenner, J. (2017, January 14). There was no such thing as "Progressive Neoliberalism." *Dissent.* Retrieved from: https://www.dissentmagazine.org/online_articles/nancy-fraser-progressive-neoliberalism-social-movements-response

Butler, J. (1997). Merely cultural. *Social Text, 52/53,* 265–277. doi:10.2307/466744

Canagarajah, S. (2011). Codemeshing in academic writing: Identifying teachable strategies of translanguaging. *Modern Language Journal, 95,* 401–417. doi:10.1111/j.1540-4781.2011.01207.x

Cook, V. (1996). Competence and multi-competence. In G. Brown, K. Malmkjaer, & J. Williams (Eds.), *Performance and competence in second language acquisition* (pp. 57–69). Cambridge, UK: Cambridge University Press.

Creese, A., & Blackledge, A. (2015). Translanguaging and identity in educational settings. *Annual Review of Applied Linguistics, 35,* 20–35. doi:10.1017/S0267190514000233

Crouch, C. (2011). *The strange non-death of neoliberalism.* Cambridge, UK: Polity Press.

Davis, K., & Phyak, P. (2017). *Engaged language policy and practice.* London, UK: Routledge.

Flores, N. (2013). The unexamined relationship between neoliberalism and plurilingualism: A cautionary tale. *TESOL Quarterly, 47*(3), 500–520. doi:10.1002/tesq.114

Flores, N. (2016). A tale of two visions: Hegemonic whiteness and bilingual education. *Educational Policy, 30*(1), 13–38. doi:10.1177/0895904815616482

Flores, N. (2017). Developing a materialist anti-racist approach to language activism. *Multilingua, 36*(5), 565–570. doi:10.1515/multi-2017-3045

Fraser, N. (1995). From redistribution to recognition? Dilemmas of justice in a "post-socialist" age. *New Left Review, 212,* 68–93.

Fraser, N. (2005). Reframing justice in a globalizing world. *New Left Review, 36,* 69–88.

Fraser, N. (2008). *Adding insult to injury: Nancy Fraser debates her critics.* (K. Olsen, Ed.). London, UK: Verso.

Fraser, N. (2015). The fortunes of socialist feminism: Jo Littler interviews Nancy Fraser. *Soundings, 58,* 21–33. doi:10.3898/136266215814379664

Fraser, N., & Honneth, A. (2003). *Redistribution or recognition? A political-philosophical exchange.* London, UK: Verso.

Fraser, N. (2013). *Fortunes of feminism: From state-managed capitalism to neoliberal crisis.* London, UK: Verso.

Fraser, N. (2017a, January 2). The End of Progressive Neoliberalism. *Dissent.* Retrieved from: https://www.dissentmagazine.org/online_articles/progressive-neoliberalism-reactionary-populism-nancy-fraser

Fraser, N. (2017b, January 28). Against progressive neoliberalism, new progressive populism. *Dissent*. Retrieved from: https://www.dissentmagazine.org/online_articles/nancy-fraser-against-progressive-neoliberalism-progressive-populism

García, O. (2017). Problematizing linguistic integration of migrants: The role of translanguaging and language teachers. In J.-C. Beacco, H. Krumm, D. Little, & P. Thagott (Eds.), *The Linguistic integration of adult migrants: Some lessons from research/ L'intégration linguistique des migrants adultes: Les enseignments de la recherche* (pp. 11–26). Berlin, Germany: De Gruyter Mouton.

García, O., Ibarra Johnson, S., & Seltzer, K. (2016). *The translanguaging classroom: Leveraging student bilingualism for learning*. Philadelphia, PA: Caslon.

García, O., & Kleyn, T. (2016a). Translanguaging theory in education. In O. García & T. Kleyn (Eds.), *Translanguaging with multilingual students: Learning from classroom moments* (pp. 9–33). London, UK: Routledge.

García, O., & Kleyn, T. (Eds.). (2016b). *Translanguaging with multilingual students: Learning from classroom moments*. London, UK: Routledge.

García, O., & Seltzer, K. (2016). The translanguaging current in language education. In B. Kindenberg (ed.), *Flerspråkighet som resurs* [Multilingualism as a resource] (pp. 19–30). The Hague, Netherlands: Liber.

García, O., & Wei, L. (2014). *Translanguaging: Language, bilingualism and education*. London, UK: Palgrave.

García, O., & Wei, L. (2015). Translanguaging, bilingualism, and bilingual education. In W. E. Wright, S. Boun, & O. García (Eds.), *The handbook of bilingual and multilingual education* (pp. 223–240). London, UK: Palgrave.

Harvey, D. (2014). *Seventeen contradictions and the end of capitalism*. London, UK: Profile Books.

Herdina, P., & Jessner, U. (2002). *A dynamic model of multilingualism*. Bristol, UK: Multilingual Matters.

Hooks, B. (2000). *Where we stand: Class matters*. London, UK: Routledge.

Kubota, R. (2016). Neoliberal paradoxes of language learning: Xenophobia and international communication. *Journal of Multilingual and Multicultural Development*, 37(5), 467–480. doi:10.1080/01434632.2015.1071825

Larsen-Freeman, D., & Cameron, L. (2008). *Complex systems and applied linguistics*. Cambridge, UK: Cambridge University Press.

Lau, S. M. C., Juby-Smith, B., & Desbiens, I. (2017). Translanguaging for transgressive praxis: Promoting critical literacy in a multiage bilingual classroom. *Critical Inquiry in Language Studies*, 14(1), 99–127. doi:10.1080/15427587.2016.1242371

Lublinmer, S., & Grisham, D. L. (Eds.). (2017). *Translanguaging: The key to comprehension for Spanish-speaking students and their peers*. New York, NY: Rowman & Littlefield Education.

MacSwan, J. (2017). A multilingual perspective on translanguaging. *American Educational Research Journal*, 54(1), 167–201. doi:10.3102/0002831216683935

Mazak, C. M., & Carroll, K. S. (Eds.). (2017). *Translanguaging in higher education: Beyond monolingual ideologies*. Bristol, UK: Multilingual Matters.

Otsuji, E., & Pennycook, A. (2011). Social inclusion and metrolingual practices. *International Journal of Bilingual Education and Bilingualism*, 14(4), 413–426. doi:10.1080/13670050.2011.573065

Paulsrud, B., Rosén, J., Straszer, B., & Weden, A. (Eds.). (2017). *New perspectives on translanguaging and education*. Bristol, UK: Multilingual Matters.

Sandhu, P., & Higgins, C. (2016). Identity in postcolonial contexts. In S. Preece (Ed.), *The routledge handbook of language and identity* (pp. 179–194). London, UK: Routledge.

Sayer, P. (2013). Translanguaging, TexMex, and bilingual pedagogy: Emergent bilinguals learning through the vernacular'. *TESOL Quarterly*, *47*(1), 63–88. doi:10.1002/tesq.2013.47.issue-1

Snell, J. (2010). From sociolinguistic variation to socially strategic stylisation. *Journal of Sociolinguistics*, *14*(4), 618–644. doi:10.1111/j.1467-9841.2010.00457.x

Snell, J. (2013). Dialect, interaction and class positioning at school: From deficit to difference to repertoire. *Language and Education*, *27*(2), 110–128. doi:10.1080/09500782.2012.760584

Streeck, W. (2016). *How will capitalism end?* London, UK: Verso.

Taylor, C. (1994). The politics of recognition. In A. Gutman (Ed.), *Multiculturalism: Examining the politics of recognition* (pp. 25–73). Princeton, NJ: Princeton University Press.

Urciuoli, B. (1996). *Exposing prejudice: Puerto Rican experiences of language, race, and class.* Boulder, CO: Westview Press.

Vertovec, S. (2007). Super-diversity and its implications. *Ethnic and Racial Studies*, *30*(6), 1024–1054. doi:10.1080/01419870701599465

Wei, L., & Hua, Z. (2013). Translanguaging identities: Creating transnational space through flexible multilingual practices amongst Chinese university students in the UK. *Applied Linguistics*, *34*(5), 516–535. doi:10.1093/applin/amt022

Williams, C. (1994). *Arfarniad o Ddulliau Dysgu ac Addysgu yng Nghyd-destun Addysg Uwchradd Ddwyieithog* [An evaluation of teaching and learning methods in the context of bilingual secondary education] (Unpublished Doctoral thesis). University of Wales, Bangor, UK.

Wright, E. O. (2015). *Understanding class.* London, UK: Verso.

Mixed-income schools and housing: advancing the neoliberal urban agenda

Pauline Lipman

> This article uses a social justice framework to problematize national and local policies in housing and education which propose to reduce poverty and improve educational performance of low-income students through mixed-income strategies. Drawing on research on Chicago, the article argues mixed-income strategies are part of the neoliberal restructuring of cities which has at its nexus capital accumulation and racial containment and exclusion through gentrification, de-democratization and privatization of public institutions, and displacement of low-income people of color. The ideological basis for these policies lies in racialized cultural deficit theories that negate the cultural and intellectual strengths and undermine the self-determination of low-income communities of color. Neoliberal mixed-income policies are unlikely to reduce inequality in education and housing. They fail to address root causes of poverty and unequal opportunity to learn and may exacerbate spatial exclusion and marginalization of people of color in urban areas. Building on Nancy Fraser's model for social justice, the article concludes with suggestions toward a framework for just housing and education policy centered on economic redistribution (economic restructuring), cultural recognition (cultural transformation), and parity of political representation.

Introduction

Chicago, Philadelphia, Denver and a number of other cities in the USA are purposefully creating mixed-income schools. In Chicago and elsewhere, this policy is linked with federal initiatives to dismantle or rehabilitate public housing for very low-income people and replace it with privately owned or managed mixed-income developments. Advocates claim these policies will reduce poverty and the inequitable educational opportunities and outcomes affecting low-income students. They contend that mixed-income schools are important to attract working- and middle-class families to mixed-income developments and to build relationships across class lines. They also maintain that income mixing in the classroom improves the educational performance of low-income children. Socio-economically integrated schools are discursively linked to the democratic purposes of the common school, racial desegregation, educational equity and justice. Thus, mixed-income policies seem, on the surface, to be common-sense and egalitarian solutions to intractable educational and social problems – a possible way out of the morass of concentrated poverty, economically devastated inner city neighborhoods, dysfunctional public housing, and failing public schools that have become iconic for urban poverty in the USA.

However, in this article, I problematize the common sense of mixed-income strategies from the standpoint of social justice. As a starting point, I draw on political philosopher Nancy Fraser's (forthcoming; Fraser and Naples 2004) framework for a social justice agenda. Fraser proposes three essential, interrelated dimensions of social justice: economic redistribution (economic restructuring), cultural recognition (cultural transformation), and political representation (parity of participation). I use this model to assess mixed-income strategies, recognizing that Fraser is part of a global dialogue about a social justice agenda for the twenty-first century.

I am not suggesting that mixed-income schools and communities are inherently counter to social justice. Reducing race and class segregation in housing and education has been a target of progressive policy and social justice movements in the USA. However, my reading of the evidence suggests that current policies to create mixed-income schools are unlikely to reduce inequality in education and housing for the majority of low-income people of color. They do not address the root causes of poverty and unequal opportunities to learn and may exacerbate spatial exclusion and marginalization for the majority of low-income people of color who are affected. That is, they perpetuate inequitable distribution of resources. I also argue that they are rooted in deficit notions that negate the cultural and intellectual strengths and undermine the political participation of low-income communities of color. I suggest that mixed-income strategies can best be understood in relation to the construction of neoliberal social and economic arrangements. Specifically, they contribute to an urban agenda which has at its nexus capital accumulation, racial containment, exclusion through gentrification, de-democratization and privatization of public institutions, and displacement of low-income people of color. To illustrate this argument, I turn to Chicago where these housing and school policies are joined, discursively and practically.[1]

To examine intersections of education and urban development, I draw on critical scholarship in urban policy and planning, urban sociology, political economy, and race and education policy. My analysis is grounded in a review of research and archival documents on federal housing policy and mixed-income schools, archival data on Chicago's housing and school policies, and data collected through qualitative research (interviews, conversations, participant observations) in collaboration with community organizations and teachers related to Chicago's school policies, beginning in July 2004.[2] Interviews with parents, teachers, administrators, school staff, and students for a study on the effects of school closings (Lipman, Person, and KOCO 2007) also inform this analysis.

I begin by situating mixed-income policies in relation to neoliberal urban development and briefly describe the Chicago context. I go on to discuss the racialized assumptions and ideological roots of neoliberal mixed-income policies in the USA and the ways in which they limit democracy, and particularly the self-determination and voice of communities of color. I then summarize arguments for mixed-income schools and question the efficacy and opportunity of mixed-income schools for low-income children of color. Finally, drawing on the work of Nancy Fraser, I conclude with thoughts toward an alternative framework for social justice that centers on redistribution, recognition, and representation.

Neoliberal urbanism

Brenner and Theodore (2002) argue that 'cities have become strategically crucial geographic arenas in which a variety of neoliberal initiatives … have been articulated' (351). Beginning in the 1970s, 'roll-back' neoliberal policy (Peck and Tickell 2002) reduced federal funding for cities, pushing city governments to cut back public services and disinvest in public institutions and infrastructure. Then, driven by market ideologies, 'roll out' neoliberal policy (Peck and Tickell 2002) replaces Keynsian welfare state institutions with public–private ventures, municipal tax laws that subsidize development,[3] and privatization of public services as a way to make up for federal funding shortfalls. These policies are shifting governance and ownership of public institutions and spaces to private interests (N. Smith 2002). Neoliberalization of cities is also driven by economic deregulation and globalization which weaken the tight coupling of urban and national economies that characterized the industrial era. As cities compete directly in the global economy for international investment, tourism, highly skilled labor, and production facilities, including the producer services that drive globalization (Sassen 2006), marketing cities and specifically their housing and schools has become a hallmark of urban development. Downtown luxury living and gentrified neighborhoods, as well as new 'innovative' schools in gentrified communities and choice within the public school system, are located in this inter-city competition (Lipman 2004).

Facilitated by municipal government, gentrification has become a pivotal sector in neoliberal urban economies (Fainstein 2001; N. Smith 2002; Hackworth 2007) and a critical element in the production of spatial inequality, displacement, homelessness, and racial containment.

> Gentrification as a global urban strategy is a consummate expression of neo-liberal urbanism. It mobilizes individual property claims via a market lubricated by state donations and often buried as regeneration. (N. Smith 2002, 446)

As cuts in federal funding pushed cities to rely more on property tax revenues, cities have become more dependent on, and subsidizers of, the real estate market through public giveaways of land and subsidies that funnel public tax dollars to developers. Real estate development is a key speculative activity with properties essentially operating as financial instruments. Speculation, in turn, causes increases in property values and rising property taxes, driving out low-income and working-class renters and home owners.

Within this urban dynamic, Hackworth (2007) argues that the 'inner city' has become a site of extreme transition and a 'soft spot' for neoliberal experimentation. An icon of vilified Keynesian welfare state policies (e.g. subsidized public housing, public health clinics and public hospitals), the 'inner city' is now a focus of 'high profile real estate investment, neoliberal policy experiments, and governance changes' (Hackworth 2007, 13). Areas of the central city that were home to low-income communities of color are the focus of public–private partnerships, gentrification complexes, privatization, and de-democratization through mayoral takeovers of public institutions and corporate-led governance bodies. This context defines the stakes involved in creating schools to market new mixed-income developments to the middle class as well as to legitimate what community residents I have interviewed in Chicago call a 'land grab'.

In the USA, race is pivotal to this process. Racialized discourses of pathology legitimated dismantling the Keynesian welfare state and instituting policies that mandate individual responsibility as an antidote to 'dependency' (Katz 1989; Barlow 2003). These discourses have helped rationalise destruction of public housing, displacement of communities of color and gentrification of their neighborhoods, and new patterns of spatial containment and expulsion of people of color from the city center and out of the city entirely (Haymes 1995).

The Chicago context

In 2004, Chicago launched Renaissance 2010 (hereafter Ren2010), a radical reform that will close 60–70 public schools (all so far are in low-income communities of color) and open 100 new schools of choice, two-thirds of which will be run by outside organizations as charter or contract schools. Ren2010 opens up the third largest school system in the USA to a market model of school choice, privatization, and elimination of school employee unions and elected local school councils. I have argued this reform is linked to the neoliberal development of the city and the exclusion of working-class and low-income people of color (Lipman and Haines 2007; Lipman and Hursh 2007). At the same time, Chicago launched a $1.6 billion transformation of public housing – the Plan for Transformation (PFT). One of the most extensive revamps of public housing in the USA, the PFT has nearly completed demolition of 22,000 units, including all the remaining 'family' units of three, four, or five bedrooms. On paper, most are to be renovated or replaced, many as mixed-income developments (Bennett, Smith, and Wright 2006c). However, some research estimates that less than 20% of former residents will be able to return to the new developments (Venkatesh et al. 2004; Wilen and Nayak 2006).

Chicago's housing plan is a local implementation of the federal HOPE VI Act (Housing Opportunities for People Everywhere). Launched in 1992, HOPE VI devolved federal responsibility for public housing to local authorities and replaced government housing provision with privatized management of public units. The state essentially moved from being a provider of housing to an agent of the housing market (Smith 2006). The theory driving HOPE VI is that the concentration of very low-income people in dense public housing units has been a major contributor to pathological behaviors and the inability of poor people to rise out of poverty. The Act calls for revitalizing or demolishing 'distressed' units and relocating public housing residents in scattered site housing, giving them vouchers in the private housing market, and financing mixed-income developments as public–private partnerships. These partnerships draw on public tax dollars to subsidise developers. HOPE VI requires self-sufficiency of public housing residents and promotes home ownership. A key revision in 1995 eliminated the requirement of one-to-one replacement, meaning residents can be displaced without guarantee of return to new or revamped units. Public housing is one of the few remaining obstacles to gentrification, and this revision eliminated a significant barrier to its demolition (Hackworth 2007), thus opening up public housing sites to large-scale private, market-rate development.

The national impact of Chicago's PFT was summed up by the MacArthur Foundation, which provided $50 million in support, including loan guarantees for investors: 'Chicago ... has the potential to demonstrate, at scale, the impact of mixed-income housing on neighbourhood revitalization' (MacArthur Foundation 2005). Ren2010 promises mixed-income schools in these communities. Chicago Public Schools (CPS) launched Ren2010 in the African-American Midsouth area with the goal to 'reinvent the area's 25 schools and make them a magnet for the return of middle-class families' (Olszewski and Sadovi 2003). The MacArthur Foundation underscores the importance of schools in mixed-income developments: 'The city has made a commitment to improving the local schools, without which the success of the new mixed-income communities would be at great risk'. However, some scholars question whether class integration is actually the goal (Bennett and Reed 1999; Bennett 2006; Bennett, Smith, and Wright 2006a), or whether it simply masks (and facilitates) neoliberal urban development and displacement of public housing residents. A telling example is the redevelopment of the ABLA public housing development located in a prime gentrifying area of Chicago. The Chicago Housing Authority was removing ABLA residents at the very time the area was becoming mixed income (Bennett, Hudspeth, and Wright 2006).

Viewed through the lens of neoliberal urbanism, the PFT is part of a development agenda which merges local, national, and transnational capital, in partnership with city government, to make Chicago a first-tier global city (Lipman 2004). The heart of that plan is downtown development, tourism, and gentrification of large sections of working-class and low-income Chicago, particularly communities of color (Demissie 2006). The city's aggressive support for capital accumulation and corporate involvement in city decision-making extends to incentives to developers and corporate and financial interests, public–private partnerships, the city's bid for the 2016 Olympics, cuts in funding for social welfare, control of labor, and privatization of public assets. If downtown development and gentrification are the 'icons of the neoliberal city' (Hackworth 2007, 78), Chicago epitomizes this agenda as working-class communities and public housing have been replaced by condominium developments, refurbished homes, and upscale shops and restaurants.

Although cast as a positive strategy for urban decay and the achievement of social stability, critical urbanists argue that present-day 'third wave' gentrification is driven by finance capital at multiple scales and is a means for the middle and upper-middle classes to claim cultural control of the city (e.g. Smith 1996; Fainstein 2001; Hackworth 2007). The class and race contours of this process are, as Neil Smith points out, hidden in the language of 'mixed income communities' and 'regeneration'. A global city driven by neoliberal economic and social policies simply has no room for public housing as devised in the 1950s and 1960s (Bennett 2006) or for low-income African Americans who are, from the standpoint of capital, largely superfluous in the new economy and 'threatening' to the corporate and tourist culture. Indeed, public housing and education policies are critical components of Chicago's bid to be a first-tier global city and to restructure its economy on neoliberal lines.

Racialised poverty discourses, and 'democratic deficits'

Underpinning mixed-income school and housing policies is a common set of assumptions about poverty and race rooted in culture of poverty theories (Brophy and Smith 1997) and racialized claims on the city (see Lipman 2007 for a more developed discussion). These theories substitute behavioral explanations of poverty for structural and political causes, 'pathologize' people of color, and promote individual responsibility and market solutions. In the late 1980s, sociologist William Julius Wilson's (1987) theory of 'underclass culture' as a barrier to African-American labor force participation captured the imaginations of neoliberal policy makers. Bruce Katz, of the Brookings Institute, and others (see Massey and Denton 1993) cited Wilson's concentration of poverty theory to support dismantling public housing. The narrative linking spatial concentration of poverty with welfare dependency, single-parent families, and crime and the salutary effect of middle-class role models is pervasive in HOPE VI literature (Brophy and Smith 1997; Popkin et al. 2004).

> [T]he intentional mixing of incomes and working status of residents [will] promote the economic and social interaction of low-income families within the broader community, thereby providing greater opportunity for the upward mobility of such families. (US Dept of Housing and Urban Development, in Bennett, Smith, and Wright 2006c, 20)[4]

The argument for mixed-income schools is rooted in a similar set of assumptions. Richard Kahlenberg (2001), key advocate for mixed-income schools, argues, 'Money does matter to educational achievement, but research – and common sense – tells us that the people who make up a school, the students, parents, and teachers matter more' (3). As with mixed-income housing, Kahlenberg argues the putatively superior values and behaviors of the middle class (greater motivation, better language skills, more positive attitudes about school and better behavior) will have a positive influence on low-income students. He makes similar claims for the beneficial influence of middle-class parents who, he asserts, are more involved and effective advocates for their children. They are expected to serve as role models for low-income families, and the school improvements they obtain by virtue of their political power and social capital are expected to benefit low-income students.

The construction of poverty as social pathology is linked to the supposedly restorative and disciplining effects of the market to promote individual responsibility and initiative, self-discipline, and regeneration of decaying public institutions. According to this neoliberal logic, while public housing and public schools breed dysfunction and failure, private management, the market, and public–private partnerships foster excellence through entrepreneurship, competition, and choice. In the USA, 'public' and 'private' have become racialized signifiers, with the private associated with what is 'good' and 'white' and the public associated with what is 'bad' and 'black' (Haymes 1995, 20). Black public spaces are constructed as pathological and in need of social control, and mixed-income schools/housing perform this function. This logic is operationalized under the 1998 Quality Housing and Work Reform Act, which institutionalises the policing of low-income tenants in new HOPE VI mixed-income developments through rigorous applicant screenings and strict work and behavior rules (Wilen and Nayak 2006).[5] Similarly, racially coded mixed-income schools with a majority of middle-class students are assumed to provide the work ethic and behavior standards necessary to transform and discipline low-income students.

In Chicago and other cities, the transformation of public housing and schools is designed without real input from the communities affected. This reflects the coercive and de-democratizing tendencies of the neoliberal state, both to streamline the process of implementing neoliberal policy without 'interference' from a democratic polity and to squelch potential resistance (Gill 2003; Harvey 2005). The plan for Ren2010 originated with the Commercial Club of Chicago (an organization of the city's most powerful corporate, financial, and civic elites). Public hearings about school closings have been called with less than one week of notice and have had no impact on decisions, despite the fact that at every school hearing I observed, parents and students argued to keep their schools open (see Lipman and Haines 2007). Ren2010 also eliminates elected Local School Councils in favor of appointed boards, and a corporate body created by the Commercial Club partners with CPS to select new Ren2010 schools and evaluate them. Exclusion of communities and teachers from Ren2010 decisions is a major theme in my data from community meetings and teacher interviews (Lipman and Haines 2007; Lipman, Person, and KOCO 2007).

Data on experiences of public housing residents in Chicago show a similar pattern. Bennett, Hudspeth, and Wright (2006) write in their study of the transformation of public housing in Chicago: 'From the standpoint of the city and the Chicago Housing Authority (CHA), effective dialogue with public housing residents appears to be consultation in which the residents, at the outset and throughout the process, agree to premises advanced by city and public housing agency officials' (202). CHA resident organizations had to pry their way into participation in the PFT through demonstrations, noisy public hearings, persistent tenant organizing, law suits, and even the intervention of the United Nations Special Rapporteur on Adequate Housing (Wright 2006). The Chicago experience mirrors reports from other HOPE VI cities (e.g. Pitcoff 1999). The state's superficial solicitation of community input, its creation of appointed advisory boards, and the exclusion of parents and residents from genuine participation in decisions reflect the 'democratic deficits' of neoliberal regimes (Fraser forthcoming). In the case of mixed-income school and housing policy, these democratic deficits particularly disenfranchise low-income people of color who are the primary residents of public housing and are 92% of the school population.

At the same time, the seemingly democratic and inclusive discourse of mixed-income communities and schools masks the nexus of racialized public policy and investment decisions that produced deindustrialization, disinvestment, unemployment, and degradation of public health, the built environment, and education in inner-city neighborhoods and schools over the past 30 years. Our interviews with teachers and administrators in Chicago's African-American Midsouth area produced a narrative of declining resources and lack of support from district officials that exacerbated problems in schools in disinvested communities (Lipman, Person, and KOCO 2007). Once devalued, schools are identified as failing, closed without community input (Lipman and Haines 2007; Lipman, Person, and KOCO 2007), and reopened and rebranded with distinctions that mark them as middle class (e.g. Montessori schools) and that appeal to whites even when initial 'gentrifiers' are African American, as in the Midsouth (Boyd 2005). This process is facilitated by an urban mythology 'that has identified Blacks with disorder and danger in the city' (Haymes 1995) and African-American schools with discourses of violence and dysfunction.

In this process Black urban communities are viewed simply as sites of capital accumulation (investment and real estate development), emptied of their meanings as spaces of identity, solidarity, cultural and political resistance, and material survival (Haymes 1995). Not only does displacement disrupt the material places in which people live, learn, and work, but also what

Fullilove (2005) calls a human ecosystem, 'a web of connections – a way of being' (4). This is what is at stake when families, students, and teachers are uprooted and relocated to communities and schools not of their own choosing. The cavalier attitude of policy makers who presume to know what is best for communities of color is illustrated by Alexander Polikoff, senior staff council of Business and Professional People for the Public Interest, a policy group backing mixed-income development in Chicago: '… so persuaded am I of the life-blighting consequences of [William Julius] Wilson's concentrated poverty circumstances, that I do not view even homelessness as clearly a greater evil' (quoted in Wright 2006, 159–60).

Evidence for mixed-income schools

Richard Kahlenberg (2001),[6] a leading proponent of mixed-income schools, asserts a good education 'is best guaranteed by the presence of a majority middle-class student body' (1) to whom, as I note above, he attributes a range of behavioral and attitudinal virtues. Evoking the democratic aims of the Common School, Kahlenberg proposes large-scale reform of public schools to create mixed-income schools with a majority of middle-class students and 'ability grouping' for 'faster' students. The evidence for this proposal rests on the correlation between academic achievement and social class (or in USA literature, socio-economic status – SES). Kahlenberg also extrapolates from research on peer influence to argue for the positive impact of middle-class students on their low-income classmates.

Research generally supports a correlation between social class and educational experiences and outcomes (see Knapp and Woolverton 2004; Sirin 2005 for a review), but the evidence for benefits of moving low-income students to low-poverty schools and to suburbs is actually mixed. Studies show a strong correlation between family SES and the school and classroom environment the student has access to (Reynolds and Walberg 1992), school quality (e.g. teacher quality, instructional resources, teacher–student ratio) (Wenglinsky 1998), and the relationship between school personnel and parents (Watkins 1997). The specific correlation between poverty and low academic performance, school completion, and other education indicators is also well-documented (Anyon 2005), as is the relationship between race/ethnicity and educational outcomes (Darling-Hammond 2004). These correlations are, however, moderated by various factors such as school location, race, and school level (Sirin 2005). Some research found positive effects of moving low-income students to suburbs under the Chicago Gatreaux housing desegregation program (Rubinowitz and Rosenbaum 2002). However, results from the national Moving to Opportunity program appear to show no significant increase in test scores at any age for students who were assigned housing vouchers to move from public housing to lower poverty neighborhoods (Sandbonmatsu 2006).

Although there may be student social class composition effects on educational outcomes, we do not know why. Kahlenberg and others contend the benefits for low-income students of being in a middle-class school are due to the positive influence of middle-class students and parents; however, they might just as well be attributed to the superior instructional and material resources, better prepared teachers, and higher academic expectations in these schools. If the latter is the case, then equitable funding (rather than income mixing) would seem to be an important remedy for educational disparities due to social class, particularly given stark disparities in school funding in the USA between affluent school districts and those with a high percentage of low-income students.[7] In fact, studies published in the past 15 years show that higher school funding has a positive effect on student learning, regardless of school composition, particularly when funding is used to obtain better quality instruction and resources for instruction (Darling-Hammond 2004).

The contention that lower income students will benefit from proximity to middle-class students evokes cultural deficit theories that situate educational outcomes in the characteristics of students rather than the constellation of structural, cultural, and pedagogical factors that perpetuate race and class inequalities in educational experiences and outcomes (Darling-Hammond 2004; Knapp and Woolverton 2004). Evidence of the persistence of these factors (e.g. tracking, teacher attitudes and expectations, and eurocentric curricula) in mixed-race, mixed-income schools indicates that they continue to produce disparities in academic achievement, assignment to academic tracks, and punishment between white students and students of color despite strong pro-school attitudes among students of color (Minority Achievement Network; Lipman 1998; Ferguson 2002). Indeed, academic tracking is built into Kahlenberg's proposal. In particular, 'mixed-income' proposals deflect attention from the centrality of racial subordination and marginalization in the production of educational inequality, although race and putative deficiencies of low-income children and families of color are quite clearly the subtext of proposals for 'economic integration' (Henderson 2001; Orfield 2001). Mixed-income proposals neither acknowledge the intellectual and cultural strengths of low-income students of color nor consider the extensive literature on the importance of culture, language, race, and ethnicity in schooling. Proposals to reform low-income students (in fact largely students of color) by exposing them to middle-class norms and behaviors run counter to 30 years of critical scholarship on multicultural, multilingual education and on the role of racial and ethnic subordination in the perpetuation of educational disparities and inequities (Banks and Banks 2004).

The assumption that the presence of middle-class parents will benefit low-income students is also questionable in light of evidence showing that middle-class families deploy their material and cultural resources to secure educational advantages for *their* children (McGrath and Kuriloff 1999; André-Bechely 2005), particularly in the context of school choice (Ball, Bowe, and Gewirtz 1995; Fuller with Orfield 1996; Ball 2003; Butler with Robson 2003). There is also evidence that middle-class parents seek to insulate their children from lower achieving students and lower income students of color (Sieber 1982; Oakes et al. 1997). Evidence from HOPE VI reveals a similar pattern of social segregation in mixed-income developments. Bennett, Hudspeth, and Wright (2006) could identify only a 'smattering of evidence' that mixed-income communities improve the life chances of low-income people. Studies of HOPE VI mixed-income developments indicate little social interaction across class, little inter-class or inter-racial 'mixing' with low-income students, and in some cases conflict between public housing residents and homeowners (Raffel et al. 2003; Varady et al. 2005). In the most extensive study of mixed-income housing, comparing seven mixed-income developments, there were low or very low levels of 'neighboring' and few market-rate tenants attending building activities (J. Smith 2002.) In the Orchard Park development, adjoining Cabrini Green public housing in Chicago, developers erected a fence to separate market rate from African-American occupied public housing.

In sum, the contention that mixed-income schools will benefit low-income students because of proximity to middle-class students conflates correlation and causality. The correlation of educational experiences and outcomes with social class and race is in fact a multifaceted phenomenon that can be attributed to an array of sedimented equalities, school structures, ideologies, and cultural practices that advantage middle-class students and schools. Framed in the language of class, the argument that low-income students will benefit from exposure to middle-class students is fundamentally a cultural deficit argument about students of color. Mixed-income solutions do not account for persistent low achievement of students of color and working-class students in mixed-income settings.

Exclusion of low-income students and families from mixed-income housing/schools

A larger question is whether mixed-income schools and housing are actually aimed at benefiting low-income families and children. Displacement, housing and school policies, and informal social and cultural mechanisms may work to exclude low-income students of color in substantial numbers from new mixed-income schools. Chicago illustrates this point. Unlike regular public schools which must admit neighborhood students, many Ren2010 schools accept applications city-wide, limit enrollments, use selection procedures including lotteries or charter school criteria, do not reserve seats for displaced students, may not offer the same grades as the closed school, and set admission deadlines– a factor that disadvantages low-income families who have less certainty about their housing (see Cuchiarra, this issue, for similar processes in Philadelphia). Informal selection mechanisms also benefit middle-class school consumers who deploy their cultural capital and social connections to secure places for their children through school choice plans (e.g. Ball 2003; André-Bechely 2005).

The discourse of opportunity to move to better performing new mixed-income schools conceals the reality of displacement and exclusion in Chicago and elsewhere. Plans to link mixed-income housing and schools make it clear that guaranteeing middle-class families slots in mixed-income magnet schools is a priority, and marketing schools to these 'consumers' is taken for granted (Raffel et al. 2003). This is evident in discussions about schools in HOPE VI reports (Varady and Raffel 1995; Raffel et al. 2003). In Chicago, most displaced public housing students have been relocated to schools academically and demographically similar to those they left, with 84% attending schools with below the average district test scores and 44% in schools on probation for low test scores (Catalyst Chicago 2007). In the Midsouth area, most low-income students are attending neighborhood schools that are overwhelmingly low-income while two schools that were closed and have been reopened as new Ren2010 schools have significantly fewer low-income students than the original schools. Concerns about mixed-income schools as a tool of permanent displacement are a central theme in my field notes from community meetings, public hearings, press conferences, and rallies opposing Ren2010 across the city (see also Nyden, Edlynn, and Davis 2006). Research on HOPE VI developments elsewhere suggests these fears may be well founded as original residents' children are not attending the new schools because of displacement (Raffel et al. 2003; Varady et al. 2005).

While HOPE VI has transformed some public housing units into more attractive buildings and communities and improved living conditions for some public housing residents, many original residents have not benefited (Popkin et al. 2004; Venkatesh et al. 2004). Most significantly, elimination of the one-to-one replacement requirement means many displaced residents do not have access to new mixed-income housing in HOPE VI developments (Pitcoff 1999; Raffel et al. 2003). In Chicago, demolition has far outpaced replacement construction, and Chicago Housing Authority (CHA) officials admit they do not have funding to replace all public housing units (Sharon Gilliam, CEO of CHA, Gateaux at 40 Forum, field notes, 3 March 2006). About 19,000 units of public housing were demolished, but in the first six years of the PFT (up to September 2005), only 766 public housing units were constructed or rehabilitated in mixed-income communities (Wilen and Nayak, 2006, 219), and the CHA's 2006 annual report lists only an additional 304 for that year (Chicago Housing Authority 2006).

This outcome is driven by the interwoven logics of capital and race – the inexorable drive to maximize returns on real estate investments and the 'pathologizing' of African-American public housing residents. In the 1990s, private developers exerted pressure to change the formula from one-to-one replacement to a 'tipping point' of one-third public housing residents. They claimed a larger percentage would drive away market-rate and affordable housing buyers (Bennett, Hudspeth, and Wright 2006). Renée Glover, CEO, Atlanta Housing Authority (Glover 2005) said, with competition to attract market rate renters the priority, 'the long-term success of mixed-income communities must be driven by the same market factors that drive the success of every other real estate development' – in this case that means the principle of keeping public housing residents below 40%. Chicago's developments follow the formula one-third public housing, one-third affordable, and one-third market rate units. Janet Smith (2006) concludes, 'We can expect poverty to go down in some of these new mixed-income communities but not necessarily because poor people have escaped poverty – rather because poor people have been moved out and replaced by higher income families' (277). Public housing residents are mainly relocating to racially segregated, low-income communities, out of the city altogether, or they are going homeless (Bennett, Hudspeth, and Wright 2006). An official report on CHA relocation in 2003 stated that 'vertical ghettos from which the families are being removed are being replaced with horizontal ghettos, located in well-defined, highly segregated neighbourhoods on the west and south sides of Chicago' (Bennett, Smith and Wright 2006b, 307). Thus, displacement and relocation due to the PFT maintains racial containment and exclusion despite a discourse of mixed-income development.

Families in areas experiencing mixed-income development have few real choices. The majority will not be admitted to new developments and must negotiate an extremely tight market for affordable housing. Children are transferred from one school to the next with few good schools available and no guarantee of a place in new mixed-income or charter schools. In short, the discourse of mixed-income housing and schools reframes the reality of disinvestment, displacement, subsidies to developers, and racial exclusion as opportunity for low-income people of color.

> [I]nequitable real estate development in cities is the knife-edge of neoliberal urbanism, reflecting a wider shift toward a more individualist and market-driven political economy in cities. Gentrification, publicly funded projects for private benefit, and the demolition of affordable housing are part of this knife-edge ... (Hackworth 2007, 192)

Closing schools in gentrifying areas, displacing students, and opening mixed-income schools of choice that appeal to new middle-class residents are also part of this knife-edge.

Conclusion: toward a social justice framework

Connecting unemployed people and low-income families to new educational opportunities and jobs is essential if we are to reduce poverty, as is upgrading and expanding the deplorable stock of affordable housing and reinvesting in communities that have been profoundly disinvested in for the past 30 years. That youth and their families need excellent health care and schools, good housing, rich opportunities for leisure and recreation, safe neighborhoods, and inexpensive and easily accessible transportation is a truism. But neoliberal plans for mixed-income schools/housing are distant from these goals. The contrived mixed-income developments spawned by neoliberal national and local policy are a far cry from organic and egalitarian communities. Nor are they an outgrowth of greater racial tolerance or reduced poverty or equalization of resources. In fact, they codify and institutionalize social separation and stigma through separate sets of rules and surveillance, educational tracking and magnet schools, and formal and informal selection mechanisms.

The evidence on HOPE VI and plans for mixed-income schools raise questions about who is served by projects that are framed as race and class uplift. They disperse and thus dilute the political power of low-income people of color and attract middle-class consumers of gentrification while legitimating the displacement of those who formerly lived there, on the premise of bettering them. They shift millions in tax dollars to developers and investors and fuel the speculative financialization of the urban economy. The centrality of real estate development and gentrification to capital accumulation in urban areas and the politics of racial exclusion and containment are rationalized by pathologizing African-American urban spaces and denying the humanity of people dislocated from their homes, schools, and communities.

These policies discursively shift the terrain of public policy from economic redistribution to behavior modification. This obligates the state to do nothing about the root causes of poverty, racism, substandard and scarce affordable housing, and failing schools. Like education standards and high stakes accountability, mixed-income schools and housing, as well as vouchers in the private housing market, require no additional outlay of funds to repair decades of disinvestment and inequality. Nor do they require critical examination of dominant ideologies that perpetuate poverty and educational inequality and marginalization of low-income students of color. Moving students into mixed-income schools is a strategy that leaves unquestioned the curricula, pedagogies and school structures, cultures, and practices *within* schools that have been shown to produce unequal opportunities to learn and that reproduce broader social inequalities. Similarly, HOPE VI mixed-income strategies do not account for the economic and social forces that have historically shaped where poor people live– that is, race and class exclusion and market forces that obstruct affordable and mixed-income housing (Smith 2000).

Challenging neoliberal explanations of poverty and educational 'failure' is an important step toward an alternative policy agenda. Darling-Hammond (2004) proposes a shift from presumed student deficits to policies that guarantee every student the right to equitable education.[8] More broadly, Ladson-Billings (2006) argues that we need a paradigm shift from the 'achievement gap', which focuses on students, to the 'education debt' owed to African Americans and other people of color. She argues this debt, which has accumulated over time, can only be rectified by collectively addressing its full spectrum of historical, economic, socio-political, and moral components. The same can be said for neoliberal education and housing policies which shift the discussion from the social debt to individual behaviors (naturalized to racialized social groups). These policies frame the right to quality affordable housing and education as choice in the education and housing marketplace.

Counter to claims that nobody knows how to fix poor schools (Kahlenberg 2001), significant redistributive remedies have never been tried. There has been no substantive effort to equalize school resources or transform structural aspects of schools that reproduce inequality and marginalize students of color. This is also true for providing quality housing and other basic human needs and eliminating poverty, although these remedies are well within the scope of the productive resources of the USA and other advanced capitalist societies. Anyon (2005) argues that to get to the roots of inequitable educational opportunities and outcomes we need an expanded education policy paradigm.

> What *should* count as education policy would include strategies to increase the minimum wage, invest in urban job creation and training, provide funds for college completion to those who cannot afford it, and enforce laws that would end racial segregation in housing and hiring. (13)

However, the roots of educational inequality, mis-education, and subordination are also located in cultural and political marginalization. Returning to Nancy Fraser's (forthcoming; Fraser and Naples 2004) framework, social justice requires three interrelated dimensions: (1) economic redistribution through political-economic restructuring; (2) cultural recognition which extends beyond recognizing cultural differences to transforming what counts as valorized culture and knowledge for all (cultural transformation); and (3) political representation (parity of participation) through radical democratization. This framework resonates with demands of working-class parents and communities of color in Chicago who call for equitable distribution of material resources and challenge who benefits from public resources, valorization of their cultural identities and centering their collective knowledge in policies about school and youth development, and genuine democratic participation in the decisions affecting their lives (Lipman and Haines 2007; Lipman, Person, and KOCO 2007).

Drawing on Fraser's framework, to rectify gross inequalities in educational resources requires economic redistribution policies that expand educational funding to ensure the highest quality education for everyone *and* that reduce poverty. This is quite different from remedies that move students around but leave economic inequalities in place. Counter to the colonizing cultural deficit approach of improving low-income children by mixing them with middle-class students, cultural recognition might include culturally relevant curricula and critical examinations of difference, symbolic forms of power, and the multiple histories and experiences of peoples in the USA and globally. This would be a step toward reconstructing knowledge, curriculum, and what counts as valued cultural capital for all students. A social justice approach to reconstructing schools and housing requires the full participation and self-determination of those affected – public housing residents and families, community members, youth, and committed teachers. Fraser calls this form of political representation a 'post-bourgeois' model of the public sphere that draws on the histories of women, workers, immigrants, and 'ethnic minorities' to build alternative discursive spaces in which to develop oppositional interpretations of their needs, or 'counter publics'.

In relation to public housing, Janet Smith (2002) argues, 'the goal should be to put real control in the hands of the people we are planning with to help them identify and implement real alternatives' (3). In Fraser's terms, this is 'the politics of needs interpretation' (9) – the power of marginalized communities to define their own needs. However, the ideal of full participation runs up against unequal material and cultural resources. Thus, full political representation requires economic and cultural reconstruction as well: 'inclusion *per se* is not sufficient for democratic legitimacy; rather, *parity of participation* [emphasis original] is also required. Parity of participation, in turn, depends on two further social conditions: fair distribution of resources and reciprocal recognition of participants' social standing' (Fraser forthcoming, 11).

Such an alternative framework may seem utopian in a period in which neoliberal discourse limits policy to what is possible and 'efficient', and neoliberal solutions are posed as inevitable. From the standpoint of social justice, transcending this fatalism may be the most essential task. At the end of his life, Paulo Freire wrote against 'an immobilising ideology of fatalism, with its flighty postmodern pragmatism, which insists that we can do nothing to change the march of social-historical and cultural reality because that is how the world is anyway. The most dominant contemporary version of fatalism is neoliberalism' (1998, 26–7). Yet, the essence of an alternative vision is concretely present in Chicago in the voices of public housing residents, displaced families, and parents who have insisted on full participation in decisions which affect them, recognition of their knowledge and community wisdom, and a just distribution of resources.

Acknowledgements

I would like to thank Stephen Ball, Eric Gutstein, David Hursh, Ruth Lupton, Pamela Quiroz, Thomas Pedroni, and two anonymous reviewers for their helpful comments, and Heather Horsely for her research assistance.

Notes

1. This is reflected in various forums and symposia that convene housing and school officials, key foundations, and local political actors — for example, Building Successful Mixed Income Communities: Education and Quality Schools, Invitational forum co-sponsored by the MacArthur Foundation and Metropolitan Planning Council in coordination with the Chicago Housing Authority, 17 November 2005.
2. Between July 2004 and September 2005 we attended and/or participated in monthly school board meetings, CPS public hearings, rallies and pickets, press conferences, community organization and teacher meetings and forums, coalition meetings, planning meetings, and congressional task force meetings. We had regular conversations with teachers and community organizations. From September 2005 to June 2006 Lipman participated in monthly coalition meetings and numerous community hearings and discussions with community organization members, teachers, parents, and local school staff.
3. Tax Increment Financing (TIF) is a development tool. The city declares an area 'blighted' and unlikely to be developed without the diversion of tax revenues. Once declared a TIF, property tax revenues for schools, libraries, parks and other public works are frozen for 23 years, and all growth in revenues above

this level is put in a TIF fund. TIF funds subsidize developers directly and pay for development infrastructure costs. As of fall 2007, Chicago had created 153 TIFs, many in the downtown and areas already undergoing real estate development (Smith 2006, 291). For extensive coverage of Chicago TIFs see *The Reader TIF Archive*: http://www.chicagoreader.com/tifarchive/.
4. For a counter perspective, see Schwartz and Tajbakhsh 1997; Bennett 1998; Bennett and Reed 1999; Smith 2000.
5. Non-exempt heads of household must work a minimum of 30 hours per week and all other non-exempt family members between ages of 18 and 61 must also work 30 hours per week or be in qualified alternative activities (e.g. enrollment in education program, training, verified job search, etc.) Public housing tenants are subject to drug testing housing keeping checks, specific behaviour rules, and exclusion if there are convicted felons in the family.
6. Kahlenberg is a fellow of the Century Foundation, a liberal think tank that supports 'a marriage of capitalism and democracy': http://www.tcf.org/about.asp.
7. Funding disparities range from annual per pupil expenditures of more than $15,000 to less than $4000 (Biddle and Berliner 2002). The wealthiest 10% of school districts spend almost 10 times more than the poorest 10% (Darling-Hammond 2004, 608). Spending in Illinois varies from a high of almost $23,700 to a low of less than $4500, which is almost $2000 below the amount the state's Education Funding Advisory Board determined was necessary for an adequate education in the state (Center for Tax and Budget Accountability 2006).
8. These include: equalization of financial resources ('opportunity to learn' standards), changes in curriculum and testing (ending tracking to differentiate curriculum and reforming assessments and their use to focus on improving teaching rather than sorting students), investing in good teaching for all students (strengthening the knowledge base for teaching and ensuring that students have equal access to competent, caring, and supported teachers).

References

André-Bechely, L. 2005. *Could it be otherwise? Parents and the inequities of public school choice.* New York: Routledge.

Anyon, J. 2005. *Radical possibilities.* New York: Routledge.

Ball, Stephen J. 2003. *Class strategies and the education market: The middle classes and social advantage.* London: RoutledgeFalmer.

Ball, S.J., R. Bowe, and S. Gewirtz. 1995. Circuits of schooling: A sociological exploration of parental choice of school in social class contexts. *The Sociological Review, 1995*: 52–78.

Banks, J.A., and C.A.M. Banks, eds. 2004. *Multicultural education: Issues and perspectives,* 4th ed. Boston: Allyn and Bacon.

Barlow, A.L. 2003. *Between fear and hope: Globalization and race in the United States.* Lanham, MD: Rowman and Littlefield.

Bennett, L. 1998. Do we really want to live in a communitarian city? Communitarian thinking and the redevelopment of Chicago's Cabrini-Green public housing complex. *Journal of Urban Affairs* 20, no. 2: 99–116.

———. 2006. Downtown restructuring and public housing in contemporary Chicago: Fashioning a better world-class city. In *Where are poor people to live? Transforming public housing communities,* ed. L. Bennett, J.L. Smith, and P.A. Wright, 282–300. Armonk, NY: M.E. Sharpe.

Bennett, L., N. Hudspeth, and P.A. Wright. 2006. A critical analysis of the ABLA redevelopment plan. In *Where are poor people to live? Transforming public housing communities,* ed. L. Bennett, J.L. Smith, and P.A. Wright, 185–215. Armonk, NY: M.E. Sharpe.

Bennett, L., and A. Reed, Jr. 1999. The new face of urban renewal: The Near North Redevelopment Initiative and the Cabrini-Green neighborhood. In *Without justice for all,* ed. A. Reed, Jr. Boulder, CO: Westview Press.

Bennett, L., J.A. Smith, and P.A. Wright, eds. 2006a. *Where are poor people to live? Transforming public housing communities.* Armonk, NY: M.E. Sharpe.

———. 2006b. Epilogue. In *Where are poor people to live? Transforming public housing communities,* ed. L. Bennett, J.A. Smith, and P.A. Wright, 301–14. Armonk, NY: M.E. Sharpe.

———. 2006c. Introduction. In *Where are poor people to live? Transforming public housing communities,* ed. L. Bennett, J.A. Smith, and P.A. Wright, 3–16. Armonk, NY: M.E. Sharpe.

Biddle, B.J., and D.C. Berliner. 2002. Unequal school funding in the United States. *Educational Leadership* 59, no. 8: 48–59.

Boyd, M. 2005. The downside of racial uplift: The meaning of gentrification in an African American neighborhood. *City & Society,* 17, no. 2: 265–288.

Brenner, N., and N. Theodore. 2002. Cities and the geographies of "Actually Existing Neoliberalism". *Antipode* 34, no. 3: 349–79.

Brophy, P.C., and R.N. Smith. 1997. Mixed income housing: Factors for success. *Cityscape: A Journal of Policy Development and Research* 3, no. 2: 3–31.

Butler, T., with G. Robson. 2003. *London calling: The middle classes and the re-making of inner London.* Oxford: Berg.

Catalyst Chicago. 2007. Special report: School autonomy all over the map. February. http://www.catalyst-chicago.org/news/index.php?item=2141andcat=23.

Center for Tax and Budget Accountability. 2006. The current status of public education funding in Illinois. http://www.ctbaonline.org/Education.htm.

Chicago Housing Authority. 2006. FY2006 annual report. http://www.thecha.org/transformplan/reports.html.

Darling-Hammond, L. 2004. What happens to a dream deferred? The continuing quest for equal educational opportunity. In *Handbook of Research on Multicultural Education,* 2nd ed., ed. J.A. Banks and C.A.M. Banks, 607–30. San Francisco: Jossey-Bass.

Demissie, F. 2006. Globalization and the city: The remaking of Chicago. In *The new Chicago: A social and cultural analysis,* ed. J.P. Koval, L. Bennett, M. Bennett, F. Demissie, and R. Garner. Philadelphia: Temple University Press.

Fainstein, S. 2001. *City builders: Property development in New York and London, 1980–2000,* 2nd ed. Lawrence: University of Kansas Press.

Ferguson, R.F. 2002. What *doesn't* meet the eye: Understanding and addressing racial disparities in high-achieving suburban schools. North Central Regional Educational Laboratory. http://www.ncrel.org/gap/ferg/.

Fraser, N. Forthcoming. Introduction: The radical imagination between redistribution and recognition. In *Mapping the radical imagination,* N. Fraser. .http://www.newschool.edu/GF/polsci/faculty/fraser/.

Fraser, N., and N.N. Naples. 2004. To interpret the world and to change it: An interview with Nancy Fraser. *Signs: Journal of Women in Culture and Society* 29: 1103–24.

Freire, P. 1998. *Pedagogy of freedom: Ethics, democracy, and civic courage.* Lanham: Rowman & Littlefield.

Fuller, E., with G. Orfield, eds. 1996. *Who chooses, who loses? Culture, institutions, and the unequal effects of school choice.* New York: Teachers College Press.

Fullilove, M.T. 2005. *Root shock: How tearing up city neighbourhoods hurts America, and what we can do about it.* New York: One World Books.

Gill, S. 2003. *Power and resistance in the new world order.* New York: Palgrave Macmillan.

Glover, R.L. 2005. Making a case for mixed-use, mixed-income communities to address America's affordable housing needs. Renée Lewis Glover presentation by Chief Executive Officer, Atlanta Housing Authority to Center for American Progress, October 12. http://www.americanprogress.org/kf/glover.pdf.

Hackworth, J. 2007. *The neoliberal city: Governance, ideology, and development in American urbanism.* Ithaca, NY: Cornell University Press.

Harvey, D. 2005. *A brief history of neoliberalism.* Oxford: Oxford University Press.

Haymes, S.N. 1995. *Race, culture and the city.* Albany: State University of New York Press.

Henderson, T.J. 2001. Socioeconomic school integration. *Poverty and Race,* November/December. Poverty and Race Research Action Council. http://www.prrac.org/full_text.php?text_id=740anditem_id=7782andnewsletter_id=59andhead.

Kahlenberg, R.D. 2001. *All together now: The case for economic integration of the public schools.* Washington, DC: Brookings Institution Press.

Katz, M. 1989. *The undeserving poor: From the war on poverty to the war on welfare.* New York: Pantheon Books.

Knapp, M.S., and S. Woolverton. 2004. Social class and schooling. In *Handbook of research on multicultural education,* 2nd ed., ed. J.A. Banks and C.A.M. Banks, 656–81. San Francisco: Jossey-Bass.

Ladson-Billings, G. 2006. From the achievement gap to the education debt: Understanding achievement in US schools. *Educational Researcher,* 35, no. 7: 3–12.

Lipman, P. 1998. *Race, class, and power in school restructuring.* Albany, NY: State University of New York Press.

———. 2004. *High stakes education: Inequality, globalization, and urban school reform.* New York: Routledge.

———. 2007. Mixed income schools/housing – a racialised discourse of displacement, exclusion, and control. Paper presented at the Annual Meeting of the American Anthropological Association, Washington, DC, Nov. 28–Dec. 2, 2007.
Lipman, P., and N. Haines. 2007. From education accountability to privatization and African American exclusion – Chicago public schools' "Renaissance 2010". *Educational Policy* 21, no. 3: 471–502.
Lipman, P., and D. Hursh. 2007. Renaissance 2010: The reassertion of ruling-class power through neoliberal policies in Chicago. *Policy Futures in Education* 5, no. 2.
Lipman, P., A. Person, and Kenwood Oakland Community Organisation (KOCO). 2007. Students as collateral damage? A preliminary study of Renaissance 2010 school closings in the Midsouth. Chicago: Kenwood Oakland Community Organisation and http://www.uic.edu/educ/ceje/index.html.
MacArthur Foundation. 2005. Revitalizing Bronzeville: Mixed-income housing is key to community strength. Newsletter, spring. http://www.macfound.org.
Massey, D.S., and N.A. Denton. 1993. *American apartheid: Segregation and the making of the underclass.* Cambridge, MA: Harvard University Press.
McGrath, D.J., and P.J. Kuriloff. 1999. They're going to tear the doors off this place: Upper-middle-class parent school involvement and the educational opportunities of other people's children. *Educational Policy* 13, no. 5: 603–29.
Minority Achievement Network. n.d. http://msan.wceruw.org/.
Myerson, D.L. 2001. Sustaining urban mixed-income communities: The role of community facilities. The ULI/Charles H. Shaw Annual Forum on Urban Community Issues, October 18–19. ULI Land Use Policy Forum Report. Washington, DC: Urban Land Institute.
Nyden, P., E. Edlynn, and J. Davis. 2006. *The differential impact of gentrification on communities in Chicago.* Chicago: Loyola University Chicago Center for Urban Research and Learning.
Oakes, J., A.S. Wells, M. Jones, and A. Datnow. 1997. Detracking: The social construction of ability, cultural politics, and resistance to reform. *Teachers College Record* 98, no. 3: 482–510.
Olszewski, L., and C. Sadovi. 2003. Rebirth of schools set for South Side. *Chicago Tribune,* December 19, Section 1, 1.
Orfield, G. 2001. Response. *Poverty and Race.* November/December. Poverty and Race Research Action Council. http://www.prrac.org/full_text.php?text_id=711anditem_id=7761andnewsletter_id=58andhead.
Peck, J., and A. Tickell. 2002. Neoliberalizing space. In *Spaces of neoliberalism: Urban restructuring in North America and Western Europe,* ed. N. Brenner and N. Theodore, 33–57. Oxford: Blackwell.
Pitcoff, W. 1999. New hope for public housing? *Shelterforce online* 104, March/April. http://www.nhi.org/online/issues/104/pitcoff.html.
Popkin. S.J., B. Katz, M. Cunningham, K. Brown, J. Gustafson, and M. Turner. 2004. *A decade of HOPE VI: Research findings and policy challenges.* Washington, DC: Urban Institute and Brookings Institution.
Raffel, J.A., L.R. Denson, D.P. Varady, and S. Sweeney. 2003. Linking housing and public schools in the HOPE VI public housing revitalization program: A case study analysis of four developments in four cities. http://www.udel.edu/ccrs/pdf/LinkingHousing.pdf.
Reynolds, A.J., and H.J. Walberg. 1992. A process model of mathematics achievement and attitude. *Journal for Research in Mathematics Education* 23, no. 4: 306–328.
Rubinowitz, L.S. and J.E. Rosenbaum. 2002. *Crossing the class and color line: From public housing to white suburbia.* Chicago: University of Chicago Press.
Sanbonmatsu, L., J.R. Kling, G.J. Duncan, and J. Brooks-Gunn. 2006. Neighbourhoods and academic achievement: Results from the moving to opportunity experiment. *Journal of Human Resources* 41, no. 4: 649–91.
Sassen, S. 2006. *Cities in a world economy,* 3rd ed. Thousand Oaks, CA: Pine Forge Press.
Schwartz, A., and K. Tajbakhsh. 1997. Mixed income housing: Unanswered questions. *Cityscape* 3, no. 2: 71–92.
Sieber, R.T. 1982. The politics of middle-class success in an inner-city public school. *Journal of Education,* 164, no. 1: 30–47.
Sirin, S.C. 2005. Socioeconomic status and academic achievement: A meta-analytic review of research. *Review of Educational Research* 75, no. 3: 417–53.
Smith, J.L. 2000. The space of local control in the devolution of US public housing policy. *Geografiska Annaler* 82B, no. 4: 221–33.
———. 2002. HOPE VI and the new urbanism: Eliminating low-income housing to make mixed-income communities. Planners Network. http://www.plannersnetwork.org/publications/mag_2002_2_spring.html.

———. 2006. Mixed-income communities: Designing out poverty or pushing out the poor? In *Where are poor people to live? Transforming public housing communities,* ed. L. Bennett, J.L. Smith, and P.A. Wright, 282–300. Armonk, NY: M.E. Sharpe.
Smith, N. 1996. *The new urban frontier: Gentrification and the revanchist city.* New York: Routledge.
———. 2002. New globalism, new urbanism: Gentrification as global urban strategy. *Antipode* 34, no. 3: 427–50.
Varady, D.P., and J.A. Raffel. 1995. *Selling cities: Attracting homebuyers through schools and housing programs.* Albany, NY: SUNY Press.
Varady, D., J.A. Raffel, S. Sweeney, and L. Denson. 2005. Attracting middle-income families in the HOPE VI public housing revitalization program. *Journal of Urban Affairs* 27, no. 2: 149–64.
Venkatesh, S.A., I. Celimli, D. Miller, A. Murphy, and B. Turner. 2004. *Chicago public housing transformation: A research report.* New York: Center for Urban Research and Policy, Columbia University.
Watkins, T.J. 1997. Teacher communications, child achievement, and parent toits in parent involvement models. *Journal of Educational Research,* 91, no. 1: 3–14.
Wenglinsky, H. 1998. Finance equalization and within-school equity: The relationship between education spending and the social distribution of achievement. *Educational Evaluation and Policy Analysis* 20, no. 4: 269–83.
Wilen, W.P., and R.D. Nayak. 2006. Relocating public housing residents have little hope of returning: Work requirements for mixed-income public housing developments. In *Where are poor people to live? Transforming public housing communities,* ed. L. Bennett, J.L. Smith, and P.A. Wright, 239–58. Armonk, NY: M.E. Sharpe.
Wilson, William Julius. 1987. *The truly disadvantaged.* Chicago: University of Chicago Press.
Wright, P. 2006. Community resistance to CHA transformation. In *Where are poor people to live? Transforming public housing communities,* ed. L. Bennett, J.L. Smith, and P.A. Wright, 125–67. Armonk, NY: M.E. Sharpe.

Public education in neoliberal times: memory and desire

Jessica Gerrard

> This article reflects on the desire to defend and claim public education amidst the educational policy effects of contemporary neoliberal politics. The defence of public education, from schools to higher education, undoubtedly provides a powerful counter veiling weight to the neoliberal policy logic of education-as-individual-value-accrual. At a time of intense global policy reform centred on marketisation in education, the public education institutions of the post-war welfare state are often characterised as being lost, attacked, encroached upon and dismantled. In this paper, I contend it is important to avoid mobilising a memory of public educational pasts that do not account for their failings and inequalities. Turning to a historical engagement with the emergence of neoliberal politics, the paper explores how challenges and contestations surrounding 'the public' from multiple standpoints converged in the rise of neoliberalism. Recognition of these convergences and contestations, I suggest, assists to provide a more nuanced account of the relationship between neoliberal reform and the welfare state, and thus of the complex task of imagining, claiming and working towards a just and equitable public education.

Introduction: desiring the public

> Think about the strangeness of today's situation. Thirty, forty years ago, we were still debating about what the future will be: communist, fascist, capitalist, whatever. Today, nobody even debates these issues. We all silently accept global capitalism is here to stay. On the other hand, we are obsessed with cosmic catastrophes: the whole life on earth disintegrating, because of some virus, because of an asteroid hitting the earth, and so on. So the paradox is, that it's much easier to imagine the end of all life on earth than a much more modest radical change in capitalism.

I start here with a characteristically provocative, and now infamous, quote from Slavoj Zizek, from his 2005 film *Zizek!*. Here, Zizek paraphrases Fredric Jameson's reflection 'that it is easier to imagine the end of the world than to imagine the end of capitalism' (Jameson 2005, 199; see also Beaumont 2014). Whilst perhaps rhetorical, the claim is an important one: within contemporary political discourse alternatives, or even adaptations to neoliberal capitalism, can appear impossible, even unimaginable. This is accentuated by the rising prominence of the political landscape of terrorism, counter-terrorism and the war on terror, within which capitalist democracy is politically defended as the only viable possibility for 'tolerant' 'civilised' nation states (see Brown 2006). Slater, for instance, argues the 'subjective damage' affected in the wake of the 'war on terrorism' (and the associated surveillance and fear) 'facilitated the imposition of increased neoliberal governmentality' (2015, 5). Within this political context, alternatives to, and critical debates over, neoliberal capitalism can come to be viewed as implausible, fanciful and reckless. There is something particularly limiting and bounded in how neoliberal capitalism has become embraced ideologically, politically, imaginatively and culturally. Arguably, Zizek over-simplifies the dynamics of political debate in previous decades ('communism, fascism, capitalism, whatever'); and this paper is certainly not a call to 'return' to the political divisions and contestations of yesteryear. Nevertheless, he provides a useful reminder that debates over what sort of world (and education) we want do not have to be determined by what is administratively possible within neoliberal capitalism.

For contemporary debates over education, this has significant repercussions. Internationally, the field of educational research, and the knowledge it creates, is strongly framed by the need for evidence that can pragmatically inform policy for governments (broadly and variously) working within the logics of neoliberalism (see Lingard 2013). There is a strong administrative and problem-solving focus in this research imperative. Yet, there are no neat linear lines of connection between educational research knowledge and educational policy and practice. The relationship between research and policy is highly vexed, and not straightforward. Jill Blackmore contends, 'Policy makers have particular agendas for which they selectively seek justification, often *post hoc*, as much as "evidence" or look for simple solutions to complex problems' (2014, 504). For those of us dedicated to pursuing research agendas concerned with equity and justice, the connections between research, practice and policy can be meandering, limited and at times broken. Even when couched within (often well intentioned) notions of best practice, policy is politics and politics is ideological.

Amidst the seemingly ferocious global turn to neoliberal educational policy reform, from schooling to higher education, there is a strong desire to claim and defend public education. This support for public education is often posited as counter to various neoliberal market-based reforms. For instance, John Holmwood's recent edited collection A *Manifesto for the Public University* (2011) explicitly positions 'the public' against a market-based version of higher education based on individual value-accrual. Responding to widespread university sector reform in England by the Tory government, this collection highlights the symbolic power of 'the public' as a counter-veiling rallying call, and at the same time draws attention to and acknowledges ambiguity and diversity in the articulation of what this 'public' might be. Similarly, in the Australian context Connell (2013) rises to defend public schools in the face of the significant (and decades-long) shift towards a market-based model of the sector. In contrast to the often technicist and formulated rationalities of neoliberalism – individual benefit, cost benefit analysis, value accrual, human capital – the defence of and desire for public education recognises education as more than a practice encapsulated in numbers, measurement and capital. Education and learning are matters for and of hearts and minds. Self and community, in other words, cannot be creatively conceived or experienced purely through quantitative measures or values. The desire for 'the public', therefore, is a claim to a purpose for education that extends beyond capital and to broader notions of self and community, pointing to the limit points of contemporary policy rationalities.

In the context of neoliberal capitalism, a generalised support for public services has collectivising power, galvanising various (and by no means congruent) perspectives under a broad 'progressive' umbrella. However, what exactly constitutes just and equitable education under this umbrella is more difficult to grasp. Often, many turn to memories of public education's past in order to animate their dedicated support. In Australia, this was perhaps most clearly demonstrated in the public outpouring of emotion in response to the death of former Prime Minister (1972–1975), Gough Whitlam in 2014. Focusing in particular on his celebrated instantiation of free university education (which was then rolled back by successive Labor and conservative Liberal governments), many lamented a lost vision of the public in education in contemporary politics. Much of this sentiment was captured in the remarks of Australian actor Cate Blanchett (2014), receiving rapturous applause at his state funeral:

> When I heard Gough Whitlam had died, I was filled with an inordinate sadness. A great sorrow. ... The loss I felt came down to something very deep and very simple. I am the beneficiary of free, tertiary education.

The loss Blanchett speaks of is regularly expressed in the defence of and claim for public education in contemporary political and research debates. Neoliberalism is touted as encroaching and dismantling the public education institutions of the post-Second World War welfare states of the 'west', and it is through a claim to public education that many articulate their alternatives to neoliberalism. Connell, for instance, writes of public education being 'displaced' by neoliberal politics, whilst Holmwood introduces *A Manifesto* as a response to the 'threats' posed by market-based reform. In the US context, Lipman (2013) describes the dual process of charter school expansion and public school closures as a 'cannibalization' of public education, and of 'public' goods and services more generally, by market-based corporate models of practice.

Undoubtedly, neoliberalism has dramatically changed the practice and understanding of the public, as markets and private interests are brought in partnership with the state in the provision of education. In this paper, I turn to a consideration of the effects of this incursion on the memory of public educational pasts and the desire for public educational futures. Here, I reflect on the construction of public education as a loss, and explore what it means to support and desire a public education in neoliberal times. Thus, my intention is not to contribute a deliberation on what 'public' might mean in education. Rather, I seek to reflect more broadly and historically on the inevitable tensions that arise in desiring the seemingly elusive (alternative) practice of 'public education' in the wake of widespread neoliberal reform. I suggest neoliberalism can easily provoke a defensive position, as the fast-paced nature of reform appears to quickly erode core bases of a supposed 'pre-neoliberal' public education. In response to contemporary 'reflexivity', 'precarity', 'corporatisation', 'privatisation' and 'risk', it is common to speak of a need to 'reclaim' or 'retrieve' public education from the clutches of neoliberalism. Yet, as I explore below, the political emergence of neoliberalism reveals the failings of the previous institutions and practices of 'public education'. The history of neoliberalism cannot be simply read as a conservative assault on public institutions, but as a process of capitalist co-option of, and adaptation to, criticisms of the exclusions and injustices within these very practices of public education. I contend, therefore, that desiring public education is both necessary and troublesome: necessary, as there is a continued pressing need to think – and struggle for – forms of education that extend beyond the needs of capital and its market; and troublesome, because this desire inevitably wrestles with complex memories of educational pasts, and the fear and possibility of educational futures.

Historical laments: neoliberalism and the welfare state

> Nostalgia, it can be said, is universal and persistent; only other [people's] nostalgias offend. (Williams 1973, 12)

Loss and nostalgia are, as Raymond Williams writes, a matter of perspective. To be sure, there are multiple and at times seemingly contradictory laments of loss in education: some hold a nostalgia for a 'back to basics' approach whilst others evoke memories of a fuller practice of 'public education'. These diverse lamentations are set within a sense of perpetual fluidity of the present. We live, we are often told, in fundamentally 'new times'. Sociological analysis (including in education) is awash with terms and concepts in which to describe our contemporary condition and selves: the 'risk society', 'knowledge economy' and the 'reflexive' and 'enterprising' self. Descriptions and labels for our contemporary particularity abounds. Yet, the conceptual apparatus of these 'new times' are slippery. 'If we take the "New Times" idea apart', Stuart Hall suggests (1989 in 1996, 223), 'we find that it is an attempt to capture the confines of a single metaphor, a number of different facets of social change, none of which has any necessary connection with the other'. Particularly bandied about since the 1980s and 1990s, the notion of 'new times' has become international shorthand to distinguish the present from the historical figure of the post-Second World War welfare states. In this account, reflexivity, entrepreneurialism, markets, risk and symbolic and intellectual labour, are tied to the emergence of a variously named present (the post-industrial 'advanced', 'late', 'consumer' and now 'cognitive' or 'affective' capitalism), characterised by intensified globalisation, the apparent detraditionalisation of gender and class roles and expansive up-take of neoliberal politics.

Correspondingly, sociological and educational literature is littered with temporal comparisons and references that emphasise the particularity of the neoliberal present. There are, we often declare (and I include myself in this 'we'), 'increasing', 'growing' and 'intensifying' economic imperatives in education, 'proliferating' practices of learning and a 'rising' entanglement of education and national productivity, individual value-accrual and reflexivity. Most often, these temporal comparisons are used to demarcate the emergence of the range of practices that fall under the umbrella of 'neoliberalism'. Yet, there is a fuzziness in the ways in which neoliberalism is used as a descriptive and analytic concept and/or historical period. Recently, Rowlands and Rawolle (2013) argued that 'neoliberalism' is problematically deployed as a 'theory of everything' in educational research. They contend neoliberalism is routinely used as a descriptive marker for all the things researchers do not like about educational reform (see also Flew 2012). With Rowlands and Rawolle, I share a concern that 'neoliberalism' can take on a spectral – and arguably rhetorical – analytic/descriptive quality. If we are not careful, this can lead us into a cul-de-sac of false nostalgia for a prior public education under the welfare state, rinsed clean of the compromises and deficiencies that invariably featured in its practice.

Of course, neoliberalism can be – and has been – identified as a distinct shift in capitalist governance. Most commonly, it is used to refer to the embrace of market-based solutions and logics within state governance, and thus by extension within a range of institutions and practices deemed 'public' in the previous liberal welfare state settlements, such as education (see Connell 2013). From a governance perspective, neoliberal capitalism has involved a creative reconfiguration in the function of the state: it 're-codes the locus of the state in the discourse of politics' through changing the relationships and governance practices between the state, private agents and the market (Rose and Miller 2010). At the very least, the term 'neoliberalism' collects a number of practices that have come to determine a kind of logic in contemporary politics: competitive markets, privatisation, managerialism, competitive standardised testing and accountability measures, devolution of financial control and performance measurement. Du Gay and Morgan (2013, 2) argue,

> ... the term 'neo-liberalism' in a sense came to provide a certain rationality, a way of linking up these diverse developments so they appeared to partake of a coherent logic. And once they did so, once a kind of rationality could be extracted from them, allowing translations between them, it could itself be redirected towards both them and other objects and persons, which were able to be thought about in the same way-as for example, with the various uses of the term 'entrepreneurship', 'empowerment', 'market', and 'choice'. And such rationalities came to be embodied in or infused a range of practices for governing economic life, public management, medical care, welfare policy, and so on (du Gay, 1996; Foucault, 2008; Rose, 1999).

Du Gay and Morgan's discussion of neoliberalism highlights the variety of practices and exchanges that characterise its expression and historical development. Whilst neoliberalism has a kind of logic, there is no uniformity in the ways in which its diverse attendant practices are realised across different national, cultural and local contexts. When used as descriptive shorthand, the diversity and ambiguity of neoliberalism becomes flattened.

Additionally, it is important to emphasise that neoliberalism is not *done to* us. Undoubtedly, it has, as Harvey (2005) and many others have outlined, entailed the creative destruction of prior institutional frameworks, divisions of labour, welfare provisions and ways of thought associated with the political liberalism of the post-Second World War welfare state settlements. However, neoliberalism is not a static 'external evil' but a 'process, with incremental reforms constantly evolving and adapting' (Morley 2014, 457). Neoliberal capitalism is a diverse, contested and historically – and locally – contingent *practice*. Rendering it otherwise can over-emphasise neoliberalism as a fundamental (and external) break from previous capitalist settlements. Historically and sociologically speaking, then, there is a need to tread carefully with a narrow focus on the contemporary 'new'. McLeod and Yates suggest (2006, 4), 'the constant theoretical and political focus on "change", "New Times", and new forms of identity has been overdone and the extent of change somewhat exaggerated'. For instance, risk, precarity and reflexivity are not novel developments of capitalism wrought from the move towards neoliberalism in the latter part of the twentieth-century. Nor is the privatisation and marketisation of education particular to our contemporary times (see Reid 2005). Whilst its contemporary expansion and iteration may well be unprecedented and particular, educational policy and practice has always been mediated by complex relationship between the state and the market, and between understandings and practices of the public and private. It is important to understand present reform dynamics within the context of a longer history of capitalism that extends beyond the post-Second World War welfare state settlements. Capitalism has long required workers to quickly adapt to the needs and shifting flows of capital, and with this industry and employment. At the same time, the 'economisation' of everyday life, in which social life becomes defined by the need for capital accumulation and commodity production and consumption, is at the very centre of the diverse social relations under capitalist, past and present (see Amin 2003; Marx and Engels 2010; Gerrard 2014a). Indeed, precariousness and the need for flexibility are core features of capitalist labour relations. Capital never stands still. It constantly creates new forms of work, commodities, constantly diversifies use-values, requiring intensive, continuous, flexible labour (Marx 1976, 1033–1034).

Moreover, the reforms and development of systems of education have always been central to the work of nation state building, and with this citizenship, economic productivity, identity and culture. Systems and institutions of education are inextricably interconnected with the attempt of the state to develop administrative and military capacity, forge national identity and culture and foster economic productivity (see Green 1990). At the same time, education has long been preoccupied with developing the capability and character of citizens as workers. Historian Richard Johnson, for instance, suggests educational reforms associated with the changing economic landscape of the mid-nineteenth century were more centred on the need for 'new human beings with a new, more disciplined, sociality', than 'required' knowledge or skills (1976, 48). Similar arguments are made today regarding the contemporary policy focus on individual 'character', 'capability' and 'flexibility' (e.g. Crowther 2004). Of course, contemporary political practices and attendant policy 'settlements' of neoliberalism are not simply mirror reproductions of – or inevitable linear developments upon – previous policy state/market settlements under capitalism. Nevertheless, an over-emphasis on the contemporary particularity of neoliberalism, with no attention to the history of educational practice in capitalism, obfuscates long held tensions between the instantiation of public state education and private and market interests.

Furthermore, neoliberalism is often represented as an ultimate challenge to notions – and practices – of 'public' services and institutions (such as schools, universities and hospitals), in favour of competitive private markets. Undoubtedly, neoliberalism is an incursion into previous practices and understandings of the state in developing, and servicing, public goods and institutions. Yet, recent 'neoliberal' reforms – and the faith in markets, individual competitiveness and privatisation – were not only wrought out of the rise of conservative neoliberal ideology; such practices were an outcome of complex social and historical events and processes. The economic crises in the early 1970s, the unrest and challenge to the welfare state caused by social movements of the 1960s and 1970s and the crises in political and military authority in Chile for instance, all contributed to opening the reform window internationally into the 1980s and 1990s (see Harvey 2005; Connell and Dados 2014). The rise of neoliberalism, in other words, was part of a wider process of recuperation and regeneration in global capitalism amidst a range of economic, social and cultural challenges. Whilst the global influence of neoliberal economists, such as Hayek and Friedman, and conservative politicians, such as Thatcher and Reagan, was undoubtedly significant, neoliberalism – and its diverse practices – was born out of social and political conflict and opportunity. As Connell and Dados assert, the tendency to analytically separate neoliberal theory (as represented in the works of Hayek and Friedman) from its imperfect (and diverse) enactments, diverts 'our attention from the practical problems … to which neoliberal practices seemed to offer solutions' (2014, 120).

Neoliberalism is, therefore, a creative product of the constant and dynamic struggle for capitalist hegemony. An important part of this dynamic is the capacity for capitalism to address critiques through reform. Capitalism is capable of tolerating significant levels of critique, and at the same time has a thirsty capability of assimilating, co-opting and adapting in the face of contestation (Boltanski and Chiapello 2005; see also Slater 2015). For example, Boltanski and Chiapello (2005) assert the shift towards flexible labour, flattened management structures, sub-contracting and even teamwork, adaptability and multi-skilling are not simply results of crises in authority surrounding enterprise and profit (see also Budgen 2000). Rather, they suggest whilst economic crises are a part of the tale of advanced capitalism, so too are the subtle incorporations and adaptations – processes of gentle disarmament – of radical critiques of and struggles against capitalism. The 'personalisation' of management governance, is in part Boltanski and Chiapello suggest, a response to the progressive critiques of the bureaucratic and authoritarian work processes of Taylorism. For instance, notions and practices of creativity and individual self-realisation cannot be entirely separated from the influential criticisms of the mechanistic practices of alienated Taylorist labour. They write (2005, 98):

> The Taylorization of work does indeed consist in treating human beings like machines. But precisely because they pertain to an automation of human beings, the rudimentary character of the methods employed does not allow the more human properties of human beings – their emotions, their moral sense, their honour, their inventive capacity – to be placed directly in the service of the pursuit of profit. Conversely, the new mechanisms, which demand greater commitment and rely on a more sophisticated ergonomics, integrating the contributions of post-behaviourist psychology and the cognitive sciences, precisely because they are more human in a way, also penetrate more deeply into people's inner selves – people are expected to 'give' themselves to their work – and facilitate an instrumentalization of human beings in their most specifically human dimensions.

Nancy Fraser makes a similar point in her analysis of second-wave feminism and neoliberalism. She suggests many 'utopian desires' of second-wave feminism found their way into the 'transition of a new form of capitalism: post-Fordist, transnational, neoliberal' (2013, 211). Working from her criticism that Boltanski and Chiapello offer a gender-blind analysis, Fraser points to the disturbing (and unintended) convergences between feminism and the rise of neoliberalism. 'Endowing their daily struggles with an ethical meaning', she states, 'the feminist romance attracts women at both ends of the social spectrum: at the one end, the female cadres of the professional middle class …; at the other end, the female temps, part-timers, low-wage service workers…'. Fraser suggests, 'At both ends, the dream of women's emancipation is harnessed to the engine of capitalist accumulation.' (220–221). None of this is to suggest that there is nothing particular about neoliberalism, or that the emergence of neoliberalism did not disturb and create anew state institutions and practices. To be sure, there have been real – and identifiable – shifts in the governance and understanding of education in comparison to the post-WWII welfare state policy settlements of the 1950s, 1960s and 1970s. Nevertheless, neoliberalism was the result of capitalist reform and adaptation amidst diverse and contested political discourses, which included the adaptation and co-option of progressive critiques of Taylorite industrial capitalism and the welfare state. Despite the optimism of many of the reforms, ultimately their realisation became thwarted by the process of capitalist recuperation we now call neoliberalism. Or, to put it in the words of Antonio Negri, 'The reformist giant had feet of clay' (1989, 67). Recognition of this not only opens up the history of neoliberalism and the contradictions and complexities of capitalism. It also, as I turn now to consider, highlights the ambiguity and contested nature of the notion of the 'public' in education.

Claims to the public

The concept, practice, imagining of and desire for the 'public' have particular significance in education. In the first instance, 'publics' are variously used to mark the physical, cultural, social, discursive and imagined spaces created in and through educational practice (e.g. Schutz 1999; Greene 2000). At the same time, with the contemporary practices of privatisation and marketisation in education, 'public education' has become a powerful, and rallying, symbol: notions of public education are offered as alternatives to neoliberal educational reform, and educational practices concerned primarily with individual gain and mobility. Public education is used to demarcate (and most often herald) an education for a common or collective good. Amidst a globalising and diverse social world, this is no easy conceptual task. Ideas of the public are often conceptually and politically ambiguous and charged with the complex task of addressing the cultural and social foundations of equality and justice in diversity. Maxine Greene, for instance, argues for a public education that creates spaces of pluralism and diversity that foster 'coming in touch with the common' (1982, 9). 'The only way to learn and live', Green states, 'is to choose as durable and precious a visible common world' (1982, 9). More recently, Masschelein and Simons also draw on notions of the common and public to conceptualise a school that makes possible the playful creation of new meaning and experiences. This school, they argue, makes 'things public for common and free use, and hence, anything can happen here.' (2011, 164). Similar articulations of the value of public education are put forward politically, such as in the Manifesto of the recent and ongoing UK Campaign for the Public Education. Drawing on educational philosopher John Dewey, the Manifesto defends the import of universities to create public spaces of association (*Campaign for the Public University* n.d.).

Yet, what exactly constitutes this public will always be unsettled. Definitions, practices and imaginings of a 'common' and 'public' are essentially contentious, and are often slippery and indeterminate. Indeed, claims to the common and public in education are made from all sides of the politics, as indicated by the current international debates surrounding common curriculum and testing, in which multiple claims are made to the common, core and public. One way to understand the history of public education, then, is as a struggle over the practice and conception of the common public. From working men's colleges, to women's admissions to universities, the raising of the school leaving age and anti-sexist and anti-racist teaching initiatives, the development of the education sector is defined by the various experiences of marginalisation from, and ensuing disputes over, what constitutes public education. These struggles highlight the perennial challenges in developing truly inclusive and equitable public education. Thus, they also point to the limits of the state's institutional practices of educational equality and justice, and with this, the diverse claims to education in challenge to, or independent of, the state (see Gerrard 2014b). As feminist scholars in education have long argued, the struggle for recognition and rights in public spaces involves far more than simply stretching or widening participation and access (e.g. Luke 1992). Marginalisation, exclusion and oppression cannot be remedied simply by enlarging the public space via the state. Rather, equality and justice often requires the fundamental reconstitution of the public and the common.

Understanding the formal limits of the public raises significant questions surrounding the way in which we might understand – and conceptualise or even defend – public education. Fraser (1990), for instance, argues that a narrow focus on the 'mainstream' public sphere obfuscates a range of experiences that may appear marginal. In response, she suggests the need to understand the public as a multiplicity of practices. Developing her position in response to Jurgen Habermas' theorisation of the public sphere, Fraser argues Habermas' public sphere privileges particular (and gendered) social action that is recognisable by the state. The result of this, she suggests, is a glossing over of the diversity of social action and experience that may be excluded or misrepresented within the mainstream public sphere. Writing in 1990, Fraser draws on Mary Ryan's study of the diverse creation of alternative public spaces alongside the multiple (and often unorthodox) pathways in to public life taken by nineteenth-century North American women. She asserts, 'even in the absence of formal political incorporation through suffrage, there were a variety of ways of accessing public life and a multiplicity of public arenas' (61). Fraser continues,

> Thus, the view that women were excluded from the public sphere turns out to be ideological; it rests on a class- and gender-biased notion of publicity, one which accepts at face value the bourgeois public's claim to be *the* public. (61)

Fraser's call to consider the multiplicity of the claim and practice of the public is a timely reminder for those of us in education interested in defending and developing notions of the public. Perhaps most importantly, it calls attention to the fact that any rendering of a past public practice in education under the post-war welfare state must acknowledge that the apparent vitality of this vision was in large part a result of lively debates and contestation over the constitution, practice and imagining of this public. The activism of the 1960s and 1970s surrounding education demanded different versions of the public, not just expansions of existing public education. To describe this period as an 'expansion' of public education (as it often is) hardly captures the fundamental critique levelled at the knowledge foundations and elitist practices of the state's educational institutions. For instance, the wellspring of debate and activity surrounding higher education in May 1968 was at its heart a contestation over what constituted 'public' education:

> The important thing is to be armed against the danger of a technocratic use of the situation created: if the crisis of the university is simply an 'unease' bound up with anxieties about future employment or the frustrations imposed by a conservative pedagogic relationship, it is easy to present as solution to all these ills a technocratic planning of the development of education simple as a function of the needs of the labour market, or fictitious concessions on the participation of student sin university life. The changes that the student movement has introduced de facto in the faculties ... can only hope to have a lasting effect on university life, and social life in general, if the relations

between university and society undergo a radical transformation. (Bourdieu [1968] 2008, 41)

At the same time, it is important to recognise the level of struggle and contestation required for reform in public education, from schools to higher education. Occupations, protests and fierce campaigns had to be waged before women's, black and indigenous subjects and departments were allowed to be established at many universities (see e.g. Crowley 1999). Similar campaigning and public agitation was necessary to bring issues of gender, class, sexuality and race knowledge, access and injustice to the fore in schools (e.g. Gerrard 2013). Concurrently, alternative educational publics were formed across all levels of education as students and parents explored alternative knowledge bases and forms of authority upon which to develop educational practice (see Gerrard 2014b).

Across a number of nation states in the 'west', throughout the 1960s and 1970s, resounding and influential critiques from many on the progressive, feminist, anti-racist and trade union left were waged against the welfare state. These debates were prompted by the exclusions and limitations of the post-Second World War welfare state, including its educational institutions. We may want to lament the loss of 'public education', but it is important to recognise that this 'public' was incomplete, riddled with exclusions and contested. Feminist, anti-racist, indigenous self-determination, queer and class-based activism around education in the 1960s, 1970s and 1980s, brought issues of inequality and prejudice to the fore through criticism of educational institutions and their policies. Many of these campaigns wrought concessions and significant advances from the state and educational policies, including anti-sexist and anti-racist initiatives and free university education. Yet, at the same time, such policy reforms were – and are – always representations of contestations, compromise and multiple desires. For instance, many reforms that appear to indicate a progressive reform in education, such as the raising of the school leaving age and the move to comprehensive education, were also deeply imbricated in more conservative concerns over youth crime and the relationship between schooling and work (see Baron et al. 1981).

Thus, it is important to acknowledge the unintended convergences that can create reform windows. In the field of education, undoubtedly the activism of the 1970s and 1980s were imbued with a genuine sense of reform possibility, and from which there were significant progressive gains. Free tertiary education, recognition and attempted redress of sexist and racist curricula and teaching practices, and support for comprehensive inclusive neighbourhood schools, all expanded, augmented, challenged and adapted the previous practices and understandings of 'public' education. To be sure, the aggressive turn towards privatisation, managerialism, corporatisation have fundamentally challenged some of the – however tentative – policy reform settlements that were wrought from these critical campaigns. Yet, the emergence of neoliberalism was invariably entangled in these new projected versions of the public: progressive and feminist challenges to traditional and teacher authority, hierarchical curriculum and 'jobs for life for the boys' work cultures in academia, clashed and converged with conservative challenges to teacher and academic authority, school knowledge and a perceived lack of accountability within higher education institutions. There are complex relationships between, for instance, the push to democratise and expand university admissions and the rise of market-based solutions (see Holmwood 2014).

Similarly, crises in professional authority of teachers and academics can be seen from multiple viewpoints, including the challenge to institutionalised elitism, racism and sexism and the conservative challenge to the supposed 'embedded progressivism' of schools and universities (e.g. Cox and Dyson 1969; see Gerrard 2013). In other words, crises and challenges around professional and institutional authority and accountability in education were wrought from multiple standpoints in the post-war period. Whilst coming from distinctly divergent political positions, these discourses mutually fuelled a problematisation of the practices of accountability, professionalism and authority that had previously characterised educational institutions. I flag the messiness and contentiousness in the various claims to public education as a means to highlight the difficulty in articulating an equitable inclusive public education, and to provoke historical reflection on the contemporary desire for public education. The perception of the 'loss' of education, via the assault of neoliberalism, raises important questions surrounding the history of neoliberalism and its relationship to the educational institutions of the welfare state. Neoliberal reform therefore represents not only a re-invigorated embrace of market-based solutions to public issues, but also a process of co-option and adaptation of progressive critiques (see Chiapello 2013).

Conclusion: dream-thoughts of the public

> On the one hand, history splinters and divides what in the original may have presented itself as a whole, abstracting here a nugget of descriptive detail, there a memorable scene. On the other hand, history composites. It integrates what in the original may have been divergent, synthesizes different classes of information, and plays different orders of experience against one another. It brings the half-forgotten back to life, very much in the manner of dream-thoughts. And it creates a consecutive narrative out of fragments, imposing order on chaos, and producing images far clearer than any reality could be. (Samuel 1994, x)

The memory of the buoyant progressive reforms of the 1960s, 1970s and 1980s has had lasting impact. Particularly for the beneficiaries of free university education, anti-sexist and anti-racist initiatives and curriculum developments and countless other progressive reforms made in the name of equality and justice, the memory of a public education for the common good is strong. Against a contemporary political climate in which educational policy dilemmas are debated as administrative concerns through the lens of individual and nation state value accrual, this memory is powerful and seductive. Yet, the retrieval of this memory is in many ways creating a 'narrative out of fragments', as Raphael Samuels puts it. To be sure, in the 1970s 'the idea of public schools as places where young people from a range of varied backgrounds and experiences can mix and learn to appreciate and respect differences was starting to be recognized in public and policy discourse' (Reid 2002, 575). But this was a *start*, made possible by years of post-war economic prosperity and highly influential social movements for change. Ultimately, this was a start that was also never realised: public education has always been an incomplete and contested project, always in the making. By imagining neoliberalism as an ultimate incursion, we are in danger of reifying the previous educational institutions of the welfare state as a kind of 'dream thought', granting them greater coherence than they may ever have had.

Undoubtedly, the notion of the public is both a contested and powerful concept. In the face of widespread ideological individualism under neoliberal capitalism, in which education is posited as being primarily an enterprise for individual gain, the language and imagining of the 'public' conjures a different practice and vision of education. The desire for 'public' education is a powerful rallying defence. Yet, a defensive position can simplify both the practices of neoliberalism, and our understanding of the public. Previous policy settlements, funding arrangements, curricula, authority practices and knowledge assumptions of state education cannot be retrieved as the pearls of public. Rather, they can be understood as reform outcomes of struggle and of historically contingent political contexts, which never fully realised the potential of an equitable and just educational system or practice. The point, then, is not to 'give up' on a notion or practice of public education. Indeed, whilst it is crucial to keep 'collective memories' of public education alive, this must also include 'extending and (supportively) criticizing them' (Apple 2006, 681), particularly in relation to the complex processes of state reform. As Michael Apple states, 'romantic possibilitarian hopes cannot substitute for a more thorough analysis of the historical tensions and the role that education has played as an arena for, and at times producer of, larger struggles and movements (2007, 165). In fact, analysis of the past and present limits and exclusions of public education enrich understanding of its possibilities and potential. It assists to understand and resist the centrifugal force of contemporary politics, which constantly pulls debate towards the primary concern of what is administratively possible under neoliberal capitalism. It is necessary to conceptually and ideologically wrestle public education from these confines, historically and sociologically. Writing on the ways in which norms and assumptions can stultify the imaginings of possibility, Simone de Beauvoir's warning appears all the more important: 'Let us beware lest our lack of imagination impoverish the future' (2011, 781).

Acknowledgments

Many thanks to Sophie Rudolph for her very helpful comments on an earlier version of this paper, and to the anonymous reviewers for their constructive feedback in preparing this paper for publication.

Disclosure statement

No potential conflict of interest was reported by the author.

References

Amin, S. 2003. *Obsolescent Capitalism: Contemporary Politics and Global Disorder*. London: Zed Books.

Apple, M. W. 2006. "Rhetoric and Reality in Critical Educational Studies in the United States." *British Journal of Sociology of Education* 27 (5): 679–687.

Apple, M. W. 2007. "Social Movements and Political Practice in Education." *Theory and Research in Education* 5 (2): 161–171.

Baron, S., D. Finn, N. Grant, M. Green, and R. Johnson. 1981. *Unpopular Education: Schooling and Social Democracy in England since 1944*. London: Hutchinson.

Beaumont, M. 2014 "Imagining the End Times: Ideology, the Contemporary Disaster Movie Cantagion." In *Zizek and Media Studies: A Reader*, edited by M. Flisfeder and L-P. Willis, 79–90. New York: Palgrave Macmillan.

de Beauvoir, S. 2011. *The Second Sex*. Translated by C. Borde and S. Malovany-Chevallier. London: Vintage Books.

Blackmore, J. 2014. "Cultural and Gender Politics in Australian Education, the Rise of Educapitalism and the 'Fragile Project' of Critical Educational Research." *The Australian Educational Researcher* 41 (5): 499–520.

Blanchett, C. 2014. Cate Blanchett Pays Tribute to Gough Whitlam: Full Text. *Sydney Morning Herald*. Accessed November 11, 2014. http://www.smh.com.au/comment/cate-blanchett-pays-tribute-to-gough-whitlam-full-text-20141105-11hdb1.html#ixzz3Ids1l4eg

Boltanski, L., and E. Chiapello. 2005. *The New Spirit of Capitalism*. London: Verso.

Bourdieu, P. [1968] 2008. "Appeal for the Organization of a General Assembly of Teaching and Research." In *Political Interventions: Social Science and Political Action*, edited by P. Bourdieu, 41–45. London: Verso.

Brown, W. 2006. *Regulating Aversion: Tolerance in the Age of Identity and Empire*. Princeton, NJ: Princeton University Press.

Budgen, S. 2000. "Review: New 'Spirit of Capitalism'." *New Left Review*, 149–156.

Campaign for the Public University n.d. *Manifesto for the Public University*. http://publicuniversity.org.uk/manifesto/

Chiapello, E. 2013. "Capitalism and Its Critiques." In *New Spirits of Capitalism?* edited by P. du Gay and G. Morgan, 60–81. Oxford: Oxford University Press.

Connell, R. 2013. "The Neoliberal Cascade and Education: An Essay on the Market Agenda and Its Consequences." *Critical Studies in Education* 54 (2): 99–112.

Connell, R., and N. Dados. 2014. "Where in the World Does Neoliberalism Come from?" *Theory and Society* 43 (2): 117–138.

Cox, C. B., and A. E. Dyson, eds. 1969. *Black Paper Two: The Crisis in Education*. London: The Critical Quarterly Society.

Crowley, H. 1999. "Women's Studies: Between a Rock and a Hard Place or Just Another Cell in the Beehive?" *Feminist Review* 61: 131–150.

Crowther, J. 2004. "'In and Against' Lifelong Learning: Flexibility and the Corrosion of Character." *International Journal of Lifelong Education* 23 (2): 125–136.

Du Gay, P., and G. Morgan 2013. "Understanding Capitalism: Crises, Legitimacy, and Change through the Prism of *the New Spirit of Capitalism*." In *New Spirits of Capitalism?* edited by P. Du Gay and G. Morgan, 1–40. Oxford: Oxford University Press.

Flew, T. 2012. "Michel Foucault's the Birth of Biopolitics and Contemporary Neo-liberalism Debates." *Thesis Eleven* 108 (1): 44–65.

Fraser, N. 1990. "Rethinking the Public Sphere: A Contribution to the Critique of Actually Existing Democracy." *Social Text* 25 (25/26): 56–80.

Fraser, N. 2013. *Fortunes of Feminism: From State Managed Capitalism to Neoliberal Crisis*. London: Verso.

Gerrard, J. 2013. "Self Help and Protest: The Emergence of Black Supplementary Schooling in Britain." *Race, Ethnicity and Education* 16 (1): 32–58.

Gerrard, J. 2014a. "All That is Solid Melts into Work: Self-work, the 'Learning Ethic' and the Work Ethic." *The Sociological Review* 62 (4): 862–879.

Gerrard, J. 2014b. *Radical Childhoods: Schooling and the Struggle for Social Change*. Manchester, NH: Manchester University Press.

Green, A. 1990. *Education and State Formation: The Rise of Education Systems in England, France and the USA*. London: Macmillan.

Greene, M. 1982. "Public Education and the Public Space." *Educational Researcher* 11 (6): 4–9.
Greene, M. 2000. "Imagining Futures: The Public School and Possibility." *Journal of Curriculum Studies* 32 (2): 267–280.
Hall, S. 1996 "The Meaning of New Times." In *Stuart Hall: Critical Dialogues in Cultural Studies*, edited by D. Morley and K-H. Chen, 222–236. Routledge: London.
Harvey, D. 2005. *A Brief History of Neoliberalism*. Oxford: Oxford University Press.
Holmwood, J., ed. 2011. *A Manifesto for the Public University*. Bloomsbury: London.
Holmwood, J. 2014. "From Social Rights to the Market: Neoliberalism and the Knowledge Economy." *International Journal of Lifelong Education* 33 (1): 62–76.
Jameson, F. 2005. *Archaeologies of the Future: The Desire Called Utopia and Other Science Fictions*. London: Verso.
Johnson, R. 1976. "Notes on the Schooling of the English Working Class 1780–1850." In *Schooling and Capitalism: A Sociological Reader*, edited by R. Dale, G. Esland, and M. MacDonald, 44–94. London: Routledge & Kegan Paul.
Lingard, B. 2013. "The Impact of Research on Education Policy in an Era of Evidence-based Policy." *Critical Studies in Education* 54 (2): 113–131.
Lipman, P. 2013. "Economic Crisis, Accountability, and the State's Coercive Assault on Public Education in the USA." *Journal of Education Policy* 28 (5): 557–573.
Luke, C. 1992. "Feminist Politics in Radical Pedagogy." In *Feminisms and Critical Pedagogy*, edited by C. Luke and J. Gore, 25–53. New York: Routledge.
Marx, K. 1976. *Capital: Volume 1*. London: Penguin.
Marx, K., and F. Engels. 2010. *The Communist Manifesto*. London: Vintage Books.
McLeod, J., and L. Yates. 2006. *Making Modern Lives: Subjectivity, Schooling and Social Change*. New York: State University of New York Press.
Morley, L. 2014. "Education and Neoliberal Globalization." *British Journal of Sociology of Education* 35 (3): 457–468.
Negri, A. 1989. *The Politics of Subversion: A Manifesto for the Twenty-first Century*. Cambridge: Polity Press.
Reid, A. 2002. "Public Education and Democracy: A Changing Relationship in a Globalizing World." *Journal of Education Policy* 17 (5): 571–585.
Reid, A. 2005. "The Regulated Education Market Has a past." *Discourse* 26 (1): 79–94.
Rose, N., and P. Miller. 2010. "Political Power beyond the State: Problematics of Government." *British Journal of Sociology* 61 (Supplement 1): 271–303.
Rowlands, J., and S. Rawolle. 2013. "Neoliberalism is Not a Theory of Everything: A Bourdieuian Analysis of Illusio in Educational Research." *Critical Studies in Education* 54 (3): 260–272.
Samuel, R. 1994. *Theatres of Memory, Volume I: Past and Present in Contemporary Culture*. London: Verso.
Schutz, A. 1999. "Creating Local 'Public Spaces' in Schools: Insights from Hannah Arendt and Maxine Greene." *Curriculum Inquiry* 29 (1): 77–98.
Simons, M., and J. Masschelein. 2011. "The Hatred of Public Schooling: The School as the Mark of Democracy." In *Ranciere, Public Education and the Taming of Democracy*, edited by M. Simons and J. Masschelein, 1–20. West Sussex: Wiley-Blackwell.
Slater, G. B. 2015. "Education as Recovery: Neoliberalism, School Reform, and the Politics of Crisis." *Journal of Education Policy* 30 (1): 1–20.
Williams, R. 1973. *The Country and the City*. Oxford: Oxford University Press.

Considering Nancy Fraser's Notion of Social Justice for Social Work: Reflections on *Misframing* and the Lives of Refugees in South Africa

Dorothee Hölscher

This article explores the implications of cross-border migration for social work's normative commitment to social justice. Specifically, it interrogates Nancy Fraser's conceptualisation of social justice in guiding social work practice with refugees. The paper is grounded in an ethnographic study conducted from 2008 to 2009 in a South African church which had provided shelter to a group of refugees following their displacement by an outbreak of xenophobic violence. The study's findings reveal that various kinds of misframing created multiple forms of voicelessness amongst its foreign participants. These filtered out to justify, perpetuate and deepen other types of injustice, particularly misrecognition and maldistribution. There was some evidence of resistance, solidarity, recognition and small acts of redistribution. However, such positive practices proved difficult to sustain. The paper confirms the central importance of the notion of misframing for conceptualising and responding to social injustice in the absence of citizenship—as required of practitioners in the field of social work with refugees and indeed other groups rendered vulnerable within current economic, social, political and cultural constellations. In this regard, Fraser's contribution looks set to enrich social work's commitment to social justice both in normative and practical terms.

I. Introduction

To a considerable extent social work derives its sense of professional identity from positioning itself in normative terms (Banks 2004; Hugman 2010a). Accordingly, the Definition of Social Work (IFSW/IASSW 2000, p. 1) declares that 'principles of human rights and social justice are fundamental to social work'. The starting point for this article is the understanding that in order to provide the profession with purpose and direction, such principles need continuous interrogation vis-à-vis social work's changing economic, social, political and cultural contexts. In the following, I critically reflect on social justice as a normative framework for social work. My arguments are grounded in reflections on the lives of refugees[1] in South Africa (please refer to the footnote which explicates my choice of terminology in respect of refugees, asylum seekers and other cross-border migrants).

A number of writers have cautioned that in spite of its apparent centrality to the profession, the notion of social justice has remained somewhat under-theorised (Mullaly 2002) and ambiguous (Humphries 2008). However, some recent contributions, such as Garrett (2010) and Bozalek (2012), have offered critical introductions of the work of one leading contemporary theorist of justice, Nancy Fraser, to mainstream social work discourse, which this article seeks to extend. Beyond Garrett's (2010) detailed critique of Fraser's two-dimensional notion of justice, I provide an interrogation of her recently expanded, multi-level, three-dimensional approach (Fraser 2008; Thompson 2009). And while Garrett's (2010) and Thompson's (2009) are theoretical discussions, I add an empirical component to considerations of Fraser's (2008) relevance for social work.

Banks (2004) contends that ethical principles in social work are generally treated as middle-level principles because—rather than being regarded as foundational in a deontological or utilitarian sense—they are derived from

---

1. I believe that in the context of this paper, it is important to venture beyond dualisms according to which a refugee is understood in opposition to an asylum seeker, or another kind of migrant. Instead, my view is that taking refuge and seeking asylum are but one form of cross-border migration, which overlap and intersect with others (compare the definition of *mixed migration* put forward by the Danish Refugee Council 2008). Moreover, within their country of refuge or residence, cross-border migrants can be displaced further, for example as a result of xenophobic violence. Thus deviating from mainstream conceptualisations (compare, for example, UNHCR 2011), I speak of persons affected by *misframing* legislation, discourses and practices (Fraser 2008) as follows:

When referring to *foreigners, foreign nationals, cross-border migrants* or *non-citizens* (which I do interchangeably, depending on context), I am making a point of general relevance for all persons implied in the Danish Refugee Council's (2008) definition of *mixed migration*, including undocumented migrants, refugees, asylum seekers, and temporary work permit holders.

When speaking about *refugees*, I refer to *both* certified refugees *and* asylum seekers, for the latter are persons who claim to be refugees, which is what matters in the context of my arguments. However, *asylum seekers* do enjoy considerably fewer rights and experience considerably more status insecurities than recognised refugees, and at certain points of the argument, I use the term to make this distinction explicit.

Finally, when speaking of *displacees* or *displaced refugees*, I refer to the fact that *all the foreign participants in my study had been internally displaced* during South Africa's May 2008 xenophobic pogroms.

dialogue and agreement around which values are shared by social workers sufficiently to be able to underpin professional practice. Some of such principles can be considered primary values in that they are applicable and able to provide guidance to social workers in varied contexts, whereas secondary values are more context specific (Hugman 2010a). This article is based on the understanding that while *social justice* is a primary value of overarching relevance to social work across cultural, social, economic and political contexts, *just practice* requires us to consider the particularity of our work: it is through our efforts to understand people's life circumstances, how these interact with their ability to live well in the world (Nussbaum 2000) and how social work might contribute to their flourishing that we become able to extend the concept of social justice further—describing, explicating and critically interrogating its evolving meaning, scope and implications for practice (Hölscher et al. 2012).

According to Fraser (Fraser in Nash & Bell 2007; Fraser 2008; Fraser in Bozalek 2012), the socio-economic and political exclusion of non-citizens must be considered a pivotal form of injustice in the current phase of globalisation—a result of its attendant rise in global interconnectedness, growing socio-economic, cultural and political polarisations within and across countries, and thus, the increasingly turbulent and complex movements of people across international borders. At its most general, therefore, this article explores the implications of cross-border migration for social work's normative commitment to social justice. However, based on the data in which its arguments are grounded, the paper asks quite specifically to what extent Fraser's (2008) expanded model of justice might be helpful in guiding the sense-making endeavours and practices of social workers who have to respond to citizenship-based exclusions and intersecting forms of social injustice in the field of social work with refugees.

The data used in this article are derived from an ethnographic study conducted during the 18 months following a wave of xenophobic violence which had swept South Africa in May 2008 and displaced over 100,000 foreign nationals. The study was situated in a church which had offered shelter to a group of refugees, thus displaced, and later implemented a project towards their integration within, and through its community. I begin my arguments by summarising key points from Fraser's expanded conceptualisation of justice, drawing on her essay *Re-framing Justice in a Globalising World*, which is published, amongst other places, in her recent monograph, *Scales of Justice* (Fraser 2008). As part of this review I engage with a selection of Fraser's critics. Next, I present an illustration of how her notion of social justice might be applied to making sense of social work practice by outlining the study's context, explicating its methodologies, and presenting some of its findings.

The paper is able to demonstrate the capacity of Fraser's (2008) expanded framework to illuminate the complex structures and dynamics of social (in)justice in the project under investigation. It finds further that *misframing* (Fraser 2008) constitutes a significant factor in contemporary constellations of social injustice, which is revealed particularly starkly in the lives of refugees.

Concerning our commitment to social justice more generally, I conclude, therefore, that social work should routinely consider misframing as the framework in which other, substantive injustices unfold—affecting the lives of people who lack citizenship, be it refugees or other groups rendered vulnerable within current economic, political, social and cultural constellations. While the practice implications flowing from the study are less clear, this article ends with a call towards the creation of *enclaves of just practice*: spaces in which the structural roots of social injustice are carefully considered, practice goals set accordingly, the injustices which we may find ourselves unable to address articulated, and their corresponding hardships acknowledged.

II. Considering Nancy Fraser: Social (In)justice, *(Mis)framing* and Social Work

Nancy Fraser is a feminist political philosopher and critical theorist. Over the past two decades, she has developed a normative framework of social justice which has much to offer for social work. This is because writing in the critical theory tradition always also seeks to make a transformative contribution to society. Fraser's theorising on social justice builds on her understanding that *participatory parity* constitutes the central norm against which to evaluate how just, or unjust, particular social arrangements are. She contends that

> Social arrangements are just if, and only if, they … institutionalise the possibility for people to participate on a par with one another in all aspects of social life. This means that social arrangements are unjust if they entrench obstacles that prevent … people from the possibility of parity of participation. (In Bozalek 2012, p. 147)

Obstacles to social justice are constituted, for example, by economic inequities and patterns of social positions and power relations which privilege some groups of people, while excluding, marginalising and disadvantaging others (Fraser 1989, 1997, 2000, 2003). Thus, inequalities of participation in social life are at once the source and result of substantive injustices; just as the presence of equal participation both ensures and indicates the absence of such substantive injustices. In other words, we find at the centre of Fraser's arguments the notion of circularity between the causes and effects of social (in)justice.

On its first level, Fraser's (2008) framework engages with *first-order, substantive issues*, or what she calls *claims concerning the 'what' of social justice*. There are three interrelated dimensions within which social injustices may occur—or with respect to which social justice may be advanced. Within the *economic dimension*, social justice concerns the *(mal)distribution* of rights, opportunities and resources along a society's particular class structure. Issues of *(mis)recognition* unfold in the form of internal status hierarchies (especially along lines of race and gender) within the *cultural and legal dimensions* of social justice. These hierarchies serve to place members of specific groups in (dis)advantaged positions, thereby (dis)enabling their access to principally existing rights, opportunities and resources in a given society. The *ordinary-political dimension* of social justice regards questions of *(mis)representation*— for example, the impact of alternative electoral systems, affirmative action rules and terms of engagement in public discourse and decision taking on people's access to rights, opportunities and resources.

Garrett (2010) has provided a detailed analysis of Fraser's work on (mis)re-cognition and the ways it intersects with the dimension of (mal)distribution. Responding to his multifaceted concerns about the dangers of a de-politicised and reductionist reading of recognition theory exceeds the scope of this paper. Importantly, however, he asserts that

> One of the chief difficulties with most... theories of recognition (including Nancy Fraser's...) is that they fail to acknowledge that the state... can be a substantial source of oppression and hardship... The state... is a formation that is seemingly 'lost' as an object of analysis, critique and comment. (Garrett 2010, pp. 1529–30; parentheses in original)

The claim that Fraser does not consider the role of the state in causing and perpetuating human suffering appears unfounded when examining her original work (Fraser 1989, 1997, 2000, 2003; Fraser in Bozalek 2012). However, by introducing into her model a *second level of (in)justice* together with the notion of *(mis)framing*, Fraser does move beyond her prior arguments: She suggests that as the impact of globalisation is increasingly and disturbingly felt, the appropriateness of the nation-state as the primary context within which to conceptualise and effect social justice needs to be critiqued in and of itself (Fraser 2008; Fraser in Bozalek 2012). Constituting the *grammar* of social justice, framing issues are *issues of scope* and pertain to the *question of who* does and who does not count as subject of justice. Located within the *political dimension* of social justice, (mis)framing operates through admission criteria, procedures and the denial of membership, for example, to non-citizens in their country of residence. Fraser (2008, p. 19) asserts that

> Far from being of marginal significance, frame setting is amongst the most consequential of political decisions. Constituting both members and non-members in a single stroke, this decision effectively excludes the latter from the universe of those entitled to consideration within the community in matters of distribution, recognition and ordinary-political justice. The result can be a serious injustice. When questions of justice are framed in a way that wrongly excludes some from consideration, the consequence is a special kind of meta-injustice, in which one is denied the chance to press first order claims in a given community. The injustice remains... as long as the effect of the political division is to put some relevant aspects of justice beyond [the] reach [of those who have been excluded].

Situated on yet another level, that is operating as *third-order (in)justices*, are issues of *process*, which pertain to *the 'how'* of social justice. These, too, concern the question of what makes for a fair and equitable *grammar* of social justice. Like framing, process issues are located within the *political dimension* of social justice. They revolve around the effects that contemporary frame and boundary setting mechanisms have on the scope of social justice. It is here that Fraser introduces the notion of *transformative politics of framing* by which she means those discourses and practices directed at changing 'the deep grammar of frame-setting in a globalising world...

> The aim is to overcome the injustices of misframing by changing the boundaries of the 'who' of justice [and] the mode of their constitution, hence the way in which they are drawn. (Fraser 2008, pp. 23–24)

In other words, Fraser (2008) implies that those wishing to resist dominant forms of social injustice at the current historical juncture may need to begin by demanding political voice. This suggestion is consistent with the centrality of the norm of participatory parity in her understanding of justice. But who should be the ones to resist social injustice at this level? Which social agents have a voice audible enough to intercept? Should those who are excluded, marginalised and disadvantaged speak for themselves? Should they also be spoken for and, if so, by whom and how? What should be the terms of engagement? Thompson (2009, pp. 1084–85) notes with Fraser that

> 'Those who... [lack] political voice... are unable to articulate and defend their interest with respect to distribution and recognition, which in turn exacerbates their misrepresentation...' The same analysis can be extended to excluded outsiders... 'The result is a vicious circle in which the three [dimensions] of injustice reinforce one another...'

Fraser (in Nash & Bell 2007) argues that in order to turn this *vicious circle of injustice* into a *virtuous circle of justice*, members who already enjoy parity of voice will need to engage in critical reflection and dialogue regarding the boundaries around, and processes of deliberation within the community or association concerned. Such reflexivity might lead to reforms towards greater inclusivity and parity, and eventually translate into more just distribution and recognition as well. However, this is to assume that such privileged members have the ability and the will to critically engage with the exclusion and/or voicelessness of *Others*. And it is to assume that they also have the capacity for redress should their reflections lead them both to seeing the need and developing the desire for change—assumptions which Thompson (2009) cautions us cannot just be made.

Fraser also places her hopes for change in what Thompson (2009, p. 1088) calls 'counter-public spheres'. Noting that under current conditions of globalisation there is a widening cleavage between 'civil society processes of contestation and state centred processes of legislation and administration', she believes that 'non-state centred public spheres [might] become spaces for contesting state-centred frames' (in Nash & Bell 2007, p. 82). Thompson (2009, p. 1089) retorts that

> While... [counter-public] spheres may be able to articulate well-founded critiques of existing political boundaries, they will be unable to exert effective influence over the bodies that establish and maintain such boundaries... [After all], it is precisely because the excluded and voiceless are excluded and voiceless that they will be unable to join in a democratic debate about the decision rules and boundaries of [the associations concerned].

In so far as Fraser's model constitutes a normative framework, its validity must be established in terms of its ability to help us understand the nature of social (in)justice inherent in particular constellations, or situations, and the ethical demands this places on social work. However, in so far as her model intends to inform transformative politics, the extent to which it can translate into effective counter-discourses and counter-practices is indeed of concern. These two interrelated aspects of Fraser's work—that is, its normative and its transformative components—are explored further in Section IV.

III. Situating the Study: Context and Research Methodologies

Having discussed the theoretical framework which lies at the centre of this paper, the context, methodologies and findings of the study to which this framework relates are explicated briefly. A more comprehensive discussion of both the study's context and methodology is available in Hölscher and Bozalek (2012).

For the fifth consecutive year in 2011, South Africa received the world's highest number of asylum applications (UNHCR 2012). The country's Refugees Act (RSA 1998) affords asylum seekers some, and refugees extensive, constitutional rights. At the same time, South Africa remains one of the most unequal societies in the world (Hoogeveen & Özler 2005). As a result, profound contradictions have developed between the formal provisions of the Act and a range of ring-fencing efforts which make it difficult for its subjects to claim their socio-economic entitlements (Makhema 2009).

South Africa's traditionally high levels of xenophobia (Crush *et al.* 2008) are intrinsically related to the country's deeply entrenched race-based discourses and practices that framed black people as *Others* (CRAI 2009). Imposed on this was South Africa's post-apartheid nation-building process in which attempts to generate a spirit of national identity included an insistence on the exclusivity and superiority of South Africa's citizenship (Neocosmos 2008). In this context, a xenophobic discourse has allowed for redirecting the imagination of *Blackness as Otherness* towards black foreigners as *South Africa's New Others*. This in turn has permitted the scapegoating of the latter as being responsible for those social and economic ills which the South African state, under the current global conditions, has failed to address (Chikanga 2012). From 1994 onward, these xenophobic discourses and practices have translated increasingly into violence, which on 11 May 2008 escalated into actual pogroms killing over 61, wounding around 670, displacing over 100,000 persons and leaving dozens of women raped (Misago et al. 2010).

With the government's response to the pogroms initially patchy and slow, civil society organisations stepped in to alleviate the crisis (Misago et al. 2010). One of them, a local church, offered emergency shelter to a group of 12 families comprising 48 adults and children, all refugees from Burundi, Rwanda and the DRC, who had been referred by the US Consulate and the Council of Churches. At the time, the church had just over 800 members, with its culture somewhat dominated by members belonging to South Africa's white middle classes. Just having commenced an ethnographic study in the field of social work with refugees, I was approached by the church leadership to assist in this response. However, in view of the multiple socio-economic problems experienced by the group members over and above the crisis of displacement, I was soon asked to remain involved for a prolonged period of time. As a result, I was able to negotiate inclusion of the church as a convenience sample in my research (Gobo 2008).

This paper draws on the following data sources: From June 2008 to October 2009 I kept a diary, recording those practices, speech acts and reflections that seemed relevant to my study. Group members began holding support group meeting in June 2008. Until October 2008, this support group served intermittently as a focus group. Life story interviews (Miller 2000) were conducted between November 2008 and June 2009 with four of the displacees, purposefully selected to represent the group's diversity along the lines of gender, national and ethnic origin, education, household composition and income (Kelly 2006). Because the data quoted in Section IV feature different voices alongside one another, I offset the voices of other participants (that is, their direct speech acts) from my own voice (that is, my descriptions, interpretations and reflections) by highlighting the former in italic.

The data were processed using a combination of Constructivist Grounded Theory (Charmaz 2003) and Critical Discourse Analysis (Fairclough 2001). Interpreting the transcribed actions, interactions and reflections vis-à-vis the changing contextual conditions of the study, the analysis proceeded along the stages of open, axial and selective coding. The notions of *(mis)framing* and *voice* were introduced as the emergent core categories were developed further in relation to literature on social justice. The findings presented below have been extracted from the broader study to meet one of this paper's key purposes, which is to interrogate the relevance of Fraser's (2008) expanded notion of social justice for social work.

In keeping with the University of KwaZulu Natal's ethical clearance requirements, standard research ethical principles were built into the study's design. However, on account of my overlapping roles as church member/social worker/researcher, the extreme vulnerability of the displaced refugees at the church, and to counteract the resultant power differential between the research participants and me (Hugman 2010b), I frequently problematised my positioning in relation to the members of the refugee group. Likewise, consent giving was structured as an iterative process throughout the data collection period. This afforded the participants repeated opportunities to withdraw from the study, as well as to impact its course and practice outcomes (Hugman et al. 2011).

Trustworthiness and validity of the study have been ensured through triangulation at the stages of sampling, data collection and analysis; as well as through construction of an audit trail (Kelly 2006). I sought regular feedback from the support group with regard to my observations and field notes. All interview participants had the opportunity to read and verify the transcripts. The initial codes and categories of the Open Coding phase were confirmed against the coding of selected diary entries and interviews by an independent researcher. Two participants (one refugee and one pastor) agreed to read initial drafts of the data analysis and write-up. Their feedback has been considered in the publications which followed, including this one.

From the ethnographic design of the study flow those limitations that are common to qualitative research, in particular, a lack of generalisability. This, however, does not prevent the data from being used to critically reflect on, or seek to ground, claims made by writers in the field of social justice; which forms part of the remaining two sections of this paper.

IV. Presentation of Findings: Refugees and the Vicious Circle of Social Injustice in South Africa

In the following, some of the study's findings are presented and discussed within the framework provided by Fraser's (2008) notion of social justice. Her claims regarding the significance of frame setting as a source of injustice in the contemporary global order (Fraser 2008) draw our interest to the extent to which the refugee participants in the study were able to have their voices heard and make substantive justice claims, as well as the obstacles they faced in this regard. In other words, focusing on the interaction and mutual impact of the political, cultural/legal and economic dimensions on the first and second levels of Fraser's (2008) conceptualisation, my analysis highlights the impact of framing decisions, that is, the inclusion and exclusion of support group members as subjects of social justice in South Africa. It is shown how, through misframing, a situation of voicelessness had been created among the refugees concerned vis-à-vis South African citizens and institutions of the South African state. This voicelessness then filtered out to justify, deepen and reproduce other substantive injustices, namely maldistribution and misrecognition, thus undermining the church's initial attempts of engaging in transformative framing practices, and illuminating pertinent aspects of the vicious circularity of social injustice (Fraser in Thompson 2009).

IV.i. The Grammar of Justice: *Misframing* and the Construction of Voicelessness

During the first support group meeting held at the church, one of the group members, Émile, spoke of his experiences of displacement:

> 'Men [were] singing, *Hamba, amakwerekwere, hamba!* [Go home aliens, go home!]' [Émile describes how] neighbours pointed out the foreigners. [The men] kicked in the door. At four in the morning, [the foreigners] were given one hour to pack their belongings. Émile [says that he] suffered flashbacks to the civil war in Burundi [and that] his heart started racing... He says, almost shouting: '*I am feeling angry! But what can I do? This is not my country.*' (Diary record 17.06.08)

This quote illustrates Neocosmos' (2008) and Misago *et al.*'s (2010) contention that the 2008 pogroms constituted an attempt by some citizens to enforce a nationalist-territorial frame around their home country when, in their assessment, the state had failed to do so: that is, to rid South Africa of those foreigners whom the government did not prevent from entering in the first place. Émile's story also expresses the sense of powerlessness and social redundancy experienced by a person who feels voiceless on account of being a non-citizen. Finally, Émile's account demonstrates that his inherited citizenship—Burundian—is a rather worthless political asset in view of his home country's decades-long civil war from which he fled.

On the same occasion, another group member, Noémie, referred to an incident which occurred two weeks after the xenophobic violence had been declared officially to be over (Misago *et al.* 2010) and related that

> She had sent her 12 year-old son to buy tomatoes at the... market. [She says that] they threatened him. They asked his name, to which he replied, '*Isaac*'... They wanted to know his surname, to which he replied, '*Mkhize*'. Then, they said to him, '*Run!*', and he ran. (Diary record 17.06.08)

The attempts of Noémie's son to misrepresent himself by using a common South African name might have failed on account of his Congolese accent. Another example of misframing of the popular kind, her story illustrates how the violent boundary setting of the pogroms developed a momentum which required little subsequent effort to maintain. As Émile, Noémie articulates, albeit on behalf of her son, the sense of fear and voicelessness generated in a situation when people's apparent lack of membership and belonging is, rather explicitly, expressed by the 'owners' of the territory which they, too, try to inhabit.

Three months on, the support group had shifted its attention from the experience of interpersonal violence to structural exclusion. In the following quote, I reflect on the role of the Department of Home Affairs in the lives of the group members. The Department is South Africa's (mis)framing institution par excellence, for it is here where residence permits, including asylum seeker and refugee permits, are awarded, withheld, or withdrawn.

> Christian... doesn't want to... talk about the past: 'It will... make me sick...' And having said that, he cannot stop talking about home... [Following a stream of indeed sickening accounts of genocide and civil war] I am beginning to appreciate... that talking... about the past is not something that everybody would want to do...
>
> [But] how do you convert a truth which is too painful to narrate into one which is exact enough to... legitimise your claim to living [as a refugee] in this... country?... Christian elaborates... 'After ten years, you are treated like a newcomer. [Every two years,] you... are asked to re-tell your story. And if you forget some parts, you may have your refugee status revoked... All we ask is to be treated fairly.'
>
> The fear of having your refugee status revoked arbitrarily is an experience... more creeping, silent and pervasive than the violent outbursts that occurred in May... All the knowledge of how Home Affairs functions, decides and implements its decisions in individual lives... is passed on through... rumours. The institution that can make or break people's existences is not well known, it is only murmured about. (Diary record 25.09.08)

Add to this another group member's account:

> Jules... is... in South Africa since 2002... had seven interviews [at Home Affairs and] remains on an asylum seeker permit [with] two-monthly extensions, awaiting appeal... During each of his first four interviews, a 'big lady'... asked him to pay a bribe... He says that... he cannot pay for what is his right. He says that several people who were interviewed at the same time as him and who agreed to paying the bribe, are now on refugee permits... Jules [says], 'Some of us... cannot go home... I cannot go home.' (Diary record 06.10.08)

In the interactions between the Department of Home Affairs and the study's participants, several types of social injustice seem to blend into one another, with practices of misrecognition emerging as an entrenched part of an institutionalised (mis)framing process around the allocation of refugee permits—creating in their wake situations of profound voicelessness amongst the refugees. There is firstly the bureaucratic imposition of an assumption that people's lives were reducible to stories against which to measure (and enforce) decisions concerning their future life courses. This imposition may be rooted in a further assumption that all refugees are potential liars who can be 'caught out' by being compelled repeatedly to re-tell their respective life stories. Finally, this system appears to have produced a breed of predator civil servants who award refugee permits in return for bribes; cynically (and criminally) endorsing, policing and subverting at once the very rules they were employed to uphold (cf. Human Rights Watch 1998, 2005).

Ultimately, Christian and Jules remind us that social injustice is a reality which undermines and curtails people's choices and life chances arbitrarily and as such is experienced as threatening and dehumanising. Christian's and Jules' stories also contain an interpretation of the nature and location of injustices to which they object, demanding fairness and voice: Aware that their life stories may at any point be used to justify the withholding, or withdrawal, of their residence permits, Christian and Jules indicate two obvious modes of resistance. Firstly, real life stories can be adjusted, changed and told strategically in accordance with known criteria for the award, or renewal, of refugee status. Secondly, money can buy what truth cannot afford. No longer voicing the truths of the lives they are meant to represent, such stories metamorphose into mirror images of the framing rules which have created them. These two accounts thus substantiate Zygmunt Bauman's (1993) warning that rules (especially those of the oppressive and exclusionary type) cannot escape being undermined and broken by those towards (or against) whom they are directed.

IV.ii. The Vicious Circle of Social Injustice: *Framing Decisions* and the Dialectics of Maldistribution and Misrecognition

At the church concerned, we took a decision to replace the citizenship frame with an alternative, apparently more accepting and inclusive (or differently divisive) type of membership; that is, membership based on faith (cf. Sen 2009, on the exclusionary structure of *all* membership frames). We agreed that having sought refuge at the church, the members of the group had, by default, also become its members. In a staff meeting soon after the group's arrival, we asked ourselves:

> Why [should] our lives continue unaltered when [the refugees] have had such major disruptions to theirs...? How did the early Christians deal with... refugees?... They would have been fully integrated. (Diary record 24.06.08)

Our initial attitude of solidarity and inclusivity translated into forms of recognition which had a healing and hope-giving effect, as one refugee, Michelle, recalled:

> When we [arrived] there [at the church]...I saw a...lady...She came through to me...She said '...There is one Bible...I bought for someone...Maybe, that someone, it is you'...From that day, I was strong. I was going to force myself to be strong...(Recorded interview 12.12.08)

But embedded in our decision there was also an acknowledgement that the violence which had brought the refugees to the church was not just interpersonal but structural as well (Mullaly 2007). Four weeks after their arrival, it had become obvious that poverty and deprivation were part of the reality from which people had fled: they were suffering an injustice of maldistribution (Fraser 1997, 2003) in their country of refuge. Much effort went into trying to solicit funding for material support, as well as trying to facilitate access to employment opportunities and affordable housing through our church networks. Émile, speaking of the dignifying way in which he had received material and practical help at a point of desperate need, suggested that

> Maybe it was my time...and for this assistance, I don't say 'thank you'... Because everything have got their time...[One day], it's going to be my time... to help those children of Dorothee...(Recorded interview 17.12.08)

In other words, our initial decision towards an inclusive construction of membership enabled small acts of recognition and redistribution which in turn helped to mend some of the injuries inflicted during the xenophobic violence. But as time went on, it emerged that our efforts, including those of trying to secure sufficiently well-paid jobs and helping to enhance the performance of survivalist businesses, remained inadequate, considering the extent of the group members' economic marginalisation. In the following, the group member Léocadie illustrates some of these challenges:

> L: *To get a job is not easy... because all companies ask for... papers* [that is, certification of previous qualifications, lost during flight]...
> *I was making bead work, selling shoes...* [Then] *they closed the Flee Market... This Flee Market was helping too many people. Now the people don't have space to go to sell... When you go to ask for licence to sell they don't want to give you.*
> D: Before, there was no licence?
> L: *The licence started when they moved* [the Flee Market] *to another site... The South Africans selling there got licence. Now us here, we do not have licence... Too much people cry.* (Recorded interview 29.11.08)

From August 2008 onwards, we tried to access support from several small business development institutions in South Africa. However, we remained unsuccessful. I noted at the time that

> Umsobomvu [a national development institution] refuses to give any answer to our written requests and weekly follow-up calls... Other agencies either state on their websites that their services are for citizens only, or tell us so when we make telephonic contact...
> Each time we stumble against another closed door, I become angry and Estelle [a group member] responds by saying that, *'If they don't want to help us, leave them...'* And when I argue towards being more assertive, pro-active and demanding of services... her view is supported, not mine. (Diary record 12.10.08)

According to Mullaly (2007, p. 278), Estelle's 'cautious, low profile conservatism' is a response typical of internalised oppression: its aim is to decrease 'visibility and social penalties' in the face of structural violence and compensate 'for a disfavoured identity'. But as established members of the church, we didn't fully appreciate the type of social injustices we were dealing with either. Efforts remained at a charitable and ameliorative level, with little time spent reflecting on the dimension, causes, nature and dynamics at the root of the refugees' marginalisation. At the time, the concept of misframing was unknown to us. Unsurprisingly, as time went on, there was a growing sense of shared powerlessness amongst those of us who had committed to assisting the group members beyond the crisis.

This sense had two main forms of expression. On the one hand, there emerged a tendency to take recourse to an imaginary well established in welfare discourse: *the deserving versus the undeserving poor.* For example, one pensioner, Irene had given a sewing machine (a cherished item that she had used through many of her working years) to one of the refugees, Juliette, in the expectation that the latter would use it to make and sell clothing. Juliette was excited as she had never been able to buy her own machine. But she failed to set up the anticipated sewing business; Juliette did not know how to sew as well as she might have led Irene to believe. Irene was disappointed, demanding that Juliette return the machine so that it could be given to somebody more deserving. Juliette refused, saying: '*But she gave it to me, and it is mine! How can she claim it back?*' (Diary record 30.01.09). Irene concluded:

> This means that Juliette is not a good person... The problem is that she cannot sew. She is untidy. And she is lazy, too. (Diary record 30.01.09)

Irene did not succeed in retrieving the sewing machine, and both women withdrew from one another feeling disappointed and hurt. Some of Irene's family and friends wound up with a categorical extension of the lessons seemingly learnt from the incident to all those carrying the same identity markers as Juliette; that is, to '*never help a refugee again*' (Diary record 30.01.09). In retrospect, it looks as though participants and onlookers on both sides were unable to appreciate how deeper, structural issues had impacted the course of events. Consequently, the two women were effectively left alone in trying (without succeeding) to resolve their dispute. In the process, negative labels and stereotypes came to crowd out opportunities for more in-depth engagement and, thus, a just resolution of the conflict. As such, this episode clearly falls within Fraser's (2000, 2003) notion of misrecognition.

On the other hand was a reaction borne out of our *witnessing* (Zembylas 2007) how unyielding the exclusionary and marginalising structures in the lives of the refugees really were. Akin to the internalised form of oppression discussed above, we directed our responses inward. Group members left the shelter at the church without ceasing to call on their newly acquired membership for remedy of their day-to-day hardships. This led to a growing sense of exhaustion on our part. For example, one of the ministers, Robert, began 'Feeling increasingly drained by this weekly string of interviews' (Diary record 29.09.08).

As time went on, exhaustion began to infiltrate perceptions. Below, I use a rather bleak metaphor to describe the sum total of misframings, misrecognitions and maldistributions we seemed unable to overcome:

> There seems to be one... barrier closing in on another—a piece of legislation, an unaffordable fee, a quota here, an exclusionary mission or vision statement there—forming a skin around society to prevent refugees from accessing the resources that they, [as] desperately [as] others, need to survive. (Diary record 30.01.09)

And some two months later, I recorded how

> The church has run out of money. I have run out of time. The group members have not run out of problems... People are starving... Even recognising people... and

responding to them empathetically—if nothing else—takes time. And time I do not have. (Diary record 11.03.09)

With hindsight, it appears that our efforts were characterised by a lack of awareness regarding the distinctly political dimension of the problems that we were responding to; that is, the pervasiveness of misframing in its ability to pre-configure and increase the refugees' vulnerability to such substantive issues of social injustice as maldistribution. Comparatively privileged, the established members of the church did not recognise the extent to which the refugees' vulnerabilities were outgrowths from structural forms of injustice which, being structural—a grammar—could have been addressed sustainably only through structural rather than through charitable or ameliorative responses, as important as these were in the aftermath of the xenophobic crisis. Such lack in critical awareness undermined eventually what we had started on so well, that is recognising the members of the refugee group as fully human. At times, we invoked essentialist images of 'the refugee as such' whom we began to label as undeserving of our help—when we could have explored more deeply the nature of the hardships that we were unable to ameliorate. At other times, we directed our feelings of helplessness and powerlessness inward rather than outward—which would have required us to frame the problem in political terms. And yet both our project's failings and gains illuminate the workings of social (in)justice in an age of globalisation, large-scale migration and implications thereof for social work.

V. Conclusions and Implications: Towards Creating *Enclaves of Just Practice* in Social Work with Refugees and Beyond

This article set out to critically interrogate the meaning of *social justice* vis-à-vis the recent experiences of refugees in South Africa. Its specific concern was the helpfulness of Fraser's (2008) recent conceptualisation of justice for social workers in this field. The arguments of this paper were grounded in findings from an ethnographic study which over 18 months investigated the relationships between local members of a South African church and a group of refugees living amongst them after being displaced by the 2008 xenophobic pogroms. The findings illustrate how the injustice of misframing translated from South Africa's legal and policy frameworks and public discourse of nation-building via exclusionary and misrecognition practices into the way the study's participants regarded themselves and one another. On the other hand, there were counter-discourses and practices which translated into small acts of resistance, recognition and redistribution, mainly on the level of encounters between individuals and groups. Such counter-discourses and practices, however, proved unsustainable in the face of the dominance of exclusionary structures and processes in which they were embedded. Moreover, lacking political understanding on the part of all research participants reinforced both internalised forms of oppression and essentialising discourses amongst the privileged about the oppressed, while preventing the development of more organised, better targeted and more collective counter-practices.

Before the background of these findings, we can now return to the two lines of criticism against Fraser's work which were discussed in Section II. Contrary to the claim that Fraser fails to consider the role of the state sufficiently well (Garrett 2010), the study applied the notions of misframing, misrecognition, maldistribution and voice successfully to illuminate the oppressive and exclusionary functions of the South African state in a context of cross-border migration. Of greater concern is the challenge posed by Thompson (2009) that Fraser's model does not help us to overcome the injustices it allows us to diagnose: The lack of sustainability of those counter-discourses and practices that our project intermittently brought to life can, to an extent, be attributed to a lack of critical reflexivity amongst us, the project's participants. Still, given the project's broader contextual conditions, we cannot conclude therefore that a deeper understanding of our implication in the interplay between misframing, voicelessness, misrecognition and maldistribution would have changed this scenario significantly.

With regard to the normative component of Fraser's work then, we may conclude the following: the fact that the study could isolate misframing as a primary dynamic behind the multiple and intersecting exclusionary processes experienced by the participant refugees suggests that we may be dealing with a concept that social workers should consider routinely as the framework in which the more substantive injustices of maldistribution and misrecognition occur. As such, understanding the workings of social injustice in the lives of refugees can model how we might conceptualise the injustice of misframing in other cases where citizenship is either absent or lacking.

With regard to Fraser's transformative intentions, the conclusions flowing from the study are less straightforward. In view of the stage of globalisation we find ourselves in at present, we must assume that some of the contradictions that social workers are confronted with in their daily practice will remain unresolved no matter how aptly they are analysed, and no matter what we do in response. This is the likely scenario for social work with refugees, and for social work with other groups rendered vulnerable in the current economic, social, political and cultural constellations.

However, one of the purposes of normative frameworks such as Fraser's is to inform and enable us to evaluate our practices in relation to the ideals they formulate, no matter how elusive these may seem. It is these kinds of ideals that inspire the reflexivity, critical discourse, counter-practices and growth of the counter-public spheres which Fraser envisages—even if the practice outcomes in individual instances appear modest at first. For the time being, justice-oriented social work may at least produce *enclaves of just practice* within an overall context that in the foreseeable future is likely to remain unjust. And yet even the limited ambition of creating such enclaves will require social workers to:

- Understand the structural roots of the particular injustices we are confronted with; and target our response on the appropriate level.
- Set realistic goals for intervention, including: ameliorating the effects of social injustice in the lives of individuals, families and communities; seeking to redress those causes of injustice as are within our reach, articulating those injustices we cannot address and acknowledging their corresponding hardships.
- Participate in public discourse around the nature, causes and possible resolution of contemporary forms of injustices.

As part of an overall political process, then, projects such as the one presented in this paper can play an important role.

Declaration

All names used in this article have been changed, as have—as far as possible in an ethnographic study—any other details which might lead to the identification of research participants.

References

Banks, S. (2004) *Ethics, Accountability, and the Social Professions*, Palgrave Macmillan, Houndmills.
Bauman, Z. (1993) *Postmodern Ethics*, Blackwell, Oxford.
Bozalek, V. (2012) 'Interview with Nancy Fraser', *Social Work Practitioner/Researcher*, Vol. 24, no. 1, pp. 136–51.
Charmaz, K. (2003) 'Grounded Theory: Objectivist and Constructivist Methods', in *Strategies of Qualitative Inquiry*, 2nd edn, eds N. K. Denzin & Y. S. Lincoln, Sage, Thousand Oaks, CA, pp. 249–91.
Chikanga, K. (2012) 'Xenophobia's Turmoil Rages On', *The Sunday Independent*, 6 May, p. 4.
Citizenship Rights in Africa Initiative (CRAI) (2009) *Tolerating Intolerance: Xenophobic Violence in South Africa*, available at: <http://www.citizenshiprightsinafrica.org/Publications/2009/CRAISAReport.July2009.pdf> (accessed February 2011).
Crush, J., McDonald, D. A., Williams, V., Lefko-Everett, K., Dorey, D., Taylor, D. & Sablonniere, R. (2008) *The Perfect Storm: The Realities of Xenophobia in Contemporary South Africa*, SAMP Migration Policy Series no. 50, Southern African Migration Project, Kingston and Cape Town.
Danish Refugee Council (2008) *Policy on Mixed Migration, Revised May 2009*, available at: <http://flygtning.dk/fileadmin/uploads/pdf/Om_dfh_PDF/Det_mener_DFH/policy_on_mixed_migration.pdf> (accessed March 2012).
Fairclough, N. (2001) *Language and Power*, 2nd edn, Pearson Education, Harlow.
Fraser, N. (1989) *Unruly Practices: Power, Discourse and Gender in Contemporary Social Theory*, Polity Press, Oxford.
Fraser, N. (1997) *Justice Interruptus: Critical Reflections on the 'Postsocialist' Condition*, Routledge, London and New York.

Fraser, N. (2000) 'Rethinking Recognition', *New Left Review*, no. 3 (May–June), pp. 107–20.
Fraser, N. (2003) 'Social Justice in the Age of Identity Politics: Redistribution, Recognition and Participation', in *Redistribution or Recognition? A Political–Philosophical Exchange*, eds N. Fraser & A. Honneth, Verso, London, pp. 7–109.
Fraser, N. (2008) *Scales of Justice: Reimagining Political Space in a Globalising World*, Polity Press, Cambridge.
Garrett, P. M. (2010) 'Recognising the Limitations of the Political Theory of Recognition: Axel Honneth, Nancy Fraser and Social Work', *British Journal of Social Work*, Vol. 40, no. 5, pp. 1517–33.
Gobo, G. (2008) *Doing Ethnography*, Sage, Los Angeles, New Delhi & Singapore.
Hölscher, D. & Bozalek, V. (2012) 'Encountering the *Other* across the Divides: Re-grounding Social Justice as a Guiding Principle for Social Work with Refugees and other Vulnerable Groups', *British Journal of Social Work*, Vol. 42, no. 6, pp. 1093–112.
Hölscher, D., Sathiparsad, R. & Mujawamariya, C. (2012) 'Interpreting Refugee Women's Life Stories: Towards a Human Capabilities Framework for Social Work with Cross-border Migrants', *Social Work Practitioner/Researcher*, Vol. 24, no. 1, pp. 48–65.
Hoogeveen, J. G. & Özler, B. (2005) *Not Separate, Not Equal: Poverty and Inequality in Post-apartheid South Africa*, William Davidson Institute at the University of Michigan, Ann Arbor.
Hugman, R. (2010a) *Understanding International Social Work: A Critical Analysis*, Palgrave Macmillan, Houndmills.
Hugman, R. (2010b) 'Social Work Research & Ethics', in *The Sage Handbook of Social Work Research*, eds I. Shaw, K. Briar-Lawson, J. Orme & R. Ruckdeschel, Sage, Thousand Oaks, CA, pp. 149–65.
Hugman, R., Pittaway, E. & Bartolomei, L. (2011) 'When "Do No Harm" is Not Enough: The Ethics of Research with Refugees and other Vulnerable Groups', *British Journal of Social Work*, Vol. 41, no. 7, pp. 1271–87.
Human Rights Watch (1998) *'Prohibited Persons': Abuse of Undocumented Migrants, Asylum-seekers, and Refugees in South Africa*, available at: <www.hrw.org/reports98/sareport/> (accessed March 2006).
Human Rights Watch (2005) *Living on the Margins: Inadequate Protection for Refugees and Asylum-seekers in Johannesburg*, Human Rights Watch, 17 November, A1715, available at: <http://www.unhcr.org/refworld/docid/43ba84a54.html> (accessed November 2012).
Humphries, B. (2008) *Social Work Research for Social Justice*, Palgrave Macmillan, Houndmills.
IFSW/IASSW (2002) *Definition of Social Work*, available at: <http://ifsw.org/resources/definition-of-social-work/> (accessed May 2012).
Kelly, K. (2006) 'Calling it a Day: Reaching Conclusions in Qualitative Research', in *Research in Practice*, 2nd edn, eds M. Terreblanche, K. Durrheim & D. Painter, University of Cape Town Press, Cape Town, pp. 370–387.
Makhema, M. (2009) Social Protection for Refugees and Asylum Seekers in the Southern African Development Community (SADC), Social Protection and Labour Discussion Paper no. 0906, World Bank, Washington, DC.
Miller, R. L. (2000) *Researching Life Stories and Family Histories*, Sage, Thousand Oaks, CA.
Misago, J. P., Monson, T., Polzer, T. & Landau, L. B. (2010) *May 2008 Violence against Foreign Nationals in South Africa: Understanding Causes and Evaluating Responses*, Forced Migration Studies Programme at the University of the Witwatersrand & Consortium for Refugees and Migrants in South Africa, Johannesburg.
Mullaly, B. (2002) *Challenging Oppression: A Critical Social Work Approach*, Oxford University Press Oxford, New York.
Mullaly, B. (2007) *The New Structural Social Work*, 3rd edn, Oxford University Press, Oxford.

Nash, K. & Bell, V. (2007) 'The Politics of Framing: An Interview with Nancy Fraser', *Theory, Culture and Society*, Vol. 24, no. 4, pp. 73–86.

Neocosmos, M. (2008) 'The Politics of Fear and the Fear of Politics: Reflections on Xenophobic Violence in South Africa', *Journal of Asian and African Studies*, Vol. 43, no. 6, pp. 586–94.

Nussbaum, M. (2000) *Women and Human Development: The Capabilities Approach*, Cambridge University Press, Cambridge.

Republic of South Africa (RSA) (1998) *Refugees Act No. 130 of 1998*, Government Gazette, Pretoria.

Sen, A. K. (2009) *The Idea of Justice*, Belknap Press of Harvard University Press, Cambridge, MA.

Thompson, S. (2009) 'On the Circularity of Democratic Justice', *Philosophy and Social Criticism*, Vol. 35, no. 9, pp. 1079–98.

UNHCR (2011) *Refugee Protection and Mixed Migration: A 10-point Plan of Action*, available at: <http://www.unhcr.org/pages/4a16aac66.html> (accessed November 2011).

UNHCR (2012) *UNHCR Country Operations Profile—South Africa*, available at: <http://www.unhcr.org/cgi-bin/texis/vtx/page?page=49e485aa6> (accessed September 2012).

Zembylas, M. (2007) *Five Pedagogies, a Thousand Possibilities*, Sense, Rotterdam.

Index

Note: Bold page numbers refer to tables and page numbers followed by "n" denote endnotes.

aboriginality and non-aboriginality 47
academic analysis 120
academics growth: course evaluation 66; cultural capital 65; destabilisation 66; enculturation 62; geographical proximity 66; institutional settings 65; maldistribution 62; misframing 62; misrecognition 62; outcomes 64; participatory parity 66; post-apartheid society 66; professional learning 62; redistribution 65; research-based interventions 63–4; role models 63; social arrangements 66; social mobility 62
active learners 78, 82–4, **83**
Adding insult to injury: Nancy Fraser debates her critics 41–2
'advocacy' 40
'affective equality' 108, 110
affective justice 114; 'affective equality' 108, 110; Australian jurisdictions 104; care relations 108; 'credit recovery' 110; flexible learning 104–6; 'job readiness' 111; marginalisation 107; multi-sited ethnography 106–7; non-academic students 110; non-vocational students 110; political injustices 103; 'relational care work' 108; self-respect 104; service providers 109; social practice 103; solidarity relations 108
affirmative approach 42, 61–2
affirmative politics 75, 80
affirmative postmodernist versions 18
Ainscow, M. 94
alternative education 9, 106, 108, 114, 115, 115n1, 165
Anastasiou, D. 76, 84–5
Anderson, E. 36, 42
Angus, L. 97
Annamma, S. 72–3, 85
anti-statism 119
Anyon, J. 150
Apple, M. 167
Arnesen, A. 73

Artiles, A. 73
atomistic liberal conceptions 16
Avramidis, E. 72

'back to basics' approach 159
Baker, J. 35
Banks, S. 171
Bardsley, K. 113
Bauman, Z. 181
Beach, D. 110
de Beauvoir, S. 167
Bennett, L. 145, 147
Big Picture model 107, 115n2
bi/multilingualism and bi/multilinguals 133
bivalency 123–7, 129, 136
Blackledge, A. 130
Blackmore, J. 157
Black urban communities 145
Blanchett, C. 158
Blommaert, J. 131
de Boer, A. 72
Boler, M. 60
Boltanski, L. 162
Bossaert, G. 72
Boyer, E. 58
Bozalek, V. 171, 176
Brenner, J. 128
Brenner, N. 141
British Labour Party 120
Butler, J. 42, 53, 127

Cameron, L. 130
Canagarajah, S. 130
cannibalization 158
Cape Higher Education Consortium (CHEC) 63
Carpenter, L. 73
centre-based approach 44
CHA *see* Chicago Housing Authority (CHA)
CHEC *see* Cape Higher Education Consortium (CHEC)
Chiapello, E. 162

Chicago Gatreaux housing desegregation program 146
Chicago Housing Authority (CHA) 143, 145
Chicago Public Schools (CPS) 143
Chinese identity 134
'chronic absenteeism and dropout' 48
Ciccone, T. 60
citizenship-based exclusions 172
Citizenship Curriculum 45
Citizenship, Social Inclusion and Difference (CSID) 63, 66
'Citizens' Service' 17
class politics 128
Clowes, L. 66–7
code switching 130
collaborative research project 64
Commercial Club of Chicago 145
Commission on Social Justice (CSJ) 17, 27n2
commonality 7, 19, 20
communitarianism 17
community disharmony 45
conceptualization 14–15, 21, 24, 26, 27; atomistic liberal conceptions 16
concrete arrangements 43, 48–50
Connell, R. 157
Constructivist Grounded Theory 177
contributive justice 114; Australian jurisdictions 104; dignity 112; disruptions and poor behaviours 113; economic justice 112; 'emerging societal contexts' 113; flexible learning 104–6; multi-sited ethnography 106–7; political injustices 103; political marginalisation 115; self-respect 104; social marginalisation 115; social practice 103
Conway, R. 73
Cook, V. 130
Cooper, D. 30
Costandius, E. 59
counter-public spheres 175, 176, 185
course evaluation 66
CPS *see* Chicago Public Schools (CPS)
Crahay, M. 97
'credit recovery' 110
Creese, A. 130
Critical Race Theory 72
'critical theory of recognition' 24
CSID *see* Citizenship, Social Inclusion and Difference (CSID)
CSJ *see* Commission on Social Justice (CSJ)
cultural-valuational structure 23, 24, 127
culture: authenticity 49; autonomy 15; awareness 45; barriers 41; bio-determinism 51; capital 65; criticism 46, 49; cultural injustice 105; deconstruction 26, 27n4; definition 105; diversity 22; imperialism 13, 21, 22–3; losses 20; Marxism 128; oppression 50; pluralism 46; recognition 44–5, 50
culture-based groups 22

Darling-Hammond, L. 150
debates and counter-debates 42
decision-making 5, 15, 42, 50, 143
decision rules 136n1, 176
De Jong, T. 110
De La Rosa, D. 43
democratic citizenship 8, 36, 38n9
democratic decision making 15
'democratic deficits' 144–6
Derouet, J.-L. 97
despised sexuality 23, 100n2, 127
De Vroey, A. 72
Disability Studies in Education and Cultural/Historical Activity Theory 72
Disadvantaged Schools Program 43
distributive justice 21; definition 14; equality of condition 16; *equality of opportunity* 16; *equality of outcome* 16; individualistic and atomistic 15; liberal conceptions 16; material and non-material resources 14
distributive language 35
Diversity and Inclusion in Australian Schools (Hyde, Carpenter, and Conway) 73
diversity politics: inclusive education 73–5; micro- and macro-political culture 73; multidimensional approach 73; 'normality' and 'abnormality' 73; 'pedagogies of indifference' 73
domestic violence 105
Dovemark, M. 110
Du Gay, P. 160
Dworkin, R. 30, 35
dynamic systems theory 130

Ebert, T. 18
economic: deprivation 43; deregulation 141; injustices 23–5, 48, 94, 98–100, 100n2, 103–5; injustices 23–5, 48, 94, 98–100, 100n2, 103–5; marginalisation 44, 182; oppression 50
economisation 161
Edmund Rice Education Australia (EREA) Youth + network 107
educational: disparities 146, 147; failure, naturalisation 99; inequalities 91, 92, 94, 98, 99, 147, 150; needs 45, 72, 77, 79, 82–6, 99; research techniques 63
education markets: 'choice' and school cultures 92; cultural injustices 96–7; 'despised sexualities' 100n2; educational attainment 92; educational failure, naturalisation 99; educational inequalities 91; educational outcomes 100; 'exploited classes' 100n2; 'Hidden Triumphs' 96; 'league tables' 92 (*see also* league tables); misrecognition 95; neoliberal-inspired policies 91; neoliberal reforms 100n3; professional closure 93; redistribution politics displacement 98–9; school separation 97–8; schools stigmatisation

99; socio-economic disadvantage 92; socio-economic factors 95–6; trade unions 93; vocational subjects 95
education policies support 27
education policy research 26–7; community 13
egalitarian communities 149
egalitarianism 30, 35–6
egalitarian theories 34
enculturation 62
engagement 2, 8, 32, 45, 47–9, 51, 53, 54, 67, 74, 76, 104, 108, 109, 114, 174, 175, 183
English-Welsh bilingual education 130
Engsig, T. 72
'equal citizenship' 36
equality: difference debate 29; distribution 33–6; distributive paradigm 30, 37n5; dual systems 31; egalitarianism 30; feminist theory 29; human difference and diversity 29; justice conception 30; material and social forms 31; overarching conception, justice 32; parity of participation 32–3; political concept 31; politico-economic restructuring 30; regulatory principles 30; rehabilitation 30; 'valorizing diversity' 30
equality of condition 16
equality of opportunity 16, 21
equality of outcome 16
equality of status 36
ethnolinguistic racism 119, 133, 134
Etzioni, A. 17–18
'expanded understanding of justice' 32, 33
exploitation 6, 13, 21, 94, 123, 124, 126, 129
exploited classes 23, 100n2

fatalism 99, 151
Feldman, Leonard 42
Felouzis, G. 96
feminist theory 1, 2, 29
Fitch, F. 75–6, 82
Flax, J. 29
flexible learning 103–7, 113, 114, 115n1
Flores, N. 128
Forst, Rainer 42
Foucault, Michel 119
'free-standing cultural harm' 48
Freire, P. 151
From Redistribution to Recognition? (Fraser) 41, 53, 122
Fullilove, M.T. 146
funding disparities 151n7

García, O. 130–2, 133, 134
Garrett, P. M. 171, 174
gay-identity politics 127
gender 2, 25, 46, 105, 125, 128
gentrification 10, 141–3, 149
Gewirtz, S. 98

global governance 50
globalization 141–2
global market 19
global media 50
Gomberg, P. 112
Gorard, S. 97
governmentalities 38n7
Grech, S. 80
Greene, M. 163
Greenstein, A. 72, 87
Griffiths, C. 110

Habermas, J. 97
Hackworth, J. 142
Hall, S. 159
Harvey, D. 21–2, 120–1, 160
Head Start programme 44
Hewitt (1997) 19–20
'Hidden Triumphs' 96
Higgins, C. 134
higher education 8, 58–63, 65, 157, 164, 165
Holmwood, J. 157
Hölscher, D. 176
home-based approach 44
homo–hetero dichotomy 127
Honneth, A. 31, 32
HOPE VI Act 143, 148–50
Hua, Z. 134
Huber, M. 60
Hudspeth, N. 145, 147
human rights 121
Hutchings, P. 58, 60
Hyde, M. 73

identity politics 2, 8, 18, 43, 46–50, 52, 74, 81, 82, 85, 86, 119, 128
'imagined communities' 19
immanent universalism 20
'Improving Schools' 95
inclusive education 73–5; active learners 82–4, **83**; advocacy 77; affirmative politics 75; classrooms 78–9; debate 72; definition 72; disability studies 75–6; disputation and power 73; educational needs 72; fine-grained analyses 78; informed participation 77; 'irregular' schooling 77; misrecognition 74; multicultural education 76; 'parity of participation in social life' 75; recognition (social status) **80,** 80–2; reconceptualisation 74; redistribution (resourcing) **79,** 79–80; 'redistribution-recognition dilemma' 76; 'rethink recognition' 74; social discrimination 75; 'status subordination' 74; teachers' responses 76; transnational claims 75
Indigenous culture 45, 47, 49, 51, 52
Indigenous education 43, 46, 47, 52
Indigenous theory and knowledges 47

INDEX

inequality 8, 33, 35, 41, 59, 61, 64, 66, 67, 75, 98, 99, 108, 126–7, 132, 133, 135, 141, 147, 150, 165
informal selection mechanisms 148, 149
informed participation 77
injustice conceptualization 13
institutional authority 166
institutional effectiveness 93, 96, 97
institutional matrix 47–8
institutional policies 61
institutional settings 65
interimbrication 42
inter-institutional course 63
'irregular' schooling 77
Isin, E. 31

Jan Pijl, S. 72
Jansen, J. 59
'job readiness' 111
Johnson, R. 161
Johnstone, C. 72
justice: distributional dimension 14–16; relational dimension 14–15; *see also* relational justice
Justice and the Politics of Difference (Young) 13
justice as freedom from oppressive relations 16; distributional justice 21; neo-Fabian conception limitations 20–1; oppression faces 21; political-economic analysis 21; 'unmediated face-to-face relations' 21–2
justice as mutuality: neo-Fabian versions 17–18; postmodernist versions 18–19
justice as recognition 17, 19–20

Kahlenberg, R.D. 144, 146
Kanu, Y. 47, 49
Katz, B. 144
Kauffman, J. 76, 84–5
Keynesian social-democratic formation 120
Keynsian welfare state institutions 141
Kim, J.-H. 110
Knight, A. 75
Kompridis, Nikolas 42
Kreber, C. 58, 60
Kubota, R. 128

labour market 43, 164
Ladson-Billings, G. 150
Lahelma, E. 73
'land grab' 142
language education research, political economy: academic analysis 120; anti-statism 119; bivalency 123; Black migrants 126; British Labour Party 120; "class politics" 128; contemporary societies 120; "culturalist" approach 121; cultural Marxism 128; decision rules 136n1; gay-identity politics 127; gender 125; homo–hetero dichotomy 127; human rights 121; 'identity politics' 128; inequalities and injustices 121; Keynesian social-democratic formation 120; lesbians 124–5; LGBTQ communities 120; "merely cultural" battles 127; monolingual-biased bilingual education 135; *New Left Review* 121; "paid productive labour" 125; postmodern fragmentations 119, 121; poststructuralist approach 121; "progressive neoliberalism" 128; progressive tax regimes 126; Queer theory 127; race 125; recognition and redistribution 122–3; recognition-oriented political action 127; redistribution-oriented research 129; self-esteem 127, 136; situating class and sexuality 125; social activism 120; social environments/job markets 124; transformative recognition 127; translanguaging research 129–34; "unpaid reproductive and domestic labour" 125
Larsen-Freeman, D. 130
Lau, S. M. C. 135
league tables: collateral damage 94; cultural injustice 94–5; democratic society 93; educational statisticians 93; holistic developmental process 93; 'Improving Schools' 95; institutional effectiveness 93; qualitative process 93; 'raw' performance data 93; reductionism 93; 'value-added' tables 95–6
Leibowitz, B. 64
Leonard, P. 18–20
lesbians 124–5
Levačić, R. 94
liberal welfare state 24
Lingard, B. 73
Lipman, P. 158
low-income communities 141, 149
low-income students and familes 147–9
ludic postmodernism 18
Lynch, K. 16, 104, 108, 114

McConaghy, C. 47, 48–9, 52
McInerney, P. 54
McLeod, J. 160
macrostructural variables 48
'mainstream' classrooms 86
mainstream: multiculturalism 24; public sphere 10; schools 105, 106, 108, 110, 111, 114
maldistribution 62, 104, 123–6
Manifesto for the Public University 157
Marcus, G. E. 106
marginalised cultures 46, 49
marginalization 13, 21, 27, 123, 129, 141, 147, 150
market-based reforms 157
material/cultural dichotomy 32
material–social dichotomy 37n2

Matthews, S. 59
micro-level classroom variables 47–8
Mietola, R. 73
Miles, S. 72
Miller, D. 15, 36
Minnaert, A. 72
Misago, J. P. 179
misframing 62; citizenship-based exclusions 172; counter-discourses 176; counter-practices 176; 'counter-public spheres' 175; cultural dimensions 173–4; data sources 177–8; globalisation 172, 174; legal dimensions 173–4; maldistribution and misrecognition 181–4; middle-level principles 171; normative frameworks 185; ordinary-political dimension 174; participatory parity 173; recognition theory 174; Refugees Act 176; refugees and vicious circle 178–81; social arrangements 173; social work, definition 171; third-order (in)justices 174–5; transformative politics 175; trustworthiness 178; xenophobia 172, 176
misrecognition 3, 8–10, 41, 48, 61, 62, 64, 74, 94, 95, 98–100, 104, 122–6, 135, 180, 183
misrepresentation 45, 62, 104, 175
mixed-income schools and housing: Chicago context 142–4; Chicago Gatreaux housing desegregation program 146; class segregation 141; common sense 140; de-democratization 141; 'democratic deficits' 144–6; economic integration 147; educational disparities 146; education development 141; egalitarian solutions 140; gentrification 141; low-income communities 141; low-income students and famiies 147–9; mixed-race 147; multilingual education 147; neoliberal urbanism 141–2; privatization, public institutions 141; race segregation 141; racialised poverty discourses 144–6; self-determination 141; urban development 141
Moje, E. 59
monolingual-biased bilingual education 135
Morgan, G. 160
Mullaly, B. 182
multicompetence 130
multicultural education 76
multiculturalism 47, 49
multi-dimensional approach 14, 54
multilingual education 130, 147
multi-sited ethnography 106–7
municipal tax laws 141
Murphy, J. B. 112
mutual respect 17, 36

Nash, K. 30
Nash, R. 100
National Goals for Schooling Framework 44–5
national jurisdictions 71, 73

National Partnership Scheme 44
Ndebele, C. 64
Negri, A. 163
Neocosmos, M. 179
neo-Fabian versions of mutuality 17–18
neoliberal-inspired policies 91–2
neoliberalism 50, 141; analytic/descriptive quality 159; 'back to basics' approach 159; contemporary politics 160; economisation 161; 'external evil' 160; personalisation 162; post-Second World War welfare state 161; 'public' services 161; second-wave feminism 162; sociological analysis 159; Taylorization 162
neoliberal urbanism 141–2, 143
New Labour's Welfare-to-Work scheme 18
New Left Review (1995) 121, 122
Nicolaidou, M. 94
Norwich, B. 72
Nusbaum, E. 72, 82

Olson, K. 42, 50, 53
oppression faces 13
organic communities 149
Otsuji, E. 130

"paid productive labour" 125
participant feedback questionnaires 63
participatory parity 32–3, 40, 64, 66, 105; affirmative approach 61–2; cultural dimension 61; institutional policies 61; material resources 61; misframing 62; psychological process 61; social arrangements 60–1; social justice dimensions 60; transformative approach 61–2; transnational flows and practices 62
'pedagogy of discomfort' 63
Pennycook, A. 130
"perspectival dualism" 123–7
Petry, K. 72
PFT *see* Plan for Transformation (PFT)
Phillips, A. 26
Plan for Transformation (PFT) 142, 143, 145, 148, 149
Polesel, J. 105
political-economy-based groups 22
political theory 33, 77
politics: construction 18; cultural 53; of difference 22–4; of diversity 72–5; of equality 36; gay-identity 127; identity 2, 8, 18, 43, 46–50, 52, 74, 81, 82, 85, 86, 119, 128; of language education 121; neoliberal 158, 159; queer 24; of recognition 2–3, 20–2, 92, 95–100; of redistribution 24–6
post-apartheid society 66
'post-bourgeois' model 151
postmodern fragmentations 119, 121
postmodernist versions of mutuality 18–19

post-Second World War welfare state 161, 165
"postsocialist age" 122
post-welfarist education policies 13
'post-westphalian' environment 50
poverty theories 144
powerlessness 13, 21, 23, 25, 27, 179, 182
procedural justice 15
'process–product' paradigm 97
professional learning 58, 62
progressive neoliberalism 6, 9, 128
progressive tax regimes 126
'progressive' teachers 40
public education, neoliberal times: cannibalization 158; claims 163–6; educational research 157; market-based reforms 157; neoliberal capitalism 156; 'war on terrorism' 157; welfare state 159–63
public–private partnerships 144
public–private ventures 141
Putnamm, R. 17

Quality Housing and Work Reform Act 144
queer theory 127

race 125; cultural identity 41; segregation 141
racialised poverty discourses 144–6
racism 45, 47, 126
Ragoonaden, K. 60
Rampton, B. 131
Rawls, J. 14–15, 36
Rawolle, S. 159
"real damage, real distortion" 122
real estate development 142
reconceptualisation 34, 74
redistribution–recognition dilemma 76; affirmative *vs.* transformative remedies 23; bipolar categorization 25; claims 22; class and sexuality 23; 'critical theory of recognition' 24; cultural deconstruction 26; cultural imperialism 22–3; cultural-valuational structure 24; culture-based groups 22; differences, types 24; liberal welfare state 24; mainstream multiculturalism 24; political-economy-based groups 22; socialist economics 24; task-defining work *vs.* task- executing work 23; transformative recognition 25–6; working-class culture 25
reflective essays 63
reframing justice: cultural bio-determinism 51; cultural recognition 50; democratic relations 53; economic redistribution 50; 'Indigenous culture' 52; Indigenous education 52; mis/framing 50–1; *ordinary* mis/representation 50–1; participation parity 52; 'post-westphalian' environment 50; *Reframing justice in a globalising world* 50;

social structure/institution 51; 'unburdening' minority groups 52
Reframing justice in a globalising world 43, 46, 50
Refugees Act 176
'regular' schooling 77
reification and displacement, rethinking recognition: aboriginality and non-aboriginality 47; academic achievement 47; 'chronic absenteeism and dropout' 48; 'concrete arrangements' 49–50; cultural authenticity 49; cultural criticism 46, 49; cultural oppression 50; cultural pluralism 46; economic oppression 50; 'free-standing cultural harm' 48; 'hypostatising' of culture 47; Indigenous theory and knowledges 47; institutional matrix 47–8; macrostructural variables 48; marginalised cultures 46; material benefits 49; micro-level classroom variables 47–8; multiculturalism 47, 49; non-dominant cultures 46; political claims-making 46; redistributive justice 46; scrutiny 46, 49; socioeconomic disadvantage 47; 'status model' 48; transformative justice 48
'relational care work' 108
relational conceptions 15
relational justice: cultural autonomy 15; definition 14; *justice as mutuality* (*see justice as mutuality*); *justice as recognition* 17, 19–20; micro face-to-face interactions 14–15; procedural justice 15
relational ontology 60
Ren2010 145, 148
research-based interventions 63–4
rethinking recognition 46–50
Rethinking recognition: overcoming displacement and reification in cultural politics 43
'rethink recognition' 74
Robeyns, Ingrid 42
'roll-back' neoliberal policy 141
'roll out' neoliberal policy 141
Rowlands, J. 159
Russell, L. 110
Ryan, Mary 164

Salamanca Agreement 71
Salend, S. 73
Samuel, R. 166
Sandhu, P. 134
Sapon-Shevin, M. 73, 85
Sarra, C. 43
Sayer, A. 104, 111–12, 114
sceptical postmodernism 18–19
scepticism 2, 18
Scheffler, S. 34
scholarship of teaching and learning (SoTL): academics growth (*see* academics growth);

conceptions 58; democratic communities 60; democratic dispensation 59; disciplinary discourses 67; 'evidence-led' instrumentalist paradigm 58; historically advantaged institutions (HAIs) 59, 68n2; historically disadvantaged institutions (HDIs) 59, 68n2; implications 57; injustice 58–9; institutional arrangements 67; institutional ethos 59; oppression 58–9; participatory parity 57, 60–2; research on teaching and learning (RTL) 58; social justice framework 57; societal phenomena 59; theory and practice 58; Western culture 59; xenophobia 59

schooling: 'advocacy' 40; affirmative approach 42; 'at-risk' students 44; centre-based approach 44; Citizenship Curriculum 45; cultural awareness 45; cultural/political barriers 41; cultural recognition 44–5; debates and counter-debates 42; *Disadvantaged Schools Program* 43; distributive principles 43; economic deprivation 43; economic marginalisation 44; educational disadvantage 44; education's material benefits 44; *Head Start* programme 44; home-based approach 44; institutionalised/hierarchical patterns 41; interimbrication 42; justice claims 46; labour market 43; legislation 45–6; lifelong productivity 44; moral imperatives 41; *National Goals for Schooling Framework* 44–5; *National Partnership Scheme* 44; obstacles 41; 'participatory parity' 40; 'progressive' teachers 40; racial/cultural identity 41; reframing justice 50–53; resource allocation and funding 44; rethinking recognition (*see* reification and displacement, rethinking recognition); separatism and intolerance 43; social arrangements 40–1; social democracy 53; social discontent/dysfunction 43; social marginalisation 44; socio-economic deprivation 43–4; 'sterile' arguments 53; three-dimensional model 41–2; western contexts 45

Scott, J. 30
scrutiny 46, 47, 49
second-wave feminism 162
self-determination 141, 151, 165
self-esteem 127, 136
self-respect 36
Seltzer, K. 134
Sen, A.K. 42
Singal, N. 72
single-issue social movements 19
Slee, R. 73
Smith, J. 149
social: activism 120; arrangements 23, 33, 40–1, 60–1, 66, 67, 126, 135, 173; capital 17, 144; costs and benefits 36; democracy 53; discontent/dysfunction 43; discrimination 75; esteem 32; fragmentation 45; inequalities 4, 37n2, 54, 150; liberalism 120, 123; marginalisation 99, 44, 115; mobility 59, 62, 105; pathology 144

socio-economic deprivation 43–4
socioeconomic injustice 123
Soldatic, K. 80
SoTL *see* scholarship of teaching and learning (SoTL)
status equality 32
stock-in-trade, egalitarian politics 33
Structure, Culture and Agency (S, C + A) 64–6
"struggle for recognition" 123
Struyf, E. 72
superdiversity 131

Tabensky, P. 59
Tax Increment Financing (TIF) 151n3
Taylor, C. 122
Taylorization 162
Taylor, K. A. 110
teachers' perspectives: diversity politics (*see* diversity politics); identity politics 85; inclusive practices 71 (*see also* inclusive education); justice demands 72; life-skills 86; 'mainstream' classrooms 86; 'normality' and 'abnormality' 86; policies and practices 87–8; 'special needs students' 85
Teese, R. 105
Theodore, N. 141
Thompson, S. 171, 175, 185
Thomson, P. 110
Thrupp, M. 97
TIF *see* Tax Increment Financing (TIF)
transcendent universalism 19–20
transformative approach 61–2, 76
transformative justice 48
transformative recognition 25–6, 27n4, 127
translanguaging research: bi/multilingualism and bi/multilinguals 133; Chinese identity 134; "code switching" 130; dynamic systems theory 130; education practices 129; English-Welsh bilingual education 130; ethnolinguistic racism 134; multicompetence 130; multilingual communicative practices 132; multilingualism research 129; multimodal communication 131; partial representation 129; recognition-based transformation 133; semiotic resources 131–2; social transformations 133; sociolinguistics research 131; superdiversity 131; surface level-change 133
transnational claims 75
transnational finance 50
trustworthiness 178

'unburdening' minority groups 52
United Nations Special Rapporteur on Adequate Housing 145
"unpaid reproductive and domestic labour" 125
urban development 141–3
Urciuoli, B. 133

'valorizing diversity' 30
'value-added' tables 95–6
'value-free' research 13
Vice, S. 64–5
violence 10, 13, 21, 44, 45, 105, 109, 122, 145, 179, 181, 182
voicelessness 10, 178–81, 185

Waitoller, F. 73
Walzer, M. 36
'war on terrorism' 157
Weber 128

Wei, L. 130–2, 134
Weiner, G. 73
Williams, C. 130
Williams, R. 159
Wilson, William Julius 144, 146
Winberg, C. 64
Wood, P. 31
Woods, P.A. 94
working-class culture 25
Wright, E. O. 133
Wright, P.A. 145, 147

xenophobia 45, 59, 176

Yates, L. 160
Young, I.M. 13–14, 16, 19, 21–2, 24, 26, 30, 34, 42, 53

Zembylas, M. 60